# Mind
# without a
# Home

# Mind without a Home

*A Memoir of Schizophrenia*

KRISTINA MORGAN

HAZELDEN®

Hazelden
Center City, Minnesota 55012
hazelden.org

ISBN: 978-1-61649-460-5

Editor's note
This memoir is based on the author's actual experiences. Certain
people's names and identifying details have been changed to protect
their identity. Some conversations and descriptions of events have
been compressed or imaginatively recreated and are not intended as
exact replications.

This publication is not intended as a substitute for the advice of
health care professionals.

The Big Book is a registered trademark of Alcoholics Anonymous
World Services, Inc.

The Twelve Steps are from *Alcoholics Anonymous,* 4th ed. (New
York: Alcoholics Anonymous World Services, 2001), 59–60.

16 15 14 13    1 2 3 4 5 6

Cover design: Jon Valk
Interior design and typesetting: Kinne Design
Developmental editor: Sid Farrar
Production editor: April Ebb

*I would like to dedicate this book to*
*Nancy Walker, my mother, and my grandmothers.*

*Literature is no one's private ground,*
*literature is common ground;*
*let us trespass freely and fearlessly*
*and find our way for ourselves.*

— VIRGINIA WOOLF

# CONTENTS

# ACKNOWLEDGMENTS

My life is possible because of God and the people in it. The people I acknowledge here are not in any particular order—except, of course, my life partner, Guy, will be first. Smile. I thank all here and all not named for their unconditional support over the years.

Guy, you have been my rock. You have my heart. No one could have done better by me during my low points. You never missed a day visiting me at the hospital even though it was a 45-minute drive one way. And outside the hospital, you have inspired me to have strength.

Thank you, Jan Black, my spiritual healing therapist, for the many hours you spend with me and for placing my manuscript in the hands of Mike Fitzpatrick, who actually read it and then passed it on to Hazelden editor Sid Farrar, who too read it. Many thanks to Sid, April Ebb, and the Hazelden staff for working with me to create the best book possible. The serendipitous nature of all this has been truly amazing.

Thanks to Jon Valk, who designed the cover.

Bob and Marty Christopher have been pseudo parents and have always kept me in their prayers.

Christy Strauch has been in my life for fifteen years. She has listened to me read to her over the telephone countless times. Her suggestions are good ones, and I truly appreciate all the time she gives me.

Poet and dear friend Francie Noyes, you rock, as does Dot DiRienzi. Both of you inspire me. I hold you in my heart.

Pat Bates has been my longest writing friend. She was convinced I would someday publish. She has gained my respect for her psychic abilities over the years.

Cathy Capozzoli, another poet friend, inspires me with her own writing and sense of spirituality.

Writer Kriste Peoples read portions of the manuscript when it was still a long poem. She, too, encouraged me to continue.

I remember when I first saw Sandy Desjardins, writer and professor. She adds magic to any room she walks into. After ten years of silence, I began writing again under her tutelage.

Sheila Taube, writer and spiritual counselor, and Bonnie Vatz literally saved my life when I was at my lowest. They were light that made its way through the cracks of my darkness. I also thank Victor Taube, who has always been a stabilizing influence.

Norman Dubie, poet and professor, you are a wonderment. Thank you for being the chairperson on my committee at Arizona State University. And thank you for singing Buddha songs to me over the phone. I find you very healing, and you helped me through the grief over my grandmother's death.

Cynthia Hogue, poet and professor, thank you for the time you spent with me and my writing. You said this manuscript would be my masterpiece. And thank you for sharing your experiences with love.

Alberto Rios, poet and professor and another member of my writing committee at ASU, thank you for your support.

Thank you, Saashley, Paula, and Susie. Thank you, Art Awakenings, for providing me with a place to go to outside of my bedroom, where I had been trapped by my own mind.

Thank you, Dr. Frankie Moorehead and Kathy Hernandez, for being a great psychiatric team. You did great by me.

Many thanks to the staff at Thunderbird Banner Hospital's mental health unit for always taking good care of me when I was psychotic or unable to get along in the common reality.

Thanks to Trish Scanlan for being such a good cheerleader.

My family members, Barbara and Jack Morgan, Stephanie Doller and James Loper, thank you for your love and support.

My life feels like not mine, which is good. It allows me to know that I am not the only one in the city. I am here as a result of a collaborative effort. With little daily things, sometimes simply a smile, I hope to give back a bit of what I have so freely been given. Life is fabulous, and thanks to these and so many other people, I can show up for it.

# Description of Schizophrenia

Schizophrenia may be characterized by delusions, hallucinations, disorganized speech (e.g., frequent derailment or incoherence), grossly disorganized or catatonic behavior, and other negative symptoms (e.g., diminished emotional expression and reduced drive). There is also often a deterioration in work, interpersonal relations, or self-care.

People with schizophrenia may display inappropriate affect, depression, anxiety, or anger as well as a disturbed sleep pattern and a lack of interest in eating or food refusal. Depersonalization (a sense of detachment from oneself), derealization (the external world appears unreal), and cognitive deficits in schizophrenia are also common.

The lifetime prevalence of schizophrenia appears to be approximately 0.3–0.7 percent with the psychotic features of schizophrenia typically emerging between the late teens and the mid-30s.

Approximately 5–6 percent of people with schizophrenia die by suicide, about 20 percent attempt suicide on one or more occasions, and many more have significant suicidal ideation.

Adapted from American Psychiatric Association. *Diagnostic and Statistical Manual of Mental Disorders.* 5th ed. Arlington, VA: American Psychiatric Association, 2013.

# Prologue (September 1993)

*I am twenty-nine years old.*

At eleven years of sobriety, a heavy cloud drops on my head. Voices from other realities plague me like a gaggle of hurt geese that can't find their way home. Men and women in black suits appear in my home and at my front door and in the grocery store aisles where cans neatly line the shelves, and boxes of cereal promise to make me an Olympian. Their presence is a plague. In three months' time, I overdose seven times. The intensive care attendants get sick and tired of bringing me back. They refuse me cups of soda and stop washing my forehead with soft cloths in the ICU.

I move three times within these three months. People don't want to rent me a room. Taylor comes to my rescue, as she has done many times before. She converts her living room into a bedroom.

There are three of us living in a small two-bedroom apartment along with Taylor's two large dogs. No one complains while I am there. And no one kicks me out after I get drunk.

\* \* \*

## Again, I decide to kill myself.

Obviously, I haven't been good at dying by overdosing on drugs. So I decide I will jump off a cliff. I know I need to be good and drunk to do this.

I go to the grocery store and buy many bottles of booze to include liquor that has come out during my sobriety, like wine coolers. I really want to try Zima, but forget to buy it.

Early evening comes and I march up to Signal Hill from my apartment. *Hill* is the key word here. It is not a cliff; it is a hill.

I get horribly drunk. The mixture of all the different kinds of alcohol makes me throw up. After throwing up, I realize if I jump from this hill I will probably break a wrist and slowly roll to the bottom of it. Dying is not possible at the height I am at with no overhang.

When I stand up to walk back to the apartment, I fall. I am too drunk to find my feet.

Here comes this guy. He says he is on the hill with his prayer group and notices me not doing so well. He offers to drive me home. I mutter a thank-you and accept the ride. During the ride he tells me I was the reason he needed to be with his prayer group on Signal Hill that evening. He felt destined to help me. I am too drunk to do much more than listen. I do tell him the government is after me, though, and ask him what he thinks about this. He says, "No worry, my car can outrun them." It was like he was a part of the frequency I was listening to. He says, "You don't need to be in an airplane to get rid of them. They can fly too. In fact, they can enter any room you're in without opening the door." I look at him while he sends these messages to me. His mouth is not moving as I hear his words. *Have they infiltrated him?* I ask myself. Before I can answer myself, we arrive at my home.

He gives me his phone number. He says, "You will probably want to telephone me in the morning to thank me." His mouth is moving as he says this. "The little shit you are—you couldn't even get home by yourself tonight and you nearly wet your pants." My eyes widen. His mouth is not moving again. I will lose his number.

The miracle of waking up in the morning is that I didn't crave alcohol and realized I was in love with the Twelve Step program and could not live without it. At least for that morning, I did not want to die, I just wanted to start over. I was upset that I had destroyed my sobriety date. I could no longer brag that I had gotten sober at eighteen and stayed sober. The point is not to brag. The point is that we stay sober one day at a time. I say fuck the day, I just lost eleven years.

Audrey, my therapist, says that this is the most self-destructive thing I could have done. She at one time tells me that I am the most destructive person she has ever worked with. I suppose so. There is much damage I have done to myself, to include taking a razor blade across my stomach while in session with her.

Then, she telephoned the police. They came and handcuffed me and took me to the hospital to be stitched up. From there, the police took me to the psych hospital, where I was admitted against my will.

All I remember from the hospital stay is that there was a woman named Jane Doe. I was sorry I had given them my name because I too wanted to be a Jane Doe.

\* \* \*

*This hospital,*
*the sharp edge of the earth,*
*confines me.*

The air pushes me to act out. My mouth doesn't stop saying *fuck*. My body bangs itself into walls. I don't know what wound my clock.

Isolation, one bed in a room, cuffed. It's useless to pull against the straps. They are unlike the butterfly that brushes the top of my hand—red wings, there and gone.

Once released from the isolation room, I pace, the corner of a long corridor echoes my name. I no longer say *fuck*, but use my name like I would a rusted wrench.

# Family

### Resemblance (February 2011)

I often felt adopted. It's not because I wasn't loved. Later, I would even resemble my mother and two sisters. We all have dark hair and Roman noses, high cheekbones, and plump lips. Mom, Rose, and Hunter are tall at five feet eight, but I am taller at six feet. My feet I attribute to my father: wide with a large big toe.

I like my pancakes with no butter. Everyone else likes butter. I love to read; aside from my father, everyone else likes television. I hate the sun. Everyone else loves to tan. I thought blue cars belonged in rain, and since it didn't really rain in Phoenix, there ought to have been fewer blue cars. Certainly, my father should have chosen red instead of blue.

Rose was doomed to sleepwalking and occasional drug usage, Hunter to using drugs often, and me to having schizophrenia. Rose's disorder was considered acceptable, though dangerous; Hunter's, bad news and life altering; and mine, tolerable.

When I learned I had mental illness, I thought the doctor was lying. I thought he was passing judgment on me for not wearing matching clothes. I couldn't bear the burden of strange without revelation. Revelation did come. Now that there was a name for what I had that came with its own set of behaviors, I could relax into it like dawn slipping into the corners of my eyes, waking me needlessly two hours before my alarm goes off. The name for my illness would not come until way late, way into my late twenties.

If I had known I was going to write about my life, I would have paid more attention. As it is, memory sits in the shadows below the olive tree. Paying attention to life today helps to flash me back to earlier times. My journey has been physically linear, but my emotional and spiritual life is a collage of fragments in rapid succession without transition. These fragments have left the book with several short journal-like entries rather than traditional chapters. I have attempted to put a narrative together with time as linear, rather than bouncing all around. It has not been easy. Bringing everything together in one story rocks my boat. I see one thing from the helm, and quite another from atop the flagpole. The two things occur at different times. Maybe not even on the same day. When I go to recollect them, I may tell the second story first and come back later to tell the first story as the sun goes down and the branches of the olive tree paste themselves against an evening sky. I take a deep breath and begin with birth.

## Chocolate (August 1963)

Jeremy had not planned to marry Hannah right out of high school. It was 1963. Maybe he thought he would bump into additional pretty women who would leave him with a glow and fast heart rate. Maybe he thought college football would do more than screw his knees up, and he too would continue on to play professional football. Honestly, no one knew what was going on in his mind when Hannah told him she was pregnant. They were at an ice cream parlor. He spit chocolate milkshake all over her skirt. He folded up his dark thoughts, dumping them into the lined napkin when she mentioned she was pregnant.

"Are you sure? I mean, we only did it that one time."

There was another young man she held hands with. Johnny. But Jeremy's 200-pound body pinned Johnny's 152 pounds to pavement in a mean testimony to spaghetti when he learned that Johnny had the hots for Hannah. It was Jeremy who was with Hannah the night light caught the dip of Hannah's throat.

Hannah never got the chocolate out of her skirt.

## Identification

I was born on Good Friday, March 27, 1964. Kristina Marie Morgan. My father, Jeremy, handed out sparklers to the hospital staff. One nurse lit hers, causing a small explosion in her hand.

That day there was an earthquake in Hawaii, and Willie Mays hit another home run. Dad attributed all that went right that day and all that went wrong to my birth. I was the first grandbaby to the Morgans and the Posers. Grandma Morgan loved to tell the story of how she gave me my first bath in her kitchen sink. She said I giggled. She said I was small. I didn't remind her that all babies are small.

Grandma Morgan was my father's mother. My parents stayed with Grandma Morgan and Grandpa Morgan the first five years of my life. The second year, Rose was born. Dad was at work when his boss delivered the message that Hannah had just given birth to another baby girl. Dad thought to make a conscious effort to bring tulips home to Mom in congratulations for Rose's birth. Not only would he forget the tulips, but he would be pulled over on his way to the hospital for speeding. When he reached for his wallet, he would discover that he left it, along with his identification, at work in his desk.

A year and a half later, another daughter, Hunter, was born.

So that was my family: Mom, Dad, and three daughters. Oh, and a dog. We always had a chocolate medium-sized poodle. The poodle's name was always Brandy.

I have an old photo pinned to my bulletin board on the wall to the left of my desk. We're all there. Dad looks like Burt Reynolds, Mom like Elizabeth Taylor, and then us kids, just kids; me and Rose with pixies, and Hunter still bald. I think Brandy has the biggest smile of us all.

## Hula-Hoop

A child shouldn't have to grab for a bone. I sit in the middle of my mother's large bed, centered so the little monsters hiding in the carpet can't reach me. Hannah rouges her cheeks and powders her nose. Usually, I am mesmerized by Mother's activities at the vanity. Today,

I become interested in the plastic left from dry-cleaned clothes. I hold the plastic up. Air can distort itself in ways we don't understand.

"Don't put that over your head, my sweet. It'll kill you."

I put the plastic over my head and wrap it around my neck like a stole. Mom leaves. I stare down the hall at her diminishing figure. Sweat breaks out on my small forehead. Panic. Then I realize I can take off the plastic myself. Taking off the plastic gives me confidence that I can also outrun the little monsters in the carpet.

I go outside to Hula-Hoop.

## Doll Shoe Magic

We moved from Grandma and Grandpa Morgan's home into a two-bedroom apartment. My dad had a job with Motorola. His father was not too happy with this. His father had always envisioned that he would go to college and get a degree. For a long time, I think Grandpa Morgan was angry with Mom, as if it were all her fault. Grandma Morgan said she was glad abortion wasn't something people often did in the sixties; she thought if it had been easy, I would have been aborted.

I really like the ease of the two-bedroom apartment. It isn't expensive; Mom and Dad seem less stressed because of this. Later would come the mortgage and frown lines.

All three of us sleep in the one bedroom. Hunter still needs a crib, although Rose and I taught her how to escape by placing her feet correctly on the bars. I catch her as she comes down the outside of her crib. Fortunately, she only escapes while I am in the room. I don't think Rose is big enough to catch her.

Rose and I share a queen bed. I think it is here that we bonded for life. I slept on my stomach, and Rose would fall asleep with her head on my back. I swear I could tap into some of her dreams. I would ask her in the morning what she dreamt about. She would tell me she didn't remember. I would tell her a wild story and exclaim, "This is what you dreamt. Jiminy Cricket really didn't starve in the wintertime. He heated up TV dinners over a fire, and saved the cherries for last!"

Money was still tight. Mom got creative at Christmas and at birthdays. For example, Dad wanted a new pair of golf shoes. So Mom borrowed my Barbie doll shoes and put them inside a little square ring box. Dad opened it and was happy to learn that eventually he would get new golf shoes, just not right now.

There was always money for Easter candy. All three of us girls always got a foot-tall chocolate bunny, marshmallow chickadees, chocolate eggs, and M&M'S. The chocolate bunnies would stand at attention in the refrigerator. Slowly we would break off ears, eat eyes, then make our way to the feet and eat those too.

I had no idea that Easter was a religious holiday until late into my teens.

We did not speak about God, much less Christ. Somehow I knew there was magic in the world, but I didn't attribute it to anything in particular. It was simply a deep feeling I had that things were always what they were supposed to be, even the bad things; there was a reason for those things too.

## Commercials

Hannah was a sober mother by day and a three-margarita mother by night. She slept through Rose's, Hunter's, and my tears. We learned that crying was pointless in the dark. The dark would stay dark like a splotch of engine oil on pavement, and there would be no one to carry us into the light where moths could be heard fluttering against lampshades to the hum of the refrigerator.

Hannah was great at throwing open the closet for us to pick our clothes. She could fry eggs and make toast and offer us chewable vitamins, but by lunch, she was distracted by the motion of the world. The world called to her like the ringing of a telephone does the ear. She forgot that she really had wanted her own babies and sought the company of female shoppers, sought the long afternoons of cocktails and hors d'oeuvres, and the attention of friends.

Teenage girls keep many secrets. Not dangerous secrets, just things that belong to teenage culture—who is drinking, Les made out with

Mary, Mary gave it up, Sarah cheated on her British literature test, and Gene is failing algebra. Hannah longed for vanilla milkshakes at the diner at midnight with girls who wore makeup and swore on occasion.

Hannah thought marriage would free her, but babies climb out of cribs and suck on marbles when no one is looking.

Bring the baby to the bar if the bar won't come to the baby. Hannah had more sense than this. She didn't slip from the house until the kids learned to sit through commercials.

Where was Jeremy? Jeremy traveled with his job and was away most of the time. Being a sales representative for Motorola kept him busy and provided good income for his family.

Who's to say if he would have hugged us tight to his chest and wiped away our tears when the monsters under our bed really did get us? These monsters whispered terrible things like, "If you close your eyes, we will claw at your eyelids until you have none and are left to permanently stare at the ceiling." Rose thought a fly was going to fly up her nose and lay eggs. Hunter simply cried randomly and often.

Mom was missing out. I think consoling a child creates a stronger bond. Maybe Mom really didn't hear us crying when she was home. Maybe the television was simply too loud. Or maybe she was afraid that she wouldn't have the right words to say to us. Maybe she thought an "I love you" was outdated. She never read the baby books. Neither have I. Maybe the baby books say, "Stay away when your child cries at age four or older; this will build strength of character." Somehow, I doubt they really say that.

Rose and I learned to console each other. One day, Hunter just stopped crying and that was it. Hunter never cried past the age of two. In her case, this was not a good thing. She grew to lack compassion for anyone or anything.

## Cake

The first time I lied I was six years old. My parents had gone out to dinner and I'm certain there must have been a babysitter. I just don't recall. The presumptive babysitter did not stop me from doing what I did. It was my father's birthday, and Mom had baked him a chocolate cake with chocolate buttercream icing. I love buttercream icing of any flavor.

Here sat this cake on the kitchen counter, so lovely and tantalizing. Deep, rich, brown. A little lopsided, but still amazing. The cake was at my eye level. Perfect. I simply couldn't resist taking a finger to it, licking the icing off my finger. Now, if I had been clever, I would have stopped with one lick and tried to fill up the gully I had created. But it was too delicious to stop. I licked the icing off the entire cake with just one finger. I didn't feel sick for having done so. I was at peace. I had indulged in one of my favorite things.

My parents came home. We rushed them at the door. And Dad yelled, "Cake time!" Uh-oh. They walked into the kitchen and eyed the cake, seeing what remained. Dad was furious. I guess he really liked chocolate birthday cake. He looked to me and asked, "Who did this?" Without hesitating, I said Rose.

Rose denied this, of course, so she was in even more trouble for having told an assumed lie. She started crying on the spot, and was shunned to the bedroom.

I felt awful. I couldn't believe I hurt Rose like that. That same night, I told the truth. Rose hadn't done it. Father was flabbergasted. I started crying and said I would never lie again, and to this day, I rarely lie. And when I do, it festers, creates this large, poisonous boil inside me that always explodes, forcing me to right what I've wronged, like the time I said I picked up the dog poop and pulled weeds from the yard all morning long. Mom gave me five dollars for this, which was quite a lot at the time. I hadn't thought that she might actually notice that the weeds and the poop were still there. I tried to tell her it was new weeds and new poop. Anyway, I am a bad liar. I almost always get caught when I do lie. Even when the truth hurts, it is better to tell it than to drag the ball and chain. On most occasions. I actually lied today. I called my supervisor and said I was throwing up and couldn't come in. In reality, I am waiting for a couch to be delivered. I didn't think it would sound good to tell the truth. The red alert of my conscience says to make right. My brain says, *Don't be stupid, what's done is done. No one got hurt.* Sigh.

## Zebras (1970)

I hated beef stroganoff. The meat was cheap and tough, and it seemed like I had to chew each piece a hundred times before swallowing. Brandy could take a nap by the time I was done eating. Being the dog that she was, I'm certain she would have liked the challenge of eating that meat. Maybe I could somehow pass it to her. Mom smiled at me from across the table. Nothing doing.

My sisters were just as challenged by the meat as I. Maybe Mother made us eat this because she needed a break. Some peace and quiet so she could watch her soap operas. *Days of Our Lives* was her favorite. We had a small black-and-white television that often did not pick up a signal, snowing through *Gilligan's Island.* No television left us plenty of time to chase each other around the family room.

We were still living in that small, two-bedroom apartment. Dad had yet to be promoted. Aside from the two bedrooms and two bathrooms, there was only one main room, which contained a dining table with chairs, a zebra-striped couch, two La-Z-Boy chairs, and a television on a stand. We would spend hours playing chase around the zebra. Mom tried to make it okay for herself by saying at least we weren't running amok in the streets.

Dad would come home tired and claim a La-Z-Boy. I would untie his shoes for him and slip them off, making certain to put them away in the closet so Brandy couldn't chew on them and Hunter, age three by now, wouldn't undo all the laces.

## Superman

In front of the television. Age seven. A man is painting a mountain and a sky. He writes "God, my father" in the sky. I am fascinated by this, the kind of fascination that grabs a person, makes them want to do something right now. Catch a butterfly. Play with a ladybug. Dance a hole in the carpeting.

I find my crayons in the drawer with my socks. I hide them there so Rose and Hunter won't use them. Hunter still likes to chew on them. Not bite, just gnaw and then spit out the color. The light carpeting is collaged in crayon.

I take the crayons, find paper, and sit at the little green table in our bedroom. I draw the mountains and the sky, add clouds and birds. I scatter a few daisies at the foot of the mountain. I like daisies as much as I like ice cream.

Then, in my seven-year-old scrawl, I write "God, my father" in the clouds. The drawing is done. I tape it to the window above my bed. It breathes in and out. I feel its pulse and in that moment sense God. Or something. Something caused my mind to be still. Something caused me to listen hard. I could hear God, but could God hear me? I needed something to hear me even if something was beyond the bedroom. Beyond the house. Stuck in the clouds, but able to look down and spot me below the roof. Like Superman, God could see through anything.

Later that day, I return to my bedroom and find my drawing ripped up, lying on the bed. Fear drops its hand, taking me in its palm. All I can think is that my father had found it and got mad that I had another father. I never did find out who ripped up my drawing.

That was the last time I thought of God for a very long time.

## Out of Town

Dad did get promoted. We moved into a four-bedroom house, two-and-a-half baths, kitchen, family room, dining room, all of it, even a swimming pool. Initially, Rose and I shared a bedroom. We each had our own twin bed. Hunter, for reasons I didn't know, got her own bedroom with Mom and Dad's old king-size bed. Maybe this was the start of Hunter growing away from us. Maybe Hunter felt adopted too. Maybe I should have made an effort to invite Hunter to play alongside Rose and I. As it was, as Hunter aged, she became independent and drug riddled.

When Hunter was thirteen, I got a call at ten at night, informing me that Hunter was drunk and in a ditch. She was so drunk her friends left her behind, calling me to come pick her up. I found her in an orange grove. I was sixteen at the time. I had just gotten my driver's license.

Once home, she passed out on the toilet seat. I had to wipe her butt, pull her pants up, and get her to her room. I pulled a chair up and sat beside her in bed the whole night, afraid that she would drown herself in vomit. I had heard such stories.

Our parents weren't there for any of this. Out of town. Maybe Vermont.

## Tooth Fairy

I do remember second grade. It was filled with Dick and Jane and see Spot run. I loved reading. And I loved being read to.

It was this year that I lost my first tooth. I was not very happy about it because it just hung in my mouth, the root half buried in my gum and half not. Mom decided to let Grandma pull it out because I seemed to trust Grandma more. It didn't matter how much I trusted anybody. I didn't want it yanked out. Pull on a dog's leg and he'll try to bite you; pull on my tooth and I'll try to kick you.

Mom came up with this brilliant idea of tying a string to my tooth and the other end of the string to the knob on the open door in the room. Slam the door and the tooth comes out. This is one of the miscellaneous things that mothers share with each other at the park. My mother didn't go to the park, but she did go to the bar.

Grandma finally got me to settle down in her lap to have the tooth pulled out by bribing me with a root beer float. She was good at making root beer floats.

The next tooth I lost came out after one of my classmates elbowed me while we stood in line. I was standing there, minding my own business, when *bam*. I was certain to pick it up because I knew the tooth fairy would come if I left it under my pillow. It was good for a quarter or maybe fifty cents. Money was worth a great deal more then. Can a candy bar be purchased with a quarter or not? That is how I looked at it. I didn't understand inflation yet.

My second-grade teacher read us *Where the Red Fern Grows*. I loved that story. I was not the only one who cried when the dogs died. I was, though, the only one who wiped snot on her arm. I was always wiping snot on my arm. When it dried, it became scaly. Other kids noticed this and harassed me. All I had to do was start using tissues, and they would stop harassing me. It didn't occur to me to do this.

I made myself popular by being the one to push the merry-go-round at recess. I felt powerful running in this circle. My body was strong and the kids screamed as I pushed them around.

## The Blob

Third grade. I watch *The Blob* starring Steve McQueen. I don't know anything about Steve McQueen, but I do know about horror movies. They make me leap outside of myself. I love living outside myself because the real fears and vulnerabilities that weave through my brain paralyze me a great deal of the time.

However, watching *The Blob* was a mistake. It stayed with me. At night, I was convinced the blob was spreading on my carpeted floor. I would listen for slime, wondering if it was possible to hear this. It was too dark at night for me to be able to tell if the blob was really there. But then, I thought the blob could be invisible. I didn't want the slime to eat me.

Finally, sleep would take me. I would wake in the morning exhausted. And then I still was concerned that the blob was on the floor, hiding in the orange shag carpeting. Thank God for athletic ability. I could jump from my bed to the door without touching the bedroom floor.

Out in the kitchen, Mom would make pancakes. I asked her if she thought the blob could be in my bedroom. She laughed and said absolutely not. She said many things I didn't believe, but this I did. I walked back to my bedroom, stood in the doorway, and put one foot forward. No slime, just shag. What a relief. I was able to go to my closet to get clothes for the day. I was able to look under the bed and see nothing hiding there. I was able to pull socks from the drawer and put shoes on. Converse shoes, always Converse.

The day would move forward as days do and then night would come and the eighth hour would approach. As kids, my sisters and I had an eight o'clock bedtime. Lying in bed again in the dark, I would swear the blob came back. I can't tell you how many times I would ask my mother in the morning if she thought the blob would find me. She patiently said no. I loved her for this.

## Serenity

I loved pretending I was a mermaid. Being a mermaid and reading were two of the greatest things in my life. I was good at both of them.

Under water, the world dissolved. My lungs got stronger. I got better and better at holding my breath. I looked up from the bottom of the pool and the world swirled. And there was a kind of rushed quiet. I loved the feel of my body in water. Once I'd broken the surface for breath, I'd breathe in deeply and return to the bottom of the pool. I could do this for hours. Frogs are lucky to be able to live on lily pads, their small bodies rhythmic with the way the water moves in wind.

## Heart Necklaces and Liquid Soap

Rose wears fluid dresses, her socks frothed over her plastic heels. She clicks around corners, announcing her coming before she enters any room that might get up and walk away. I tell Rose a room exists only if I'm standing in it; otherwise it is simply a memory of clothes hanging in closets, an unmade bed, a bowl of oatmeal on the counter getting cold.

I slip sideways through doors the older I get. My tilt to the world doesn't keep Rose from running through sprinklers. She rarely pauses to ask me what I mean by what I say, just lets the words fall into the grass as she plays, spraying me with the hose. I don't appreciate getting wet. It's always a hazard to be around Rose when she commands water.

Dad tosses Rose in the air. Her dress parachutes out as she floats back into his arms. He also tosses me in the air. Unlike Rose, I fall fast with gravity thick in my boots. It doesn't hurt my bones much to land hard on the floor.

I read books after school, in the evening, through the diminishing moon. My bed glows beneath the sheet because of the flashlight I hold there. The light not only allows me to read in the dark, but also warms me.

Rose on the other side of the room is surrounded in soft sleep that will fuel her for the next day, while I sleep on the picnic table at recess.

Rose wears ankle bracelets and small heart necklaces. She hangs with friends who giggle over boys in teen magazines. When anyone in her group is threatened, they are ferocious, like small radios turned up high.

I want to be a part of them, Instead, I usually wind up watching Hunter for Mother. Hunter is not a well-behaved child. She eats or sucks on everything we play with. Play-Doh. Barbie dolls. She especially likes to put army men in her mouth; she says she doesn't want them firing at each other. I tell her gun control can't be achieved that way. I might as well be talking to my Mrs. Beasley doll.

Mom likes Rose and her friends gathering at our house. She likes to have Rose in sight. Rose is not always to be found. I know she sneaks away in the middle of the night. A firefly flies deep into the middle of a bush. Rose's spirit extinguishes long enough to hide.

Mom doesn't like Rose to be bold and free and not afraid of the dark. Mom's first thought is of safety. Then she gets jealous of all the fun Rose has roaming the streets in the gauze of streetlamps, chattering with friends who too are not afraid of a bit of darkness.

By this time, vodka begins to affect Mom's mood. I believe the animosity Mom begins to show toward Rose is due to the drinking.

Rose begins to cuss. Mom doesn't recognize herself on the tongue of Rose. Mom squirts liquid soap into Rose's mouth and instructs her to not spit it out for fifteen seconds. In that fifteen seconds, a single ant roams into the kitchen and carries a bread crumb outside to his hill.

## Red Eyes

I was on a camping trip with my Girl Scout group. It was my first time camping. The older girl, the leader, helped us to pitch our tent. There were two to a tent. I thought *pitching* was a weird word to use when putting up a tent. Even then I was playing with words, letting them bounce around in my brain, having them land in a sentence sometimes spoken, sometimes written, and sometimes simply hoarded in my mind.

Anyhow, I laid my sleeping bag on the ground. The ground sloped. For no reason at all, I laid down with my head at the bottom of the slope and my feet at the top. The leader girl came around to check on us all and to say good night. She laughed when she saw me and told me that all my blood was going to rush to my head and leave my eyes permanently red. I didn't say anything. And I didn't change positions. I spent the whole night awake, waiting for my vision to darken because of the flow of blood. I believed her. As simple as it would have been to turn around, I didn't. I was glad when morning came, and I asked my tentmate if my eyes were red. She said of course not, and left me in the tent to sigh.

I returned from that trip glad to be home until Mother said something to me that really upset me. To this day, I don't recall what I said, but I do remember how she responded. She told me that she wished I had stayed away and never come home. I went to bed and cried. She woke me sometime in the middle of the night. I was crying in my sleep loud enough for her to hear from the hall. She shook me and said she had no idea I was going to take her words to heart. There it was again, words taking on the weight of iron balls. I did slowly stop crying as she rubbed my back. But I never forgot how vulnerable I could be when a single sentence like "I don't want you" stung me.

## Cologne Bottles

It's Christmas and Grandma Poser is crying quietly in the front room of the house looking out a big window to the cul-de-sac. It hurts to see my grandmother crying. Mom and Dad had both yelled at her for being late again. I didn't see why it was any big deal. Christmas will still be Christmas an hour later.

I leave Grandma to her sadness, thinking that if I went up to her now she would be embarrassed. At eleven years old, embarrassment is being called a boy when I am really a girl. I have a pixie haircut and am taller than anybody else in my class. And there is the beginning of a mustache. It already hurts to be me. But not all the time.

This Christmas I had shopped for gifts and wrapped them all in aluminum foil. They look very shiny mixing with the green of the pine and sparkling against the other gifts. As usual, my parents went all out. The presents spread from beneath the tree to four feet in front. We all find a seat and Dad plays Santa Claus.

Grandfather Poser sits next to me. I'm embarrassed. My mother had bought me a bra and wrapped it up as a Christmas present. I thought I'd die. Now Grandpa would be looking at my boobs to see if anything is poking through my shirt. And there is. I'm not ready for my body to be changing. I'm not like Rose, who wants boobies bad. She told me so.

I put the lid back on the box as quick as I can. Everyone wants to see. Sharing our gifts is a part of our Christmas tradition. "Really," I say, "it's nothing to share. Really. It's a bogus gift. The box is empty. Please. I'll open another. Dad, pass me another. Please."

And he does. A small one. Too small for another bra to fit in. I lift a Fred Flintstone necklace from the box. I love Fred. He is in a running stance on a gold necklace. Fabulous. Grandpa helps me put it on by hooking it behind my neck.

Hunter is a show-off. She wants center stage all the time. I'm the exact opposite. I want to fold into the couch and be a witness to all without participating. As a witness, I still live some kind of life. I am gone when reading a book. I am gone when practicing to be a mermaid. I am gone when I go on long walks beside the canal. So I make up for all that gone time by watching others live their lives.

Both grandmas get charm bracelets, with little hearts and stars attached. There is plenty of room for them to add more charms, which they will do over the years. When Hunter is eighteen, Grandma Morgan still has her bracelet. When Hunter is eighteen, she steals the bracelet and pawns it. Grandma Morgan tries to buy it from the pawn shop, but it has already been sold.

Mom gets a watch. I think great, now we will be on a "minute schedule." She would call to us to come *this minute*. I know Rose and Hunter will be lousy at it. And myself even worse than lousy if I am zoned out, which I often am. Schizophrenia has yet to clutch me in a tight grip. Maybe zoning out is a precursor for me. The wind shifts, and I float with it.

Dad gets Old Spice. Every Christmas he gets Old Spice aftershave. Later, he has better and better jobs, and his portion of the bathroom counter becomes littered with bottles of cologne. The bottles are beautiful. I ask for the empties. He gives them to me. I keep them until I am in college. Then, I toss them out, wanting to rid myself of everything that meant anything to me.

Both grandfathers receive a bottle of champagne. This too is a tradition. The bottles will be opened at dinner and a toast called for. "To Christmas, hallelujah," and that's all I say when asked to make the toast.

Rose received bracelets that jingle along with her heels. Gold and silver. It's a relief for me to know that my parents know me well enough not to give me items that jingle and jangle and bring unnecessary attention to myself. And too, I think any attention brought to myself is unnecessary unless I am given cash for chores well done.

Hunter gets a Nerf football and a yo-yo. I figure Mom and Dad are trying to channel her energy. She's a minor monster, always playing tricks. Once, she brought me a glass of milk, which was nice, but she also added orange juice, which curdled the milk. I spit it everywhere. She just laughed.

That night, I dream of a purple horse to ride off on. Another Christmas has come to its end. I barely have enough room to put away my new belongings: green and blue-colored socks, three large sweatshirts, a pair of red boots, a new doll that I'm glad when squeezed says nothing, several stuffed animals, books, and a deck of cards.

## Martini

We loved huddling on the bed with my parents when there were going to be surprises. Dad called Rose, Hunter, and me into the bedroom. Then he shouted out for Mom. She yelled, "Just a minute," from the kitchen. It was early evening. A good time for cocktails. Dad made a martini for Mom.

"Yes, you called." My breath was taken away as it often was when I noted how beautiful my mother was. Tonight she wore a pair of blue pants and a glittery top that made her face seem to glitter also. Her hair was down, long and black.

"I made you a martini," Dad said as he handed her the glass.

"Mmmm, my favorite." She paused and looked at us all on the bed. "Did you all think I was going to turn into a monkey or something? Is that why you're all here to watch me as I drink?"

"Drink, drink, drink," we all shouted. "Olive first," Hunter said.

"Olive first," Mom agreed. She lifted the toothpick that stabbed the olive from the glass and gasped. On top of the olive sat a diamond ring.

"Yeah!" all three of us girls shouted.

"What do you think, hon?" asked Dad.

Tears in Mom's eyes, "I don't know what to say."

"I never did get you an engagement ring. It only took eight years of marriage."

We probably had many moments like this together as a family. It's just that I recall very few.

## Caterpillars

Rose was the jewel in Dad's crown, his princess in the velvet dress with the satin bow in the back. Hunter was his baby, the young one. The young one could do no wrong because she was simply the young one acting the part of the young one. Rose and Hunter would drift wildly in the house. Their fury knocked framed photographs from the walls and lamps to the ground. Nothing ever broke, but everything got rearranged. Their excitement went cool when Dad entered the house; he was a sturdy stick of wood they would glue themselves to.

Rose was a doll with long brown lashes whom Dad would tuck in at night while my feet wrestled at the bottom of my twin bed. My blanket did not fold neatly beneath my chin. Sometimes, I would throw the heavy blanket over my head, hoping that Dad would pull me from the darkness.

Rose dreamt of little ballerinas who pivoted on music boxes. I dreamt of being caught in the branches of a tree, unable to place my feet on the ground to pirouette beside Rose.

In my dreams, Dad sat on an ivory chair with a high iron back, applauding Rose as she danced. He never looked up to see me in the tree. I would cry big tears that fell on the leaves, decorating them with a glassy shimmer. One day it would not matter that I missed conversations with Dad that might have grounded me in a common reality.

Common reality is a place of love and friendship; it has postal workers and supermarkets, hardship and sorrow, electric bills and green arrows. It is human experience lived in a place of mind common to all who gain sustenance from its light.

Later, other realities push themselves into my consciousness like water slapping against rock hard enough to leave its mark—putting a period at the beginning of my sentence. I will hear voices that no one else can hear and see things that no one else can see. I will spend years photographing people in my dreams where caterpillars wrap around my upper arm, creating bracelets of strength out of their bodies.

## A Passion for Waking

Boys show up by seventh grade. They knock at the front door and enter the gate into the backyard. They push through the shrubs in front of our bedroom windows and knock on the glass, whisper "come plays" through the screen. Mom doesn't like all the attention Rose gets from these boys. She threatens to BB-gun them, but they still come like lint to tape.

Dad is proud. He loves that he has a beautiful daughter who charms people into buying her ice cream sodas and barrettes for her hair.

I am not like Rose. I continue to read books, forgetting to pay attention to my clothes or hair. My hair hangs in ratty strands down my face, blocking my deep-set eyes from onlookers. I wear boys' pants because I have no hips and like how they slide from my waist to the heel of my shoe in one straight line without a belt. The pants are plain, with no fancy stitching or embroidered flowers. No peace signs or glitter or bell bottoms. Just black pants allowing for no hips.

Rose wears T-shirts that hint at her emerging breasts and training bras. I wear loose cotton with long sleeves that cover my hands. Rose wears beaded sandals and platform shoes. I, Converse sneakers with dirty laces and scuffed rubber. Rose has flair. I have mystery.

Dad loves flair. Later, I would learn from him that the reason he favored Rose wasn't because I was mysterious and androgynous well into my thirties, but because he believed Mom favored me.

Rose moves into life, a drop of dye in a colored T-shirt, blue mingling with other blues and not being afraid of purples and greens. Wash the T-shirt in cold or hot and all the colors retain their distinct lines or curves around the shoulder. Pull on too many threads and the pattern unravels. The boldness of the blue suffers, as it is easier to see threads aligned on a spool than rolled across the floor.

Rose's spool has never been without thread. Her passion for waking keeps her knotted to the bone. This is something I might have learned from her before my first overdose, how to hang in like a lit wick in a candle when a wind blows fierce. Rather than lose her spool to fire, Rose does remain dampened by drugs; maybe there is something to be said for marijuana maintenance. However, Rose's drug use never reaches the height of Hunter's.

## Fog

By the time I was twelve, I sported hair above my upper lip and on what was becoming a unibrow. I started to hang my head, eyes to the ground, with dark lanky hair hiding a good portion of my face. I did not mind feeling the swing of my hair on my cheeks as I walked. By not looking at the world that so intimidated me, I thought to create my own. I imagined I was surrounded by fog with one star descended from the sky to light the path ahead of me. The path was cobblestone, so I could hear little other than my own shoes kissing rock. I was not lonely locked in my own privacy. My peers could poke fun at me all they wanted to, and they did.

I wished I didn't have a mustache. There was no easy way to get rid of it. Plucking it would just cause it to grow in more coarsely and darker. A neighbor suggested I see an electrologist. And I did. Mom took me once a week to have a thin wire inserted into each of my follicles and zapped with electricity. The treatment was painful. I felt like a big head with no body attached.

Mom took care of my bushy eyebrows. She pinned me to her king-size bed one day. She hovered above and plucked one hair after another. That hurt too. Bee stings felt better and bothered me less since they could only sting once. The king-size bed became a raft. I floated, listening to the sound of water lapping around me. Pluck, pluck, pluck. I don't remember caring much about my overgrown eyebrows. It was then I began to wonder if I was an embarrassment to my mother. Pluck. Pluck. She said it wouldn't hurt as bad the second go-around.

## Plenty

Mom and Dad, Rose, Hunter, and I, and our poodle, Brandy, were on our way to the dog park.

First stop after leaving the house for the park was McDonald's. At twelve, I was a new vegetarian. Dad poked fun and said, "Is that like being an Aquarius?"

"That's the zodiac, Dad," I said from the backseat of the station wagon. I liked to look out the rear window, pretending that I was traveling backward to a less populated time in history. And I liked to stare at the drivers in the following cars so much that they usually sped up to pass us whenever possible. This made Dad think he was driving too slowly, and he too sped up.

"I've never known a vegetarian," Dad said. "Have you, Hannah?"

"No, darling, I haven't. I think it's weird."

"That's Kristina for you," Rose replied from the seat next to me. "Weird with a capital W."

"A capital W," Hunter repeated.

"See, even Hunter agrees," Rose said.

"I agree," Hunter said.

"What, are you a parrot?" I asked Hunter.

"Of course not, silly," Hunter said. "I'm eight."

"I'm not weird. I'm just eccentric."

"Whoa, there's a word for you. Where'd you find that one, Kris?" Dad asked.

"The dictionary," Rose responded as she blew steam on the window and then drew her initials onto it.

"Yes, I catch her reading the dictionary at the breakfast table," Mom said.

"What do you mean, you catch me? I do it in the open," I said. "I don't have anything to hide."

"You have plenty to hide," piped up Rose.

"Plenty," said Hunter.

"Do not."

"Do too."

"Like what?" I asked.

"Kristina has a rat in a cage under her bed," Hunter sang.

"I know about that," Mom said.

"And you didn't make her get rid of it? You won't even let me have a hamster," Rose complained.

"You don't spend enough time in your room," I said as I turned and looked at Rose.

"Huh," Rose said.

"Hamsters need attention too," Mom said.

"Oh yeah? How do you know that, Hannah?" Dad joined in. It was known that Dad would always support Rose when he could, just as it was known a penny is copper.

"I just know," Mom said.

"Love, love the hamster," Hunter sang.

"I would too be good to it," Rose said.

"I didn't say anything about your being good to it, Rose. I just mean you wouldn't play with it enough."

"That's crazy. Hamsters sleep. That's what they do best. I know that. Sheila has a Teddy Bear hamster, and it's always sleeping every time I'm at her house," Rose provided.

"Well you can't have one," Mom said.

"Kristina has a rat. Dad—"

"Mom's decision." Dad surprised everyone by saying this so quickly. "Why do you let Kris have a rat?" Dad asked.

"It's Kristina," I corrected my father.

"Kristina," Dad returned.

"Kristina," Hunter said. "Yeah, why does Kristina get to have a rat? I want one too."

"You don't," Rose said. "You just want to create trouble."

"Everyone needs company," Mom said.

"Yeah, Kristina reads the dictionary to the rat. Instead of playing outside," Rose said.

"Do not."

"Do too."

"Nothing wrong with learning words, rat or no rat," Dad said.

"But she doesn't even use them, Dad, except for *eccentric*. How often do you really hear her talk?" Rose asked.

"I talk," I said.

"In your sleep," taunted Rose.

I went for it. "My sleep? What do I say in my sleep?"

"All sorts of stuff," Rose responded.

"Like what?" I asked.

"I don't know. Just stuff."

"You sleepwalk, Rose," Hunter added to the conversation.

"I know, Hunter. Everyone has already told me that."

"One of these days you're going to find yourself in the street in your pajamas," Mom said.

"No I'm not," Rose said.

"How do you know that?" Mom asked.

"You won't let that happen to me."

"How do I help you when I'm sleeping?" Mom asked.

"You'll wake up. I'll knock something over and you will wake up. Or you'll sense that one of your kids is in trouble."

"Your mom sleeps too heavy for any of that," Dad said.

"You're doomed," I said.

"Shut up, Kristina."

"Watch your language, Rose. We don't tell each other to shut up," Mom said.

"Shut up," Hunter piped up.

"HUNTER!"

"When the neighbors are screaming at each other on the front lawn, you tell them to shut up," Rose said.

"They shouldn't bring their business outside. It's not right," Mom explained.

"Charlie says his mom is a drunk," Rose said.

"That doesn't excuse her behavior," Mom said.

"Charlie says she falls asleep on the couch with a cigarette burning. He's afraid she'll burn down the house. We saw it in a movie. It happens," Rose exclaimed.

"You can't always believe movies, Rose," Dad said.

"Mom does, don't you, Mom?"

"Sometimes."

"All the world's a stage," I offered.

"What do you mean by that?" Dad asked.

"Shakespeare said it," I replied. "Ask him."

"Right," Rose said. "He's dead."

"Here we are, McKee Dee's," Hunter announced.

"Good," Rose said. "We don't have to listen to Kristina talk about the dead as if they are still around. Dead is dead."

"People don't really die in the movies," Hunter said.

"Don't encourage her, Hunter."

"Okay. I want french fries and a chocolate shake. A big one," Hunter said.

"Stay here, Brandy. We'll be right back," and I slid from the back, back to the back, and stepped out the door.

The McDonald's man who took our order turned out to be a friend of Mom's. "I know him from the club," she said to Dad on the way back to the car.

"He's a member of the club?" Dad asked.

"What, you don't think people who work at McDonald's can be members of the club?" Mom asked.

"I didn't say that."

"Yes you did. You inferred it."

"To infer and to say are two different things."

"Really," Mom said.

"Yes," Dad said.

"Mom knows lots of people, Dad. She's very popular," mentioned Rose.

Mom didn't comment to this. Dad was suspicious of Mom's popularity, as if she were doing things behind his back. She wasn't. I just knew this about her. She and Dad both liked flirting. That's all.

"I know," Dad said. "Isn't it nice to be popular?"

"Kristina doesn't think so," Rose said. "Remember her best friend is a rat."

"I want a rat too," piped up Hunter.

* * *

At the dog park, Dad spread the blanket on the grass. Mom passed out the food. "Cheese for Kristina. Pickles and ketchup for Rose. Double meat for Dad. Double meat for me. Shake and fries for Hunter. Nothing for Brandy but the ball."

Everyone else at the dog park stared at our family on the blanket. Everyone knows you don't come to the dog park to picnic. Even Mom and Dad know this. They just chose to ignore everyone else.

"What a beautiful day," Dad said. "I've got my wife and my kids and my dog, what more could I want?"

"PLENTY," Rose, Hunter, and I say simultaneously and laugh. Every time at the dog park, Dad would say what he says and we would respond with *plenty*. It was another one of the many little rituals we had.

## The Ocean at Her Feet

I line items in the refrigerator in straight rows, drawing a map for what goes where, and tape it to the refrigerator door. The milk is always on the same shelf as the eggs, and the ketchup stands boldly next to the mayonnaise.

My parents continue to bicker with each other and snap at us even in my effort to organize things. How does a child organize "I hate you" alongside "I love you" with indifference in between?

I rearrange the family room furniture each time my parents leave town so they won't tire of the furniture. The furniture seems to be refreshed by the relocation. Couches move to the center of the room, chairs into corners, and the television edges against the wall, screen facing out.

I set the clock on the coffee table beside the hourglass to time commercials and how long it takes for us to talk with each other. Thirty seconds pretty much kills the interest Dad has in us during football season and beer, and forty-five seconds for Mom between martinis and telephone conversations she has with girlfriends complaining about her sex life.

I document my early years by recounting the dust settling on the heads of everyone, but is it not true that we occasionally bathed each other in Murphy's Oil Soap, waxing love into the layers of our skin?

I stand on my wood floor today. It is clean of dust bunnies. I remember I feel safe with my dolls, and anything outside of that is simply extra.

Hunter bangs a hammer on the floor in the next room. She is nine and loud. Sometimes she is like a little dog biting ankles; a person wants to shoo her away. Mostly she is ignored.

Rose paints her toenails blue. I think of the ocean at her feet.

## Twelve

Solitude in my closet of pants wears heavy. I pray for someone to find me. I stave off hunger by dreaming of avocado while the smell of hamburger wafts from the kitchen.

I tell my father that I am exhausted. He laughs. He says that one can't be exhausted at twelve. Father says twelve-year-olds have an easy walk. *Easy walk,* I think. *Run for thirteen before twelve suffocates me.* It's easier to stick pins into my doll than to comb her hair. Just as people's hair mats from no conditioning, so does Dolly's. I think if I wet her hair, it may all fall out. Dolly didn't come with instructions. Like many things, I haven't a clue as to how to take good care of her. Rose offers to help, offers to trim her bangs. I say thank you, but no.

Hunter says I am too old to have a doll. Having a doll makes me a baby, she says. She takes Dolly and hides her in the bread box. I find her when I go into the kitchen to make a bologna sandwich.

I put Dolly in the corner of my dark closet hoping she feels safe, not scared. Brandy finds her, carries her into the hall, and chews on her face. Her mauled body haunts me for weeks. I place her in a box and bury her in the backyard near the water sprinkler. The ground will stay soft enough so that I can dig her out with my hands should I need to.

## Wilted Silence

In my teens, I take to lying on the carpet in heavily traveled rooms. *Someone please say something is wrong with me.* Mom says, "Get up off the floor, we are going to the doctor."

I am ready, my laces knotted, my socks pulled up straight.

* * *

The doctor taps on my knee, looks in my eyes with a pinpoint of light, never asks me what is wrong. I'm not going to voluntarily tell him that another reality invades my fifteen-year-old existence on planet Earth. I want to shove his light up his nostril, which is wide and hairy.

I sit in wilted silence.

Mom examines herself in the small mirror above the sink. A doctor's mirror provides no additional truth if he is too fat with opinions to see.

The doctor says I am faking illness because I want attention. Rather than get angry, I cry, "But it's not true."

Then I stop crying, preferring apathy to the clumsiness of tears.

* * *

I continue to grow apart from the common reality. One night it is all too much and I overdose on pills. It is a simple thing to do and one I would repeat hoping against hope that death will swallow me.

Death continues to spit me out with painful disregard.

## Low Sun

Bald men and bald women stand guard over me in my bedroom, formal in their black suits like a maître d' at an expensive steakhouse. They stand stiff as dried taffy. Puncture my room with their presence or their voices.

I think I have stopped being afraid of the men and the women in suits that have hung around for months. Mostly, I just hear them. Their voices are low, as if coming from the floor. I don't think of hell when this happens. Clearly, they are from some other reality. I doubt there is religion where they are from. They are so invested in the mind and how they interact. Like the collective unconscious Mrs. Lane sometimes talks about in class. She says some people believe that no one really ever dies. People's minds end up in some kind of collective pool that floats above us somewhere. Or at least that is what I hear her say. It is all pretty confusing to me. Sometimes I am glad they are here. They like being around me. I just wish they would take off their dark glasses. I can't see their eyes, but I bet they're flat, without fire.

I have stopped trying to be a part of the kids at school. They're cruel, like low sun on the windshield of cars.

## Echo (1979)

I can hear Mom and Dad talking. They're sitting in the family room with the window open just below my window. They talk loudly in order to hear each other over the television set. I don't know why they just don't turn the TV down. Maybe they want me to hear them talking. Maybe they're like the kids at school, and they think my mind is not listening. Ha. I am starting to think of myself as a fist—a mind sitting on top of a tall body. I think I don't really feel much anymore, and I am always running into things, as if I forget that I even have a body. I think the Suits are preparing me to join them. Maybe tonight is the night. I am not afraid anymore.

I sit at my desk and stare out the window. The other houses are dark. It is late. One of the Suits stands to the left of me. I wait for his instruction. And I listen. I listen to Mom and Dad love me. They tell me their worry is just a sign of their love. I ask them not to worry. I don't want people loving me anymore. There is freedom in this. I can just walk away from them without anyone caring. I don't want to hurt anyone. Or maybe I don't even care about that anymore.

"Kristina and I baked cookies all afternoon," Mom says.

"Oh yeah." I imagine Dad drawing on his cigar as he says this to Mom. "Kristina left school again." It's a statement my Dad makes, not a question.

"Same deal. The hives spread to her face. The kids teased her about being a monster, about being so ugly not even a mother could love her."

"I hope you made it clear that we love her," Dad says.

"Of course. I hate when you say things like that to me. I'm the one loving her all the time. You're the one who avoids her."

"I resent that, Hannah. She's the one who brushes off my attention. It's not that I don't try to connect with her."

"You're too wrapped up in the television when you're home, Jeremy. Maybe you could do more with the girls when you're home."

"Did you get her drunk again today?" Dad asks.

"I told you that was just a onetime thing. I thought a drink might relax her a bit and the hives would leave."

"I'm still not convinced that she's not allergic to something. I know the doctor said they were due to stress, but I can't imagine what would stress a fifteen-year-old."

"You don't remember being fifteen?"

"Of course I do. Dirt bikes and dogs. My parents bought me both for my fifteenth birthday. I had a blast riding in the desert with Teacup chasing after me."

"Fifteen is hard on girls," Mom says.

"Rose is almost there. She's sailing through."

"Rose has girlfriends to talk to and do things with."

"Well, tell Kristina to join a club or something. Lock up her books. See if she doesn't leave the house then," Dad says.

"Maybe she should cut her hair."

"What's that got to do with the price of rice?"

The TV volume goes up. I shudder with the thought of being locked away from my books. Reading is the only thing that takes my mind off things. Reading sometimes even keeps the Voices from the other reality away.

"But you don't want to keep us away any longer," the Suit says. I hated when they read my mind like that.

"We're your worst nightmare and your best friends, Kristina. We are everything to you. We don't care that you're weird. We don't care that you're ugly. We'll accept you just as you are, Kristina." His mouth doesn't move when he says any of this. It's all telepathic. I try to remember if I had ever seen any of their mouths move.

I shut my eyes with the thought that maybe if I couldn't see him, I wouldn't be able to hear him, either.

"I think you're desperate, Kristina. I think you want out of this little life of yours. No one will miss you. I promise. You'll have us. Go ahead, Kristina. Swallow those pills you've been hiding in your desk drawer. It's so easy, Kristina. You won't know that you've even died. You'll wake up with me and the others. And I told you we can go anywhere. Do anything. Our world is beautiful. It's not polluted with emotion. You won't have hives anymore. People won't tease you anymore."

I know he is right. Tonight, I know he is right. I look around my room. There isn't anything especially different. Books surround my bed, making a wall so that when I slept, if anyone tried to sneak up on me, they would knock over a stack of books and I would wake. Black-and-white photos I had taken of the city and the people in the city collaged one whole wall. Another wall had a poster of a single sunflower. I love how the sunflower bends toward me, as if trying to tell me something. My desk is covered with single-line poems. I can't concentrate enough anymore to write anything longer. My favorite for the moment is *the blind woman knows when the hummingbird pauses*. I wonder if I will be able to write in this other reality.

"Do you have any books where you are?"

"Everything you need you will have."

I think again about whether or not I am afraid. I have never overdosed before, so I'm not sure what will happen. This kind of scares me. I mean, I don't want to end up in a coma or anything like that. I don't want to end up waking up and having something wrong with me because of the pills. Like a bad brain, or something.

"Will it hurt me?" I ask him.

"No." The word seems to echo in the corners of my room. I think I might be able to catch the sound and throw it out the window. Let *no* echo around the world.

"Okay," and I am calm. I get up and shut the window. I don't want anything from the outside world to interfere. I don't want to hear the television or my parents talking.

I pull the bag from my desk drawer. There are a bunch of bottles I have snatched over the past six months from my mother's medicine cabinet. There are also bottles I have bought at the grocery store. Aspirin. Tylenol. Stuff like that. I line them all up. Slowly and with great attention, I pop the lids off the bottles. I pour the pills into a tall plastic glass I have saved for just the occasion. Everything around me fades to black. All I can see are the pills and my Coca-Cola can. I think about Rose finding me in the morning. I imagine it will be she who comes to wake me. And I begin to swallow. A mouthful of pills and a drink of Coke. A mouthful of pills and a drink of Coke. It takes about five minutes to get it all down although it literally feels like hours. The first minutes feel like summer. I lay my head on my desk and wait. Voices. They talk to me all at once, so I can't make out anything they say. I don't want to make out anything they say. I am so tired.

Within a half an hour, my body begins to spasm and my mouth goes dry. My breathing becomes more and more shallow. I don't know that my eyes are closed, but I do know that it doesn't matter; I can't see anything but mist. I fall from the chair. I know my head hits the wood floor hard. I hear it but do not feel it.

And then there are snowshoes.

## The Tube

Mother finds me on the floor when she comes to say good night to me. She immediately calls 911. I am not completely out of it. I respond when they give me charcoal to drink in the ambulance by spitting it up.

"Good gag reflex. If you don't drink this, we are going to have to pump your stomach."

I don't know what they mean by all of this. All I know is that my brain has been hurt, and that I can't keep the charcoal down.

My body is shaking and convulsing. Another reaction to the amount of pills I took. It hurt. *My brain is hurt, my brain is hurt*—a mantra inside my head. Maybe if I can keep putting words together, my brain will recover.

At the emergency room, they put me in a bed and close the drapes. A nurse shoves a tube the circumference of a nickel down my nose, down my throat, all the way to my stomach. I have never known such pain, or such panic. The nurse is not kind. Tells me how self-centered and selfish it was for me to have tried suicide. I can't tell him about the other realities. I can't tell him that if I left my body, I would be well taken care of.

Hours later, I am still in the bed. The tube has been removed. My throat is sore. My nose hasn't fallen off like I thought it might.

I am waiting for the arrival of the psych person on call. I am terrified. What does a psych person do? I can't imagine what next. There isn't supposed to be a "what next."

## The Number

The psych person shows up wearing high heels that I imagine pinch her toes. They make a pleasant sound as they click on the linoleum floor of the hospital. She is tiny, maybe five feet. Her long, dark hair is pulled back in a ponytail. The light blue dress she wears is flattering. I'm not good at guessing ages, but I do think she is still in her twenties. Late twenties.

I don't want to talk to her and turn in the bed, my back to her. My throat still feels raw from the tube.

She begins. "Kristina. How are you? My name is Sara."

*What a stupid question that is.* I am too polite to say this to her.

"I need you to talk with me. The sooner you talk, the sooner you go home. Would you like to go home?"

*Where else would I go?* I thought. I do know, though, that home isn't the root of my problems. I don't want to die because I have a bad home life. My parents are real people. They bicker, yes. They aren't perfect, yes. But I believe they try to give my sisters and me a good home. I want some kind of emotional connection to them. The fact that I don't have it is not their fault. I know, somehow I know, it is my fault.

I roll over and face the psych lady. "What's wrong with me?" I ask. "I know that's a big question to ask a stranger, but maybe you know someone just like me and you can tell me what is wrong with them. I mean, I guess I have to talk to you, but I don't want to."

She smiles. "It won't hurt. I promise." That breaks the air. I relax.

"Were you trying to kill yourself?" Here we go, I get all tense again.

"I don't know," I reply. I'm not about to tell her that swallowing the pills was a command from another reality. No way am I going to say this. It is my secret. I would hang on to this secret for a long time.

"Okay. So do you think you can be safe at home?

"Yes. I want to go home."

"And what will prevent you from hurting yourself again?"

I look at her hard. I kick at the sheets as if I can kick out an answer. "I don't want to turn purple," I said. Ehhh. Wrong answer. Her right eyebrow rises.

"You know, when people don't get enough oxygen, they turn colors. I don't want to be permanently blue or purple. And I don't want to hurt my brain. It was an accident. Really."

I find myself pleading with her. I don't want to get sent to the loony bin. I guess that is why she is here, asking me questions, trying to figure out if I am crazy. "I'm not crazy," I blurt out. "Please."

"Please—"

"Please let me go home."

She reaches into her pocket and pulls out a card. "Do you promise you will call this number if you should find yourself contemplating hurting yourself again?"

"Of course," I say. Her eyebrows rise again. I realize I am too ready with my response. *Slow down, Kristina,* I tell myself. *Breathe.*

"I will, I will call the number."

I think, *there is no way I will call the number. I would sooner die than call the number.* This thought makes me smile. She smiles back at me.

## Bones

One of my father's friends suggested to him that I have my nose done. I had a typical Greek-Roman nose that was too large for my face. My father agreed. My father also felt that I needed to cut my hair so I would stop hiding behind it and would wash it more often. I guess he felt shorter hair was easier to wash and take care of. This proved not accurate. I would spend hours straightening my hair and then recurling it. It didn't stop with the nose job and new haircut. My father paid for me to take self-improvement classes. In these classes, I was transformed so that at sixteen, I modeled clothes. I was a runway model. My frame was able to pull off a size twelve, although I had dieted down to a size six. At six feet tall and with large bones, this was no easy task. I was almost horribly thin. I thought the agency wanted me this way. As it turned out, they asked me to put on some weight, but then lie about it when asked.

Modeling made me a nervous wreck. Actually, having to leave my house made me a nervous wreck. At sixteen, it usually took a couple shots of rum to get me moving. However, I could not drink anything before a modeling shoot. I had to show up stone-cold sober. I don't know why I thought this, but I did.

Before a shoot in July, I tried breaking my arm by pounding on it with a hammer. I didn't want to leave the house and thought I needed some excuse other than "I don't want to go. I don't want to do a shoot today." Of course, not wanting to go would never be accepted, thus, the hammer. I tried to break a bone and couldn't do it. I packed my clothes, belts, hats, shoes, makeup, and jewelry and headed out.

Mac, the photographer, had no idea I was strung out emotionally. I had "the look." I could plaster the exotic stare or the girl-next-door smile on my face. I had heard you can't hide from a camera; this I knew was not true. I could hide from the camera as easily as I could hide from the people in my life. I could look in a mirror and not know that it was me looking back. I was a single flame in a pool of fire.

My modeling career ended when we moved from Phoenix to Morgan Hill, California. I wasn't sad to let go of it, nor was I sad to be moving away from what I knew. What I knew was life was painful, and I thought a change of environment might make it less so. I didn't understand that wherever you go, there you are.

## Interacting

Mom's green eyes cast low in the dark made her sultry. She enjoyed dressing in gowns for dinner parties, her cleavage a clean line beginning from the bottom curve of a sparkling necklace that spoke to the fire in her hands.

Her hands liked to rest on the shoulders of men she trusted not to make a pass at her. These men cast back the warmth she sent them by engaging her in conversation while Dad watched the ballgame with others in the next room.

Mom disliked being left with her own thoughts, which picked at her like a seamstress pulling out a hem. She was raised to seek engagement with others as a spiritual necessity. Life is about interacting rather than reflecting in isolation. When time finally caught her alone, like lightning catching thunder, introspection was bruised by alcohol. Then the dialogue she had with herself and others was diluted with pity, fear, and sadness, the children of Tanqueray and Jim Beam.

## Distance

Hannah pressured Jeremy to spend more money on automobiles and restaurants. He bought Hannah a Porsche and gave her a kiss. The kiss seemed odd to him. Her lips had changed. He wasn't quite certain when this had happened, only that it had. They continued to grow distant from each other. Her kiss would always be a testament to this.

### Relationships (1980)

Morgan Hill. Mom in bed drinking whiskey and eating ice cream for days on end. Dad traveled a great deal. He didn't know what Mom did with her time.

Mom asked me if she could be my friend. I needed a mother. We both started crying.

### Movement

The wild life of a woman in her thirties with teenagers at home snared Hannah. I didn't know if it was alcohol pushing Mom onto the path of reckless nirvana or the fact that she no longer had to watch her children.

Mom didn't need to be concerned with Hunter because Hunter was living with another family. The other family was a swimming family. Hunter was really good at swimming. She was staying with this other family so she could swim for a particular swim team.

Rose and I were on the road, wheels rolling. Because we drove, Mom didn't feel it was necessary to be home. She had taught us to wash our clothes, fix our meals, scrub the house clean, and make up our faces. Rose loved mascara and lipstick. I loved a thick black line circling my eyes: a detour sign; only the really sincere would want to have me as a friend.

Rose had helped shatter Mom's belief in her role of mother. Rose did not come to her when she began menstruating, but turned to friends for an explanation. Things like this led Mom to cast off her role of mother just as she did high heels after a night of dancing. Mom asked us to call her Hannah. "Whatever," was Rose's response. "How can you do this?" was mine. I knew my life was becoming unhinged. I needed someone to tell me what to do. Not that I would actually bury myself in advice, but I appreciated and sometimes was desperate for a second plan.

I felt that what a mother had to say held more weight than what a friend had to say. Hannah was weightless by Rose's account.

"Mom has nothing to say. She grew up not having to outlive trouble. How could she teach us to jump over holes? Everything she wants she gets. It's not our fault that she pisses it all away for the next drunk," Rose said.

"Quiet your piss. God finds it offensive." I threw my words at Rose's chest. Mom didn't know that we squabbled out of genuine concern for her. Maybe if she had known, she might not have collapsed.

## Fox

Mom's fascination with wealth began with television. She had grown into the habit of watching *Lifestyles of the Rich and Famous* over a two–Bloody Mary breakfast with eggs and a slice of toast. She knew it was possible to live with wealth.

Dad bought her a fur coat. It never occurred to her that the coat had been purchased with a credit card. Dad would be making payments for it over the next couple of years. Dad became itchy for things too. Mom's desire for things helped justify his extravagances, beginning with the fur coat. A fox has no idea how powerful he is dead.

The coat hung proudly between cotton sweaters with fuzz balls. Mom made it a point each morning to run her face over the fur. This relaxed her, moved her into a day of potential pleasure. Pleasure had moved beyond petting the dog.

## Aprons

A tornado's tail cuts quickly through dirt. Rose put the television in the closet. Rearranged the furniture in preparation for the party. Drunk teens could collapse on the couch while waiting for the commode. Rose asked me to pray that no one spilled Budweiser on the pool table. The refrigerator said, "Keep Out, Bacteria-Infected Food."

Insects can only see bright light when caught on the bulb of a flashlight. Scream *fuck* and *goddammit* too often, and the children come to believe these words. These words make things happen.

\* \* \*

Have you ever thrown away the instruction manual because you are certain there is a better, more efficient way of operating the toaster?

Mom and Dad left town. No parties. Just one friend at a time. Rose and I figured if one friend is fun, fifty would be outrageous. Shake up suburban life. Bring the nightclub to our Morgan lawn. Rose loved outrage. Rose liked to be the focus of a room the way a high-definition television set takes up one entire wall and hooks to speakers in each corner.

I wash the dishes, tell Rose God blesses her. Truth is as important to me as vision is to a prophet. Take vision from a prophet and you have an empty apron.

## Popularity

I did not know I grew up in an alcoholic home until I became a member of a group of sober drunks at age eighteen. Keep the rum and the ruin in the family. There was no alcoholic age limit. Our entire family drank when they wanted to, and I wanted to often enough. Alcohol was medicine. At first, it gave me the feeling that everything was all right. And then it fueled my apathy, bringing me to the place I wanted to be, not caring about anything. I felt loveless and godless and didn't even know how much both of those things would mean to me much later.

Just as my parents threw great parties, I did too. I went from being teased in school, afraid to look anyone in the eye, hiding behind greasy long hair, to a popular teen.

There was only one high school. Everybody knew everybody. I was surprised at how much I appreciated the smallness. However, I didn't appreciate the cliques; this was my first real exposure to racism and cultural differences. There were the athletes, the cowboys, the Mexicans (referred to as spics), the druggies, and the really smart kids (referred to as dweebs.) The cowboys and Mexicans were at war. I was in high school well before weapon laws were fiercely enforced at schools. It was not unusual for a cowboy or a Mexican to bring long chains or knives to school. I floated among all these groups mostly because I didn't feel I belonged anywhere even though I was popular. I wondered if my popularity had to do with the fact that I threw parties that allowed alcohol.

## Long, Greasy Hair

It was Friday night, and I was having a sleepover for the girls. The guys were allowed to stay until midnight. There was a great deal of cheese and crackers and a great deal of booze. Rose was there. Mom was there. I don't remember where Dad was.

Everybody came from the various cliques. I liked that. Some got deathly drunk. I didn't like that. Somewhere around ten o'clock, the party was out of control. I had gone to the bathroom to find peace and to cry. My mother followed me in and gave me a big hug. I told her Chloe was upstairs passed out in the bathtub, as white as cotton. And she was clammy. I later realized that she had alcohol poisoning and could have died or done real damage to her brain. I was relieved when morning came and she woke up. I fed her as many raspberry Danishes as she wanted.

Jeff was hysterical the night of the party in a pathetic kind of way. He had asked for the spaghetti pot, and I had given it to him. He walked around with it, holding it in front of him. He would begin a conversation with someone and then puke mid-sentence. The person he was conversing with usually walked away. Some asked him if he was all right. He said he had never been better. Jeff was smart, even brilliant, and his brilliance got in the way of him relating to other people. So, at the party, he was thrilled to be a part of it, thrilled that girls would talk to him, and that the guys even tapped him on the back saying, "Good to see you out." Alcohol was doing for him what he couldn't do for himself. Icebreaker. Liquid courage.

One thing missing from the party was drugs. My parents were strict about this. Drugs were illegal; you didn't do illegal things or do things that would damage a person's mind. Oddly, it never occurred to them that they let underage kids drink, or that alcohol could really do damage.

They were the cool parents that every kid wished they had. I think my parents allowed the parties because they loved to entertain. It was fun for them to see that their daughters also loved to entertain.

I had my first boyfriend at this time. I was six feet tall. He was five six. And a good wrestler. A really good wrestler. He was also an adrenaline junkie. He had a truck, the old-fashioned kind, which he kept spotless. I didn't care to drive with him because the way he drove always scared me. He would do a hundred down the hill and around the curves, screaming the whole way. We didn't last long.

The next boyfriend I had was a senior and a cowboy. His name was Casey. I didn't realize how much Casey loved me. Rose told me much later that Casey wanted to marry me. I know I broke his heart. I just didn't have the love thing in me. Nor did I have the sex thing in me. I would kiss, even passionately with a bit of tongue, but never pull my pants down. Occasionally, I would date someone who ended up calling me a cock tease. I hated this term and was glad that the label never went further.

We didn't stay in Morgan Hill very long, just a year. In that year the local paper reported that Burt Reynolds had been seen and was believed to live in town. It was my dad; people had mistaken my father for Burt Reynolds. This actually happened often to my dad when he was in his thirties. And my mother looked like Liz Taylor. I had a pretty family, aside from me, that is. No matter how many people referred to me as pretty, I couldn't accept it. I still felt like the girl with long, greasy hair.

### Senior Year (1982)

I spent my senior year in high school living with Mom and Pops Biskup in San Jose, California. They were a swimming family whom I had met when swimming for San Jose Aquatics while living in Morgan Hill. As I said earlier, it is not unusual for a swimmer to live with another family in order to swim for a certain team. The only difference now was that I was no longer swimming. I was simply desperate not to live with my mother and father. I can't recall what the desperation was about. My parents signed over guardianship to the Biskups, and I was good to go.

I attended and would graduate from Gunderson High School. There I took a psychology course taught by Mr. North. After class one day, I asked Mr. North what I could do for a friend who was suicidal. He recommended a book. My made-up friend didn't fool him. He knew that it was me who was suicidal.

Either he told Mom Biskup or I told her; either way, it was recommended that I telephone this therapist. My father thought that all therapists did was steal your money. Dad flew into San Jose and took me to dinner. At dinner, he outlined what I would do with my life after high school graduation. Of course, college was next. I got good and drunk that evening. The blush on my cheeks from the wine felt good. Everything would be all right or not.

Dad flew home and things didn't change. I was hiding booze around the house. Once, after I poured a glass of wine at dinner, I remember Pops saying to Mom Biskup to go ahead and let me drink because I was going to do it anyway. I don't know where he learned to let me drink so I would hit bottom faster and then get help.

I was miserable. Many times I would stay home, missing class. At home, I would pace and think up ways to hurt myself. I shouted at the demons that plagued me. They were either in my head or not in my head; I didn't know. The Voices had been a mere hum for years, but now they were louder and clearer. I just knew they were telling me to do things that would hurt me or the house. I would telephone Mom Biskup at work, all upset and crazed. She would come home. I remember sitting on the couch with her and her rocking me back and forth in an attempt to soothe me.

Two weeks away from graduation, I got it in my head to leave. Immediately. My parents were then living in Dayton, Ohio. I was driven to join them there, and I missed my graduation ceremony. I was fortunate that my diploma was mailed to me.

## Coop

Seventeen years old, and I didn't know anyone in Ohio. My parents hooked me up with a daughter of one of their friends, Cathy. Cathy and her friends were going to a party at some farm. Nothing was said of hayrides. I associated farm parties with hayrides, itchy skin, and gnarly hair.

Mom came through and gave me a bottle of Bacardi 151 rum. That, Diet Coke, boots, and both my hands, and I was set.

Cathy picked me up in her little Nova. I was introduced to Rick, Tom, and Jennifer—all crammed together in the backseat. I was the princess in the passenger seat and Cathy, the queen.

The farm was a great deal farther away than I imagined. I was shy and not much of a conversationalist at seventeen. At least I tied my hair back from my face so people could look at me, and I at them.

I asked if they liked raspberries. It was the first thing that came to my mind at a pause in their conversation. They had been talking about a wrestler dude named Howard asking a cheerleader named Mica out to dinner. Howard had the reputation of using and discarding. I knew raspberries were quick to be discarded because they grew mold easily, and there was never any telling at the supermarket how fresh they were. Logic led me to raspberries because they too were something often discarded.

Initially, my question was answered with silence. Then laughter. I laughed along with them as if I had made some joke. What they didn't know is that I was always dead serious. Lightening up, I thought, was for smokers. Lightening up was for mothers before they beat their kid senseless after they spit peas across the table at guests.

Next question: "So whose farm are we going to?" I thought that legitimate enough. Answer: "Matt's."

Then Cathy offered us all Quaaludes. I had never heard of Quaaludes. I didn't think taking a Quaalude from a relative stranger was a good idea. Peer pressure tumbled off my back, leaving my shoulders strong. I said, "No thank you." Later, I learned that Quaaludes made a person feel drunk without having to pee all the time. *What a beautiful thing,* I thought, years after this particular party.

\* \* \*

The farm was indeed a farm. We pulled up to the chicken coop and parked. There was a barn to the left of the coop and a big house to the right. They had a fire pit some hundred yards away. It was just getting dark, so the fire against a falling sky was marvelous, and I said so. "Marvelous," they all said together, and then laughed. Rick asked Cathy how I got hooked up with her. I didn't know if the question was meant to offend me in some way.

We pulled lawn chairs up to the fire. Matt's mom had sent Matt out of the house with bags of graham crackers, marshmallows, and Hershey's bars. I loved s'mores as much as the rest of them. I also loved burning marshmallows on the end of coat hangers.

Matt said, "You guys are on 'ludes." A statement, not a question.

"Man, you got it right," responded Rick. The four of them were kind of lopsided and very happy. Caution the flame. It would not be good if someone tripped and fried.

I was ready for a drink. I opened my cooler and pulled out the bottle of 151 rum. The Diet Coke was my mother's idea. She thought if you drink liquor with soda you get less drunk. I wanted drunk, not less drunk. Suddenly, I had everyone's attention. Share the bottle. That would be proper etiquette. But hell, I wasn't much into etiquette. I shared anyway, just as long as I got dibs on most of it.

I don't know how I got into the chicken coop, but I did. I came to with the clucking of all the chickens. Night, with birds surrounding me, scared the bejesus out of me. And I desperately had to pee. In the coop, with all of them watching—no way. It was dark, but I finally found the entrance and exit of the coop. Cathy was outside. I told her I needed to pee; she did too. We made our way to the house. Inside, Matt's mom led us to the bathroom. We wasted seconds trying to figure out who had to pee worse. I was fairly certain it was me, but I let Cathy go first.

Wouldn't you know she used the last bit of toilet paper. I fanned my bare ass to the best of my ability, and then pulled up my pants, hoping nothing would soak through.

Coming out, the hallway seemed twice as long as it had when I walked down it. Cathy hadn't waited for me. I freaked a bit, thinking I was going to get stuck in some sort of maze, and then caged and fed only green foods.

With great effort, I did walk straight and make my way out of the house and back to the fire. Everyone was kissing everyone. Rick asked me if I would kiss him. He was very good looking. The booze answered yes. He took my hand and led me to the barn. We climbed the ladder to the loft. He was hungry for me, or at least that is how it appeared to me. We kissed and felt each other up, and then he wanted me to take off my pants. Stone-cold sober. I told him no. That I was not interested in fucking. He got pissed, really pissed. I thought he might push me over the edge of the loft.

"Bitch," and he climbed down.

I climbed down too. After he had left the barn, I noticed an owl on the way out and thought that somehow the owl had imparted wisdom and safety. I had done the right thing.

Back at the fire, Rick was telling everyone I was a tease. Everyone looked at me. I wished my hair wasn't pulled back.

I spent the rest of the night in a lounge chair. I woke to a mangy dog licking my face. I felt dirty.

The ride home was quiet. Everyone slept except for Cathy and me. She drove erratically, but at least she drove.

Once home, I showered. Then slept. And slept.

## College (1982)

Summertime. My father and I hang out on the couch. He, with a Heineken, me with a rum and Coke. He says to me, "You need to get away from your mother." I don't respond to this, but I do think, *but why?* "You need to go to college. You should go to Arizona State University.

You can claim in-state tuition by using your grandparents as legal guardians."

I tell my dad that school starts in two weeks. In order to go to college, I would need to have applied at least six months ago. Even then, I would still need to be accepted. My grades aren't that good.

Dad says he'll make a call to the swimming coach at ASU. The swimming coach will know me. I used to be a great backstroker. Backstroker. *Back-pedaling,* I think, *I need to be back-pedaling right now.* I once thought about becoming a nun even though I had no relationship with God. Hell, I'd even thought of joining the military but realized I was only passionate about art and reading, not guns and fighting.

Dad calls the coach. The coach says come. He gets me into the dormitory and everything. Dad neglects to tell the coach that I haven't been in a pool for two years and had befriended King Alcohol.

Mom and Dad put me on a flight from Dayton, Ohio, to Tempe, Arizona. I was officially in school. My grandparents picked me up at the airport.

# Institutions

## Debris

August 1982, I move into Manzanita Hall at Arizona State University in Tempe. My room is on the fifteenth floor. The dorm is co-ed. Testosterone and raging hormones make for a mixed salad of fresh greens and stalks of asparagus. I have great plans for my room and don't want my roommate to get in the way of my decorating. I'm Baroque/Romantic period, and she's straight from the sixties, hippie and all.

After hello, the first thing she does is undo her bed, which I had made so carefully. She throws the bedspread, sheets, and pillows to the floor. She redoes it all in tie-dye. And then lights incense. Nag Champa incense.

Rather than getting all upset, I offer her a drink. She doesn't drink. Smokes a little weed here and there, but no alcohol. We can't be more different.

Her name is Martha. She is the only Martha I know. Do I befriend her or remain silent and aloof? The phone rings as I am trying to make up my mind about her.

It's my grandmother. She wants to know if I'd settled in. "Not quite," I say.

"Is your roommate there?"

"Yes. All royal and everything."

"So you can't talk freely?"

"That's right."

"I love you. Call me later."

"Love you too."

The morning moves on like a dog with broken back legs attached to a little cart so he can move about, sometimes rapidly.

I have to get to swim practice.

* * *

We are all dressed in street clothes rather than swimsuits. The meeting is just that, a meeting. We introduce ourselves to each other, stating where we're from and which stroke is our best.

The coach gives his hurrah hurrah speech and that is it.

Some months into the semester, I hear that the swim team is going to Hawaii. I want to go to Hawaii. I walk into the coach's office and let him know this. He tells me that I had been voted off the team a month ago. I'm aghast. My alcoholic brain cannot fathom why I'd been voted off. No matter that I had never attended a practice.

I say "oh" to the coach and leave without apologizing for my actions. Leave without a thank-you for all the help he had given me.

I do not like sun and chlorine. I will never get into a pool again.

Occasionally, I had moments of regret, mostly because I felt my father and I had used the coach, which really we had. When my brain was not consumed by alcohol, I cared that I didn't thank the coach. Under the influence of alcohol, I didn't give a damn; I didn't give a damn about anything. I had moved from the shy, *I don't want to hurt anyone* girl to the young woman who blasted through people's lives with no concern for the debris.

## Teeth

Martha leaves before the first month of dorm life ends. I am mixing my protein shake with a dash of rum. Breakfast. On her way out, she pauses and calls me an alcoholic and eccentric. Nobody had ever called me *alcoholic*. This I do not like. *Eccentric* I like even though I know she means crazy and unpredictable. I see eccentrics as individuals and art-ists—people who don't give a damn about what other people think of them or their actions.

After drinking my drink, I telephone my father and tell him that Martha had called me alcoholic. My dad says that as long as I don't drink in the mornings, as long as I don't drink alone, and as long as I still have a mouthful of teeth, I'm not alcoholic. One out of three. Not bad. I brush my teeth compulsively.

Another roommate comes, can't handle me, and leaves. The next roommate sleeps mostly at her parents' house. This is good, as it leaves me the whole place to myself. Earl, a young man I had grown up with playing hide-and-seek and tag, comes and builds a loft for me with stairs and everything. The loft holds the beds and the downstairs area has a small black refrigerator and two fabulous chairs imitating the Baroque period with its fabric covers. Of course, there are desks and shelves above the desks. I just don't find time to use my desk much. Dust gathers on my books.

I always have liquor. Word spreads, and students want to hang out with me. My room becomes an in-and-out party-hardy place.

This ends soon. I am too sloppily drunk at these gatherings and say uncouth things. Then one night someone gives me pot, which I've never tried. I rock in the corner, talking incoherently.

\* \* \*

It is midnight and I am totally alone. I look out the window, trying to focus on the lights, realizing that all I can really see is my face reflected back to me. The depth of my aloneness and the apathetic way I have been leading my life catch me in this reflection. I try to blink it away. The reflection persists. I blink again. Alcohol no longer drowns out the Voices I hear from the other realities. Tonight they are particularly strong and clear: *come with us, be with us, rest with us.*

For the second time, I try to take my life. I swallow all the alcohol I have on hand and a bunch of pills. Before I slip under, someone knocks at my door. I am currently in a backgammon tournament; the guy at the door is there to play. I tell him he won and go away. He goes away. He tells the residency hall supervisor, named Kat. I know Kat. I like Kat. He tells her I don't open my door. He tells her I sound wrong.

Just as I am going under, Kat enters my room and calls 911. The paramedics come. I have no idea about the timing of things. I am heading toward a place where there is no time.

A female paramedic punches my clavicle hard. Man, it hurts. In the ambulance, they try again to wake me so I can drink charcoal. The charcoal is meant to coat my stomach. I just keep spitting charcoal back at them.

Once at the hospital, they shove a tube through my nose and down to my stomach. It is as painful as I remembered. The attitude of the emergency staff is as horrible as last time. They are disgusted. "Real" people have "real" health issues. I am not a real person. A body without a heart, a mind without willingness. I run on electricity, not blood. It is a hazard to shake my hand. I will shock you every time.

* * *

After pumping my stomach, they send me on my way. Kat comes to get me. There isn't much talk as we drive to the dorm. She asks me if I am done harming myself. I do what I believe most do in this kind of situation; I swear I will never overdose again. I tell her I don't want to die. I tell her it was accidental. I tell her the same things I will tell the dean of the college.

I go back to my place as student. A student among thousands of students, and in my self-centeredness I think I am the only one who lives in the deep, unable to make it to the shore, much less to a chair in a classroom.

I overdose again two weeks later.

This time I will not return to the dorm.

This time when I finally come to, I believe for certain I had damaged my brain.

## Shallow Waters

My grandparents pick me up from the hospital and take me to the other hospital. The psychiatric hospital. Phoenix Camelback Hospital. It is just down the street from my grandparents' house, a five-minute drive at most.

The ride to Phoenix Camelback is a quiet one. A ride in the car on a hard-sun afternoon. I do not talk. One of my grandparents could insist I talk, threaten me with a pair of scissors, and I still wouldn't talk. But they would never threaten me and are probably glad for my silence. What do you say to someone who tries to throw life away as if it were a wrapper on a jawbreaker?

I see disappointment etched on my grandfather's face in the rear-view mirror. The backseat feels like a small house.

It was an intentional overdose. They found me cramped in a corner of my room, the corner a deep fist. No light. Then the soft light of the ICU. Now the stiff light of day. This is my first ride to a psych hospital. I watch a rabbit run into the road. The car misses the rabbit by inches.

My grandfather breaks the silence by telling me I have just destroyed any opportunity I would have had in becoming an FBI agent. My grandfather is a retired FBI agent. Maybe if he had told me earlier, told me he wanted to groom me, mentor me, maybe I wouldn't have been so painfully careless with life.

I don't know that *careless* is the right word. It appears to all that I could care less about life. But I don't think this is accurate. More the truth is that I care greatly. So greatly that I can never measure up. The veil between me and God has grown thick over the years. I don't want to live a shallow life. I don't realize that all life appears shallow at times. People have epiphanies. People have moments of clarity. I believe that one moment slides between work and breakfast eggs, between the mile run and the shower, between a night out dancing and the makeup removed. I think smiles are deep. All of humanity has smiled at least once.

My grandfather parks the car and they accompany me inside. The intake lady knows we are coming. She greets us. I don't look up. I don't say anything. I sense the world I am about to enter is far removed from anything I have experienced up until now.

Questions. She asks many questions. Maybe I have the answer to some of them, maybe not to most of them. Either way, I don't respond. I am only eighteen. I can't even tell you what colors I like. I've spent little time learning about myself. I have spent most of my time on basic survival in a world that is as foreign to me as a brick to a monkey.

They snap my picture, put a band around my wrist, and check my bag for contraband. My grandparents say good-bye to me, and I am escorted to the unit. They put me with the adults rather than the adolescents. Somewhere in my silence, they had thought me mature for my age. How they came to that I have no clue.

## Nine Months

Of the nine months I was to stay at Phoenix Camelback Hospital, I have little recollection. Some things, though, have never left me. And some of the people have never left me.

During those nine months, I was careful not to talk about the hum that plagued me. I was certain that if the staff knew, they would put me on medication, tell me that no one should experience a hum. Nor did I tell them of my knowledge of other realities. Again, I was terrified at the thought of having to take medication—medication that would mess with my mind. I didn't have an easy time with my mind; this I clearly knew. But I didn't want to get used to a different mind—that is what I thought medication would do. Take your real mind away and make it into something else. I was terrified of the something else.

## Bouquets

"Move the broad from my room immediately," Gladys stormed the hall, her words deadened by the glass partition separating us from the staff. *I'm no broad,* I thought. *I'm eighteen.* I had just told Gladys to fuck off. For what reason, I no longer remember.

Gladys was thin and frail, swimming in a night coat the color of salmon with a voice as large as the Liberty Bell at noon on a clear after-noon of quiet birds. Her slippers had lace around the ankles. She wore gloves to the elbows and sang a cappella throughout the day. She used red lipstick on her lips and brows, creating perfect arcs above each eye.

It was not my idea to put me in her room. Staff insisted. The rest of the patients were afraid of me, afraid that I would turn my stare on them, sling profanities, spit when lockdown became too hard, like it did when my mind returned to my brain after wandering the skies, taking refuge in castles that existed like a line of palm to my hand.

"She told me to fuck off," the words splintered from Gladys's mouth. They didn't fit her the way they fit my young punk self.

Staff didn't move me, and Gladys stayed. We screamed at each other long enough to become friends. She would slip me her elephant pills and I would swim in my bedsheets, my feet tangled at the foot of my bed.

I don't know how staff caught on to the fact that Gladys was slip-ping me pills, but they did. They were not happy. Gladys was forced to tip her head down, stick out her tongue, and shake it so the nurses could be certain she swallowed everything, including her voice.

That's the thing about medications. All of them have side effects. Later, I would take them. They made me forget that I am heaven. That I am as hard to know as sternum. That quiet sips from a melted glass light my hand and the stars within. That the world is swept like God in the a.m. Medication softens the blaze, although my feet continue to feel like bouquets.

I was sad when Gladys's voice lessened. I was sad to watch her shuffle down the hall, but the medication allowed her to converse with other people and respond in a seemingly sane way. And she had stories to tell. She was a master at storytelling.

## Owls

God followed me to the hospital. I sensed him fluttering between the patients and me, a sweet draft blowing my hair and pressing against my cheek, softly, like my grandmother's hand had after I was stung by a bee.

In a simple way, I did believe in God. I had never read the Bible and had only thought to read it as a book of literature that would help me understand some of the symbolism in other books. I didn't believe that Jesus Christ was any mightier than Gandhi. I didn't believe that he was a superhero, just a good man who served others and encouraged them to believe in a power greater than themselves.

My God wasn't responsible for me struggling with my mind. He wasn't responsible for my torment. But I was in the right place; I just didn't know to accept that right now. My struggles would eventually aid me in having a deeper compassion for other people. I would learn to love simple things like being able to floss my teeth (dental floss was not allowed on the unit). The freedom I have with God is immense, is mightier than any locked door or clouded thinking. I come back to soft pillows and the smell of wet grass. I come back to the twinkle in the eye of a stranger whom I've just told has good-looking shoes.

My belief in God has grown with time. I have learned to really know that the darkest shadow casts the brightest light. I am not alone. I live with the whisper of owls.

## Chocolate and Popcorn Balls

And then there was Alberta, a large woman heavy on her feet who pre-ferred a ride in a wheelchair to the movement of her own brown legs.

Alberta asked for peanut M&M'S while I dreamt of revolution. A revolution that would knock me sideways and kick sense into me. Each was as important to our emotional well-being as hands to a clock, time to a city, or breezes to a bird.

M&M'S settled Alberta's scorn like paste smoothed over the brow of a mask meant to scare the kindest of people.

I understood that revolution was a step toward peace. I had been months on the unit and was finally coming aware enough to watch things, see things, interpret things. It didn't matter that I had my own logic. It simply mattered that I had a logic. Some of the staff were able to follow my sentences, some not.

I thought revolution would ignite me, tear me down, allow me to rebuild—my body a redwood, my mind a platter of beads or a kaleidoscope of God.

Alberta didn't need a revolution. She blazed outside herself, kindled fires in others that left her alone at a round table, her mouth filled with fierce words.

Medication didn't tame her belligerence. She was the iron ball of a catapult that would launch itself onto the patio of smokers who clicked like biddies. In that moment, their self-examination would focus on the wrath of Alberta wanting a cigarette and being offered none.

Staff brushed her cornrows out and washed her housecoat the morning the marshal and two security guards came from the state hospital. They were unprepared for her size; she couldn't fit into the back of the police car. I thought that even if she were thin, she would not have been able to fit in the seat. She was no criminal. She was a suffering woman whose rage stole the best of her and scared other patients into wishing she would be taken away and lobotomized, ensuring her a docile life, one that would not disturb theirs.

I think Alberta is in me. I too see with the unbroken gaze of psychosis, but am somehow able to come back to palm trees and swimming pools.

Alberta doesn't know I am in her. I am in her like dust in a tornado, night in a star, ice in a glacier. Too small to be heartfelt. Too small to pull Alberta out of illness.

They wheel her back to the unit to await a van that will steal her away to the state hospital.

Staff gives her a chocolate bar. She sits on the patio in her circle of one. I watch her eat, slowly, deliberately. I wonder if the moment is as significant to her as it is to me.

I will go grocery shopping someday, will pick from many chocolate bars, thank God for the quiet that comes after the revolution, be glad that the pavement is hot beneath my feet and I have shoes that prevent me from blistering as I walk to my car.

The marshal and security guards did return in a van. Alberta pushed herself out of the wheelchair and walked to the locked door leading to the hall. The door was buzzed open. She pushed the door, entered the hall, and began the long walk down the hall to the van that awaited her. I would never see her again. I hope she found peace. I hope she found a plethora of chocolate. I hope she spent more time walking rather than pushing herself along in a wheelchair.

* * *

At Christmas, we string the tree with popcorn. One morning, Gladys is caught gumming popcorn with an empty strand of string in her hand. I ask my grandmother to make popcorn balls for Gladys for Christmas. My grandmother wraps them in red cellophane. A week after Christmas, Gladys's popcorn balls are still sitting wrapped beneath the tree. I asked her why she didn't open Santa's presents to her. She tells me she can't eat apples with no teeth. Ha. I unwrap one and show her it is popcorn. Her lipstick smile is huge.

* * *

Gladys told me that one day her son would pull up to our window in her pink Cadillac. She would drive away with her song.

Time hung in the ward as the calendar moved on. Gladys sang. The rest of us paced. We all ate three meals a day with Lorna Doones for snacks. Someone would bang her head against the wall, throw a fist into the pillar, jump from chair to chair, burst out laughing. Time read like a storyboard, the frames wavering in their ink, committed to a single story.

It was Sunday, one of the countless Sundays. Cartoons played on the television set. The psych techs wandered around the main floor checking in with the patients. I lounged on the couch, pretended I was Joan Crawford as I puffed on a cigarette. Unlike the majority of the patients, I was careful not to let my cigarette ash fall to the floor.

I thought I would be fined ten dollars if I did. I thought the hot ash might start a fire even though the hot ash of others' cigarettes didn't.

I saw Gladys step from the bedroom into the hall. She held a hard-case, pea-green suitcase in her gloved hand. "Oh darling one, where are you going? Got a plane to catch?" I asked.

She responded, "My son is bringing my car. I'm riding away at two o'clock."

I waited for her to say, "Just kidding." I waited for her to say she had stolen a small statue of the Madonna and was afraid to leave the item unattended for fear the owners would show up and recuperate the stolen statue.

"You're kidding, right?" I said.

"Of course not." She acted as if this were a common Sunday event.

She lowered herself slowly into the chair next to me, placing the suitcase on the floor. "You really should stop that."

"Stop what?" I asked.

"Smoking those cancer sticks. They're going to stunt your growth."

"Well if that's what they've done, it's a good thing I started. I was six feet tall by age thirteen."

Gladys checked the clock on the wall. It was ten of two. The nurse called for her to come to the counter. She lifted herself from the chair, grasped her suitcase by the handle, and walked on. The suitcase was light. I could tell because it was no effort for her to walk and she stood even, rather than tilted to her left. It made sense to me that it would be light; Gladys only had half a dozen housecoats, underwear, and a shower cap, unlike myself, who had many tiny little plastic jars of lotion and whatnot for my face, three pairs of shoes (all without laces), a couple of hardback books, several pairs of sweatpants, and even more Fruit of the Loom T-shirts. And I did have underwear of all different colors.

I could hear the nurse speak with Gladys from where I sat. The nurse was going over Gladys's discharge papers. To say the least, I was shocked. What was I going to do without Gladys? She was the only one I spoke with or ate my meals with. I couldn't be happy for her; I was at the point where I was still only concerned with myself. It was true, though, that Gladys had gotten much better. She was no longer speaking senselessly to no one in sight. She had stopped getting into physical fights with the staff weeks ago. She could carry on a clipped conversation, and she was bathing regularly. I took a deep breath, telling myself that it would be okay.

The nurse was done with Gladys. It was two o'clock. Gladys walked over to me and said, "Come here. I have to show you something."

I got up from the couch and followed her into the bedroom. "Look out the window," she said. The hard plastic window—of course, real glass could prove hazardous. I looked out and immediately sucked air in; a pink Cadillac was parked just outside the window. A man was just getting out of the driver's seat. He wore a striped polo shirt and dark pants. I thought he was good-looking.

"My son," she said. "And my car," she said.

"Oh, Gladys," I said, "I will try to be happy for you. I will try not to miss you. Do you really drive?" I asked.

"Not for years," she said, "but my son is good at getting me around." And she turned and left the room, suitcase in hand. I stayed staring out the window. I didn't want to see her walk away with her son. I had no interest in meeting him. I just stared out the window until they appeared. Her son took the driver's seat after putting her suitcase in the trunk. She sat in the passenger's side, and they drove off. That was it. It wasn't any more celebratory than that.

## FBI

In the hospital, there was plenty of time to think. I thought again about Grandfather telling me I could never be an FBI agent. Grandfather was the agent; I was the fish who drowned in my little bowl and was brought back to breathe air outside it. I wondered what he saw in me that he saw in himself. I mean, if he thought I might have been an FBI agent, then he saw something I never saw. I had reached for the moon and come away with a few pebbles not heavy enough to hold down my fear.

Grandfather hung his hat from Saturn's ring and faced the bull head-on. I wanted to close my eyes to the overhead lights but was too afraid to lull in a daydream where flowers rooted in clouds and the earth held me peacefully in a fold of grass. The car ride I took with my grandparents would not be my last, but it was the moment that told the truth of me for many years to come.

Each year would gnaw a bit on my heart, and eventually I would slip from my life again. I was the run in my mother's stocking that nail polish could not stop. Grandfather stopped looking for the FBI agent in me.

## Worms

"Psychodrama: an extemporized dramatization designed to afford catharsis and social relearning for one or more of the participants from whose life history the plot is abstracted" (*Webster's*). Whatever. All I know is that I was dragged to psychodramas. A patient would get in the middle of a circle with two staff trained in psychodrama. The staff would push the patient into reliving past horrors, like sexual abuse. Someone from the audience would get up and act the part of Father or Mother, or siblings. Stranger maybe. *Stranger*, that was a good word for me. I felt like an outsider. I hated the display of emotion. I often left in the middle. A psych tech would chase after me and take me back to the unit.

One time a psych tech came after me and asked me to sit a moment on the curve of sidewalk. I believe her name was Michelle. Michelle had been working with me for months. Finally, I had frustrated her enough that she lost her cool with me.

"You don't feel anything for the victim," she screamed to the edge of her temper.

"Nothing," I said. "Well, anger. Anger for making such a display of themselves."

The truth was, I couldn't handle all the emotions at odds in the room. Much later, I learned this was a component of my own mental illness.

"Don't you feel any compassion for the person?"

"Fuck off, would you." A sentence rather than a question.

"Hasn't anything over these past months softened you?"

Why would I want to be softened? What could being softened do for me? Make me cry like a dweeb? Make me befriend anyone in here? Gladys, Gladys was my friend and now she's gone. Pink Cadillac and all. Fuck anyone else here. God spoke to me and said *beware of imbeciles, they will flatten you every time.*

"You know what the doctor said to my dad? He said I would be in and out of institutions for the rest of my life. My dad got him mad and that's what he spit back. Great thing to look forward to, overdone eggs and whiners."

I stood, tall, head down behind my hair, but tall. "Take me back to the unit, would you?"

And back we went.

I kind of liked Michelle. Too bad that she had grown frustrated with me. Would she continue working with me or just write me off as one who won't or can't change? I didn't tell Michelle that I was feeling changed. It wasn't anger that chased me out of psychodrama, but fear. It was fear. I was terrified of losing control. I was terrified of becoming an emotional wreck. I was terrified of vulnerability. Isolating myself protected me from expecting anything from life. I was living on borrowed time. I never expected to make it to eighteen, and here I was, eighteen. I had spent my birthday in a psychiatric hospital, just as I had Christmas, the New Year, and Easter.

I was drowning. *Please, God, don't let me lose my mind. Take the hum from me so I can better focus.*

That night at dinner, I found a worm in my salad. The head nurse came walking by and I shouted at her that there was a worm in my salad.

"Aren't you happy that you have the whole worm and not half of it?" She flew right by me, offering no concern.

## Cigarettes

In group, there is this young Mexican dude who thinks he is tough. Gangbanger Joe.

Joe shared something with the group and I can't resist: "Oh, big Joe, I'm so scared."

He doesn't like my sarcasm. He jumps from his chair, crosses the room, and punches me on the side of my head. The group monitor can't act fast enough to stop this.

"Oh, big Joe," I say again. Joe backed up and took a boxer's stance.

"Come on chicky, chicky. I'm all over you."

Then Erica, the monitor, steps in. She gets between the two of us and asks Joe to take his seat, and he does. Surprises the hell out of me.

"Group's over. Marlene's here to take you back to the unit. Kristina, you stay."

After all leave, Erica takes a seat next to me and says, "You are just like all the women I see who become criminals. People like you spend their life in prison. Is that what you want? You're certainly working toward it."

Wow—the Voices were screaming at me, laughing at me. I manage to say to her, "Fuck you." Of course I say, "Fuck you."

She is as exasperated with me as Michelle is.

Then she says, "I need something from you. I know you are smart and that you pay attention to everything even though you want us to think you don't." She talks street talk with me. "Someone is bringing in dope. I need to know who. I know you know who."

"What's in it for me?"

"What do you want?"

"A carton of cigarettes." I had started smoking in the hospital. It didn't take me long to get up to three packs a day. My parents were pissed about this. They didn't understand why the staff hadn't stopped me. Had not banned me from smoking.

"I can do that."

"What we talk about stays at the table. Got me?" I ask.

"Of course."

So I tell her. I do know who is sneaking in dope.

* * *

The next day, Jeff and Robin are thrown out of the hospital. I am shocked that you can just be thrown out. But then, they were only here for substance abuse, not for mental illness. Rules are rules. If you use, you lose. I am not sad to see them go.

## Palm Leaves

There was a door between the adolescent and adult units. Paper could be slipped beneath the door. I got some letters before staff did. The adolescents thought I was some sort of magical hero, busting out of the place whenever I wanted to.

Truth was, I did escape weekly. I was good at timing the doors when guests came through for visiting hours. Off I went.

There was a canal nearby. I would run there and hide under palm leaves, thinking they would send a helicopter with a bright light after me. It took me a long time to learn that I just wasn't that important. The government didn't even know my name. I wasn't always convinced of this.

A few hours into the night, I would walk back to the hospital. Ring myself in. I had no place to go to. And I had no money. The psychiatric hospital had become my home. *Not so groovy,* I say. *Keep playing it cool.* And I did for some time.

## Flo

A round little woman with blue shoes and brown hair the color of fall leaves visits me in the hospital. I met her at one of the substance abuse meetings to which the hospital staff took me and the other drunks and drug addicts. I am an eighteen-year-old alcoholic at rest. My grandmother stops bringing me mouthwash when she learns I drink it. She wonders how I went through so much; she thinks I share with the other patients. Always, Grandma Morgan gives me the benefit of the doubt. I love her for her kindness, for seeing first the good in people and, much later, the bad.

The round little woman, Flo, asks me to get a pass so she can take me out of the hospital. I am on the open unit now. I refer to these excursions as field trips; Flo refers to them as Twelve Step meetings. I am still not ready to be an alcoholic in recovery. Alcohol has been my medicine for so long, I cannot imagine living a life sober outside the hospital. Plus, alcohol quiets the hum.

Flo takes me to churches, hospitals, parks, and empty warehouses. Drunks have meetings everywhere. Even on the rooftops of buildings. I imagine myself flying off the building.

At the meetings, I look mean and stand in Flo's shadow. Flo wanders away from me, leaving me alone to obsess on the door. I want out. I overhear their conversations. Flo asks the women to rally around me. She tells them I am terrified and really need their support. I think, *no, I don't want any of them coming near me.* I can't hold a conversation without saying something off the wall, like, "Your underwear is attacking your ass; you could have prevented this by ironing your pants."

An older woman with a platinum bob and long nails walks toward me, smiling. I turn my back to her and pray she comes no closer. A redhead in a black caftan two sizes too big wants to talk with Ms. Platinum. This saves me.

We drive back to the hospital in silence. I hate being heard. My voice is one of the things that is still mine. The hospital stole my dignity. Staff are always searching my room for contraband, and always after a field trip, I am strip-searched. I pretend I am a bird and my feathers need preening. This makes me laugh. They never know if I am a crow or a blue jay or maybe a greedy pigeon.

## Good-byes

Flo really lives in Los Angeles; she travels to Phoenix for business. Every time she is in town, she comes to see me. This time she shows up, I haven't bothered to get a pass. I like her attention, but I also dislike the fact that I like her attention. So in true Kristina fashion, I destroy another thing that might give me hope and a bit of joy.

Flo stands in the doorway, never enters the room. She is wearing blue jeans and a bright yellow T-shirt that says *Peace Is Cotton.* This is the first time I've seen her in pants, the first time I've seen her in sneakers. I want to get up from the bed and give her a big hug. I keep this display of emotion in check.

I can hear people puttering around in the pool yards behind Flo. The sun embraces the back of Flo. I want Flo to come in and sit down. I can't bring myself to ask this of her.

Flo looks straight at me, tosses a book on my bed beside me, and says she can't see me anymore and she hopes I read the book and find a solution.

I say nothing. She turns and leaves. I imagine the sun leaving with her and a dark pall entering the room that smells of feces.

I play her dismissal off as no big deal, like a cat that hides under the bed and claws at the person trying to pet her. Fuck her. Fine. I will soon do something that sends me back to the locked ward anyway.

## Volleyballs

I get weird feelings around Marlene, one of our group therapists. *You have to be kidding me,* I think. *I don't actually love Marlene, do I? No, not possible.*

It is real. I get excited hot flashes around Marlene. I ask my doctor if I am a lesbian because of these feelings I have toward Marlene. He says, "Absolutely not. You are not a lesbian." I am so relieved, until I see Marlene again.

As it turns out, Marlene is gay and I am picking up on it. I sit on a picnic bench with her to the left of the volleyball court where people play and I tell her I love her. She tells me she is flattered.

I ask are my feelings wrong? She says no.

I can't remember the rest of the conversation. I do remember being terrified and excited all at the same time. The volleyball bops me in the head, bringing me back to earth.

## Operator

Somebody from the hospital telephones my father and tells him that I had taken a turn for the worse by staying so long in the hospital. My parents call my doctor, insisting that I be released to their care. I don't want to go. I have come to depend on the easy rhythm of the hospital. My parents tell me I can come to Ohio for a visit and then return to the hospital. I agree.

Grandmother Morgan brings me a new pair of Levis. Size thirteen. I was a size six when I entered the hospital. Too many helpings of food, too many Lorna Doone cookies, too little activity—no wonder I had put on weight. For the past five months all I have worn is sweatpants. The sweatpants have an expanding waistband. I'm not happy to learn that I really am a size thirteen. The doctor says my weight will easily fall away once I am back in the community and making friends. Making friends, ha. I am terrified and now armed with the fact that I am alcoholic and can't drink if I wish to have any kind of life at all. No more taking the edge off with Jack Daniel's.

\* \* \*

My first night in Dayton, I panic. Although I was told that I could return to the hospital at any time, my parents had no intention of sending me back.

I am desperate for Flo. She had planted a seed that desperately needed fertilizer. I telephone the Dayton operator, who hooks me up with the Los Angeles operator. I ask for the number to Flo in Los Angeles. The operator asks me for her last name. I don't have a last name. The operator says he could do nothing without a last name. I tell him I need to find the blade of green grass in the dry hill of hay. The operator hangs up. I would be furious if I weren't so terrified.

I dial the number for Yellow Cab, thank God for phone books. The Yellow Cab dispatcher asks for my address. I don't know it. *Can't you just come get me without it?* I scream into the phone. I need to get to Los Angeles. The dispatcher tells me they wouldn't drive that far, tells me that I should catch a bus. I hang up.

I am as alone as I was the last time I attempted suicide. The room is dark. It's night and I don't want the noise of light. There is a bed and a dresser. The dresser is filled with new clothes my mother had bought me. I curl into a fetal position on the floor and cry. I wish I could still fit under the bed. I would've hidden there.

As a child, I would crawl underneath my bed hoping that one of my parents would come to my aid. They didn't know to do this. They couldn't read my mind.

Tonight, though, I want no one to come. I want the cool breeze of an open window. Finally, I fall asleep. Sometime in the night, one of my parents places a blanket over me.

## Fury

My parents and I are not well together. It is mostly me; I distrust them. They promised I was just coming for a visit to work things out between us, and here I am, stuck in Ohio not knowing the street names, not having a friend to call, not loving anything. Down the road, love was to become a huge motivating factor for me in my recovery.

My parents wanted to believe that I had an eating disorder rather than a drinking problem. We drive to Cincinnati for family counseling, and me for individual counseling, also. The gentleman that runs the family sessions says he thinks of me as wanting to bolt from the room as soon as possible. He has that right; I want to bolt from my life. I learn that he had suggested to my mother that she get individual counseling, also. I wish she had. Maybe the tragedy of her death could have been prevented. She would die an alcoholic death.

My father was very stoic, but attempting to express his feelings. This is all new to our family. We don't do therapy well. We have a hard time identifying how we are feeling. I am impressed that my father is even trying to understand me, to understand himself. He is furious with the doctor in Phoenix. The doctor in Phoenix subtly attacked my father one too many times, insinuating that he had something to do with my emotional problems.

I think we went to family therapy twice. I see the therapist they want me to see once. This therapist asks if I feel like I had an eating disorder and I say no. She asks me if I have ever squeezed a zit, having it symbolize my need to purge. I laugh. This is ridiculous to me. She asks me if I throw up after eating. I answer never. I tell her the only thing I need help with at this time is accepting my homosexuality. I catch her off guard. I guess I surprise her. I tell her my parents don't know, nor do I want them knowing. I tell her that I doubt they would want to pay for me to have sessions around this issue. She wishes me luck. I don't see her again. I think both my parents are relieved that we will not be continuing family therapy. We are only uncomfortable in therapy rather than hopeful.

In Dayton, I start going to Twelve Step meetings for alcoholism. A clubhouse is an hour-and-a-half walk from my parents' home. I can't ask for help, ask for a ride, so in a way, I walk myself into sobriety. I have no real desire to quit drinking; it's been my medicine for so long. But if I drink again, I believe I will overdose again. This fear keeps me walking to meetings. It's a blessing that I don't have to work the first few months I am in Dayton. I walk to the morning meeting, stay for the afternoon meeting, walk home, then walk back to the happy hour meeting, stay for the late meeting, and then walk back home. It's months before I ask anyone for a ride. I don't want to impose. And I still don't know how to ask for help. I don't quite get the thing of "me asking for help helps the person whom I asked."

The members of the club love that I am eighteen and getting sober. In 1982, it's rare that a young person attends meetings. The old-timers love telling me that I am really lucky that I am getting sober so young. This angers me every time one of them says it. All I see is that they came to the program and retired. I don't want to go to school, get a job, and be in a relationship with people sober. I too want to come to the program and retire, with all the stressful things behind me. I don't want to do hard things stone-cold sober. Life is too hard.

My parents continue to not think I'm alcoholic, but they support me in going to meetings. Maybe they see that meetings are changing me. I'm becoming less angry, and I am making friends. My anger initially was volatile. One afternoon, my mother tried to give me a hug and I totally freaked out. I pushed her off me, stormed down the hall, punched out the glass lights as I went, and then smashed a potted plant that stood at attention at the door, on my way out. My father searched my room while I was gone, looking for money he would take to pay for the damages. And he did find money. And he did take money from me. I was even more furious. My fury kept me from loving them. My fury kept me from loving anything. I was desperate to care. How does one begin to bring care to a rusted automobile? One panel at a time. I began by showering every day and putting on a fresh set of clothes.

At this time in Dayton, Rose is living and working for Motorola in Phoenix, and Hunter is living with a family in Cincinnati swimming with the aquatics team there and finishing up high school. I am not in touch with either of them. The stint in the psych hospital has left me feeling estranged from everyone I knew prior to entering the hospital.

## Nicotine

By the grace of God, I do what the people in the meetings are telling me to do, and my life and attitude start to change. I find fellowship and begin to thrive—like a lizard's tail, I begin to grow back beautifully. This beautiful was not always apparent to others. My internal life was still just that—mine. And I was still experiencing psychiatric symptoms that I was hiding for the most part.

The people give me things to do at the club like make coffee, empty ashtrays, clean the nicotine off the paneled walls, things like that. These activities help keep the Voices I hear at bay. I have very real things to focus on.

Sometimes I talk crazy in the meetings. Hell, I had just come from a psych hospital where everyone talked crazy. I tell the members of the group that my clock was talking to me, so I threw it against the wall to stop it. It put a dent in the wall before breaking into pieces.

I tell them that outer space is alive and it seems to me if I just jump high enough my feet would leave the ground and I'd be able to lasso a cloud, which would ferry me to outer space. Things in outer space must be easier than things on Earth.

I imagine rainbows adorning my wrists as I sit in coffeehouses whenever I want, drinking steam from a cup of hope. I pick oranges from my tree and offer them to others. The bright blaze of their smiles leaves me smiling. I hold a box of crayons in my hand, color outside the lines, creating a full page of purple.

I am above my skin, making a slight wind that helps blow other people's hair into place.

Marcus catches my breeze. He is five years sober, in his late thirties, and people at the club treat him like a guru. And he is married, separated but married. This doesn't keep him from flirting with me.

Marcus and I become a secret item. He doesn't want people to know we are seeing each other, and I don't care about this because I am simply happy to be with him when I can be. That is, until his back surgery.

He has major back surgery. I want to go to the hospital and visit him, but one of his closest friends, Tim, tells me not to go because I might run into Marcus's wife. Though separated, they were still husband and wife. The reality of this hits me hard and I decide I will not see Marcus any longer.

Marcus phones me the day he gets out of the hospital. He tells me that if ever there was a time he needed me, it's now. Sucker. I was such a sucker. I pick him up from the clubhouse and we go to the home of a friend who is out of town.

It's evening. The house is really dark. Marcus leads me by the hand to the master bedroom upstairs. He turns on a little light. Everything has a dreamlike quality to it.

We both strip naked. I am on the bottom, he, the top. He is thrusting hard when I hear it—a pop. "Marcus, stop," I say. "Something is wrong." And I am right, something is terribly wrong. The stitches in his back broke. A huge, gaping hole let me see his spine. I tell Marcus to lie still on his stomach while I call for an ambulance. I run downstairs to the phone. The operators are on strike and will not give me a connecting number to the hospital or ambulance. I'm in a strange house and have no idea where the telephone books are.

Panicked, I phone my dad. I could tell I woke him up. I tell him I need the number to the hospital. He starts to question me. I tell him I'm with my friend who had just had back surgery and that I need to get him to the hospital. My father continues to question me, so I hang up.

I run back upstairs. Marcus is standing like a child, in shock. I help him pull on a pair of shorts and do the only next thing I knew to do—I walk him slowly down the stairs, out the door, and seat him in my car.

I pray my car will start, as it sometimes doesn't. It starts and I race to the emergency room. There, I snatch the first medical person I see and explain the condition of my friend. He at once grabs another medical person and they both head to my car right outside the glass door.

They put Marcus on a gurney and rush him into an operating room. I am left to answer questions from the intake lady. She asks me if I am his wife. I say no. After that, I remember no questions. I call Tim and let him know what had happened. Tim rushes to the hospital. He asks me to leave. I feel so at fault and so ashamed that I had not listened to my intuitive self. That is the last night I ever spend with him.

## Jane

I move with my parents from Ohio to San Clemente, California. I will create a life for myself here, although the plan is for me to move to Columbia, Missouri, to attend Stephens College in the fall. The abrupt move from California to Missouri is indicative of my alcoholism. I am always thinking someplace else will be better. I still move in and out of people's lives with little consideration of anyone else's feelings.

It is beautiful here. I can walk from my home to the beach. The house was large. Upstairs, downstairs, four bedrooms, two baths, and a great bar. The bar always sold my parents on the home. This home even has a wine cellar. I dream of someday having a home with a fabulous juice bar. I can still have all the pretty bottles and crystal glasses, just a different beverage than booze.

The first Twelve Step meeting for my sobriety that I go to is in Laguna Beach. There was a clubhouse there. Laguna Beach has a large gay community. My father calls it the granola country, the place of fruits and nuts. I don't tell him that such a place is perfect for me.

The meeting I attend is for women. I introduce myself as new in town when the chairperson asks if there is anyone from out of town. Everyone claps, welcoming me.

"Don't get too crazy here," the Voices say to me. "Don't let anyone know you're human."

"Bug off," I tell them telepathically.

The Voices have been a low drone for some time. I credit this fact to my sobriety. Sobriety comes with a series of steps to live by and a group of people who can identify with the experience of being a drunk, and then the experience of getting sober and staying sober. With no alcohol tethering my brain, somehow my chemistry straightens itself out a bit. I think. I don't know. I still experience the low drone and the paranoia that accompanies that—I'm afraid of being found out. Afraid that people might learn I have a dial on my brain that turns itself, sometimes dumping me into another reality from the common reality. The other realities consist of the second reality that allows me to hear the Voices clearly. They mimic everything I do. I sit, they say you sit. I eat, they say you eat. They invite me to join them, tell me how beautiful their world is and how free from problems it is. They also command me to do things like run over that pedestrian in the red jacket with my car. The third reality leaves me catatonic. And the fourth reality is the reality that they want me to join them in. To date, I have never been to the third or fourth reality. The drug overdoses were an attempt to get into the fourth reality. But it didn't work, and I thought the Voices lied to me. Much later, when I am talking about the Voices, my therapist would remind me that the Voices always lie to me.

I am happy in sobriety just hearing a hum.

After the meeting, a woman comes up to me with a meeting list. She has circled the meetings that she likes. I intuitively know this woman is gay and wondered if that influenced the meetings she circled. It didn't. I learned by attending them that all the meetings were for anybody with a desire to stop drinking. Gay or straight, it didn't matter.

At another women's meeting in Mission Viejo, I arrive early so that I can make a beeline to the back of the room. The meeting is at a preschool, so the tables we sit around are low and the seats, tiny. The tables create a U-shape so everybody can see everybody.

In walks Flo. I blink hard, and blink again. *Oh my God,* I think, *you have to be kidding me.* I get up from my seat and approach the door; Flo turns to me and smiles. Ha. She remembers me. She gives me a big hug, welcomes me to the meeting, and says it is a miracle that I am standing there before her. Miracle, indeed.

Behind Flo is a woman who should never wear heels. She clomps in partially bent over from the height of the shoe. Flo introduces her to me. Jane is her name. Flo sponsors her in the program. Flo tells me Jane would be a perfect sponsor for me. *Great. A clodhopper,* I thought. But Jane is great. She is honest and funny and has time to give me.

That night was the first of many nights that would change my life. My dark had a shine to it that would keep me moving forward each day. An automobile rarely hits someone standing on the sidewalk, and I was becoming good at standing on sidewalks, away from the curb, crossing only on green lights. Jane helped me to do this, as well as Flo and many other recovering alcoholics. It felt good settling in. Ohio had become a distant memory.

### Girlfriend

The recovery program from alcoholism has Twelve Steps. One of the Steps asks that I make an inventory of my life, listing all my character defects, fears, and resentments and then share it with another person. I do this with my sponsor, Jane. After sharing it with another person, the list is used to make an amends list from. I had listed many girlfriends. At the height of my alcoholism and into early sobriety, my inability to love was daunting. How had I become so calloused at such a young age? My sponsor said that by noting it on paper, by bringing it into my consciousness, and by wanting to change, I would eventually soften and maybe love again. She didn't say definitely love again; she told me things would be different without promising me things would get better. I appreciated this because, sober for a good ten months, life had not gotten easier.

I saved my list, but balled it up and threw it in the corner of my desk in my bedroom before leaving for a trip to San Francisco with my girlfriend, Arielle. From San Clemente, it was a six-hour drive north. We were excited to get away for a weekend. I hadn't seen San Francisco since I was a kid.

San Francisco was amazing. We did all the touristy things: went to Alcatraz and stepped into a cell to feel what confinement there would be like; went to the wharf and ate hot sourdough bread dripping with butter; ate chocolate at Ghirardelli Square; walked the many hills and rode the trolley. And we held hands. I had never held hands with a woman in public. I didn't want to attract attention. In San Francisco, everyone was holding hands. How cool is that?

Upon returning, I find my inventory spread out on my desk. I immediately panic and then go into a rage. I ask Arielle to leave.

My mother eventually comes home, with a friend. Because she comes in with a friend, my anger is kept in check. I ask Mom, "Why?" She knows what I am talking about and informs me that if I can go into her closet for a belt, she can go into my room any time she likes, and read anything she wants to read.

She calls me sick and accuses me of wanting to be a man. This was so far from the truth. Her friend is uncomfortable and tells my mom she will call her later, then leaves.

My mother tells me she isn't certain when she will tell my father that I am a lesbian. But she will do it. I don't correct her and tell her that I am really bisexual. It doesn't matter. All she keeps in mind is that I have had many female lovers.

My parents hate gay people—one of the worst things a person could be is gay. (My acceptance of myself comes with years.) My sexuality is a beautiful thing to me, and I wasn't going to let my mother hold this over my head like an ax. I would tell my father myself.

* * *

I find my father in his bedroom stretched out on the floor watching Sunday football. I sit on the bed and ask him if he has noticed the tension between Mom and me. He says yes without turning his head and looking at me, engrossed in the game. "Well, Dad," I said, "I am bisexual, and Mom found this out." Without missing a beat or pausing, my father says without turning his head, "I don't know what I'm going to do about this yet."

And that is it. He says no more. He continues to watch football, and I leave the room.

It is two weeks before I will get in my car and drive to Columbia, Missouri, to go to school at Stephens College.

Later that day, my father corners me in the garage. I had gone down there to look for a hammer so I might hang a picture of lights on my bedroom wall. My father says, "You are dead to me, and if I hadn't promised you school already, I would not be helping to pay for it. I know you will mess up. You always do. So when you get kicked out of Stephens, remember we're done with you, and you have no home with us here." And then he walks away.

For the next two weeks, my father literally treats me as if I am invisible. He doesn't look at me; he doesn't talk to me. If I am in the room when he is talking to Mom, he talks through me.

I am glad when the two weeks are up. I am determined to make school work and finish my degree.

## Stephens

My mother would accuse me of going to Stephens because it was an all-women's college aside from fifteen men who are there on full scholarship to major in theater. Not true. I recalled one of my advisors in high school telling me that I should consider attending Stephens College. The advisor may have recommended Stephens because she saw how much I struggled simply to be in attendance and felt that a small school would embrace me and assist me more than a larger school, where I would be one of many.

Because no one had withdrawn me from my courses at ASU, I had been assigned Fs in most of my classes. I had a 1.0 GPA.

Stephens required me to write an essay about why they should let me into their college. I wish I had that essay now, to see how much further along I am than when I wrote it. I know I told them everything. I told them about being in a psych hospital and about being in recovery from alcoholism. I must have come across as sincerely wanting to change my life. I wanted a bachelor's degree. I was determined to get it. Stephens accepted me on academic probation.

Stephens College was a great fit for me because it was small, and the class sizes were no larger than twenty-five people to one professor. As I advanced in my coursework, the class sizes grew even smaller.

When it came time to choose an advisor, I marched over to Vivian Walker's office. I had been told that she was tough, and toughness appealed to me. I took it to mean that she would never lie to me. I needed that kind of support.

Her office was amazing. Dark wood, floor-to-ceiling bookshelves. Books stacked on the floor because there was no more room on the shelves. And a daunting desk that seemed even larger because Vivian was very slight. She was dressed impeccably, with reading glasses hanging from a chain around her neck.

She motioned for me to sit in the chair on the other side of the desk, facing her.

"What can I do for you?"

"I want you to be my advisor."

"And why should I do that?"

I offered her my journals. "Read them. I promise you'll find me in their pages and be moved to help me."

A few days later, she calls me into her office and tells me she will be honored to be my advisor. This is one of the best moments of my life.

\* \* \*

And then there was one of the worst moments of my life. I learned years later, after I had graduated, that Vivian had died. I learned this when I phoned her home to wish her happy Thanksgiving. Her husband answered, and let me know. It was lung cancer, and it took her fast. He said he didn't know how to contact me, so that's why he didn't. I got off the phone with him, shocked. I hadn't been able to tell Vivian again how much I loved her and to thank her for how supportive she had been of me. What do I do when I'm in grief? I write.

Dear Vivian,

I remember the last letter I wrote you in 1990. I was sitting on the corner of First and Pacific in downtown Long Beach at a coffee bar after work. The library, where I worked, was the gray cement building directly across Pacific. It was raining, and the rivulets of water were making their spontaneous Kandinsky, all in verticals, across the windows. The bronze statue of roughly twenty feet in height stood in the courtyard of the library. It was of a single man in an overcoat and hat carrying a newspaper tucked in the crook of his left elbow, extending his right to shake the hand of an invisible adult or brush the cheek of an adolescent. The statue had caught my eye as I wrote you, and I remember including it in my short note to you. I had written about what the newspaper meant to the statue and what the newspaper meant to the homeless woman who slept at the base of Mr. Bronze. The homeless woman was stretched out on her back, with newspaper covering her clothed body from her chest to her forehead, cupping itself beneath her head. Her hands were folded on her stomach. Her dirty white Keds pointed at ten after ten. The polyester pants molded against her legs, hinting at the shape of her knee in their wetness. The newspaper, also soaked in rain, plastered itself to her face, and she lay as if her head and chest were a papier-mâché headdress and breast plate, unable to protect her adequately from the rain. I imagined the ink of the paper printing onto her face as it would onto Silly Putty in dry conditions. I was awed to think that Mr. Bronze represented more freedom than the homeless woman although he was forever rooted to his base in the courtyard and could not wipe pigeon shit from his body while the woman could. She could walk into the ocean or catch a cab on a good day of panhandling, while he forever reached for that invisible person to touch. And he was more free. The freedom was in the imagining of that hand connecting with another living soul, moved by the spirit of kindness and recognition, whereas the homeless woman did not extend her hand in kindness and recognition. I saw her daily picking her teeth and her nose as she sat back on her heels having one-sided conversations with everyone who passed her. She commented on clothes and the color of a person's hair, the baldness of the woman strung out on drugs and the roundness of the youth who always seemed to swallow a cinnamon doughnut just before entering the library. She reached for babies in strollers and young mothers screeched and the babies cried. And all this I wrote you in the small space of a postcard with a cat and a fish on the front.

Walking into your office at the college president's mansion was one of the wisest things I have done. I needed an advisor and was instructed to see you by one of my friends, who felt I needed somebody brilliant with a serious disposition and direct way of speaking truths. You were not taking on any more students, but I left my journals with you to read anyhow, hoping that you would indeed read them and fall in love with the person you found in the pages. You did fall for me. I do not know that it was love, but you were interested in seeing a person with a 1.0 GPA on academic probation who strung words together like lights and silver garland on a Christmas tree succeed in college. You became my queen and I a female knight of your court.

## Fame

I have gotten special permission to move into the dormitory early, ahead of the other students. Because of my previous experience with roommates, I have also gotten permission to room alone. It is a warm day in August. I am wearing Hawaiian shorts and a white T-shirt. I park my minivan on the street across from the Physical Plant and Maintenance Building where I have to pick up my key. I climb the steps to the second floor and walk up to the counter. A young woman with a fabulously long blond ponytail gets up from her desk and asks me what I need.

I explain to her that I had gotten special permission to move into the dorm early.

"Are you famous?"

"What?" I answer.

"Are you famous?"

I assure her not. "You look famous, and I recognize your name." She had received a memo to give me the key.

I leave with the key.

\* \* \*

A few days later, as I get into the driver's seat of my minivan, I notice a piece of paper stuck under my windshield wiper. I reach for it. It says, "I want to make a peanut butter and banana sandwich for you." Nothing else. No name.

I go about my business.

The next day there is a note again. "Are you hungry? How about carrot cake?" *Ha,* I thought. *This is crazy fun.* I just knew that the person behind the notes would eventually let me know who they were.

That night, I go clubbing with a couple of women I met at Stephens. I dress in the style of the day: oversized pajama bottoms, a black men's jacket, and a T-shirt. Men's jackets have an inside pocket where I can keep my driver's license and keys. No need to carry a purse.

The room is covered with mirrors; the dance floor is wood and large. The bar is off to the right as I enter. In a back room attached to the larger room, people can sit and talk with each other without the booming of the music.

I love dancing by myself. Especially to The Cure. The Cure is playing. I dance.

In the doorway of the backroom stands the woman with the long ponytail who works at the Physical Plant and Maintenance Building. I stop dancing and cross the floor.

"Hello," I said. "Remember me?"

"You're the famous one. My name's Annie."

"Annie. Nice." The "nice" just slipped out. The woman was gorgeous.

"Would you like me to bake you a carrot cake tonight?"

"It's you who's sending the notes."

"Yes."

"How did you know it was my car?"

"I saw you park it from the window."

"I love carrot cake."

We dance that night. I do end up going to her house around midnight. And she did make me a carrot cake. I asked her months later why she did that. She said she wanted me to stay and figured I would if I had something sweet to eat. Ha. She didn't know me from Frank, and yet guessed right that I could be influenced by sweets.

## Flowers (1988)

At Stephens, I am allowed to initiate my own major; I'm allowed to pick my course of study. I decide to major in English and Women Studies with a heavy emphasis on creative writing. I decide to write a play that culminates all the experiences I have had at Stephens. This is my senior project.

I'm overwhelmed my senior year; there is so much to do in finishing everything. I begin to isolate. Annie and I have been off and on the past year. I live in a dorm that is locked at the front door, so only people living there had a key, and if a person was to be a guest, she or he would need to set up the visit ahead of time so the host could let them in. The locked door does not prevent Annie from coming in whenever she pleases. The other residents also find her beautiful and charming and think for certain I would always want her to come in when she pleased. This is not the case.

The end of our relationship comes on the eve she knocks at my door at midnight, drunk. I answer the door because she refuses to go away. She reeks of cigarettes and beer.

"What do you want?"

"You," she says.

"You can't have me."

"Why?"

I don't know how to respond to this. I really don't know why other than the fact that I believe I cannot finish my degree if distracted, and Annie is a huge distraction.

"Please go, Annie." And she gives me a hard stare—she was good at hard stares—and leaves. I am mixed about our relationship. This evening will not be the last time I see her, only the last time for a while.

I have been going to bed at 7 p.m. and waking at 4 a.m. all semester long. This doesn't make it very convenient to remain friends with people. I literally only visit with people over lunch and dinner.

Vivian was concerned for me because I was losing a tremendous amount of weight. The stress eats at me.

I visit the psychologist on campus. She is lovely and warm and wears an outrageous straw hat whenever she is outside in the sun. Mabel says I can talk with her whenever I want, but she wants me to also see someone outside the college. She tells me I am too complicated, and my problems too many, for her to handle all alone. She refers me to Justin, who used to be a student of hers long ago.

Justin is great. He has a generous smile that makes me feel comfortable right away. He appreciates that Mabel has sent me to him, but he tells me he feels I need to be in therapy with a woman and refers me to one of his colleagues.

I feel shuttled around, but do report to Helen anyway.

I hate being at Helen's. She doesn't allow smoking during session. And to top that, during our fourth session, she tells me that she is unwilling to go to the dark places my mind takes me. What the hell does that mean? She won't go where I go? I don't even know where it is I go. I remember standing on the sidewalk outside her office, which was in this great two-story Tudor house, crying because I didn't know what is going on with me or anyone else.

That was the end of therapy for me. It was nice to simply drop in on Mabel occasionally to talk of things like flowers littering a certain patch of grass.

## The Black Ant

Professor Brown, my playwright instructor, stops me outside the library below the crisp sun and says to me to stop playing solitaire. He says to me to write, tells me we need to hear what I have to say. I don't know how he knows this.

I try to imagine saying more than *tree, dog, heat*—the heat of the tree covers the dog in the shade. This is what I know. This, all I want to know. The rest belongs in the shade with the dog.

I sit really still, lean against the outside wall of the library, and forget that I know how to read, forget I used to find pleasure in books.

There is something occurring in me that is quiet. Cotton falls 500 feet to land on the back of a pigeon. Quiet. The bird takes flight. The cotton sticks. The bird is untroubled by a bit more weight.

I am the place of my feet. I am the place of my heart. I am the place of my mind. An iron pole runs up my back, forcing me to be tall. The tall forces me to see.

A giraffe looks beyond the tree to find water.

* * *

I write outside the library, *the woman is crying in her bed. Gershwin plays from the radio on the nightstand. The smell of an extinguished wick curls around her ear.*

*Beauty is being lost in her bedsheets.*

*A bottle of whiskey lies at her head, soaking the pillow. The bottle of pills is empty.*

Say *empty*—it hollows my tongue, echoes in my throat. It is not a nice word.

*Little dogs lie on the floor beside her bed. They will be forced to leave her.* I cry at this. Is this the kind of writing Professor Brown is asking me to write? A death drama in which I wish I really played a part.

* * *

The something is occurring in me. It is larger than me, pulls on my hair, lifts me to my feet.

Ten toes, an arch moving to the heel—they hold me up. I think to lie down. I am the place of my mind—it keeps me standing, climbs me up the steps of the library. I become public.

There is a book in row A, second shelf. I pull it down. It is heavy in my hands, the weight of a fat pigeon.

I thumb through it, land on the word *stay*, land on the word *be*, land on the word *color*—*stay and be color.* I cry again.

* * *

Professor Brown stops me outside beneath the moon, says to me to stop playing solitaire. I don't know that I can. The wool blanket is heavy. I don't know that I want to. The wool blanket is heavy, is red, is too large to bury. I cry again.

* * *

Is there night where you are? The kind of night that lies on your back like a wet beach towel that is hard to wring out; it stretches the length of a cactus. My arm span is just not that long.

The night living in me steals me from your voice, steals from me soft laughter in the stripe of pink painted across the foreheads of young girls heading into the library.

I pocket kind eyes as I do scraps of paper.

In night the dawn waits behind the bulletin board in the park, advertising avocados. Is there night where you are? The kind that sucks heat from your brow, leaves you kneeled in the stones of your rock garden.

The desert night is not thick with leaves. Gray wanders the side of the mountain, a silhouette of strength. I imagine you stand still. A bat is able to fly just above your head, not threatened by the smell of you.

Is this the kind of writing Professor Brown is asking me to write? The anonymous "you" whom I know to be close to me?

\* \* \*

I drop the night I'm living in. It puddles at my feet. Sticks to my soles. Challenges me to move into the exaggerated light of day. Exaggerated because it has been a long go in night with my eyes closed to any element other than visions that play across the screen in my mind.

The first vision places me on a bridge with a girl who wishes to jump. I see the bottom of her soles as she dives headfirst to the street below. There was no word or scream, only tires screeching in an attempt to miss her.

She rose on the wing of a taillight, red in her ascent. A soft red which mixed into the night—no explosion, just the last sound of a single bird on its way home.

I won't speak to the second vision, but it did move me forward, shook the dark right out of me, knowing I could rest in the silhouette of the mountain.

It is the nature of night to be dark, but then the moon gets thrown in to pull at our bellies, to pull us right out of our pants before we become lost like a black ant in the bottom of a black bowl.

Professor Brown wants to know about the black ant.

## White Roses

MTV, the music channel of music videos, began my senior year at Stephens College. I would sit for hours watching one violent scene after another. The music was screaming to be heard, and screaming to be seen. I had a reputation for being a peaceful human, dreaming of a peaceful world. Because of this, my friends and other students didn't understand why I would spend my time this way. Why I would subject my psyche to such trash.

I didn't see MTV as trash or wicked. I saw it as a cultural phenomenon. What a great way to emote. Violence. Anger. Love. Inspiration. Sex. Tenderness. MTV offered it all. As a blossoming writer, I wanted to be centered in culture. The play I was working on was an account of daily circumstance of my character, Mere Crayon. In one scene, she is eating an apple. In another scene, she is contemplating joining the army. The newspaper articles she read on stage were violent. The personal letters she read, loving.

The one-night showing of *Mere Crayon* filled the theater past capacity. People actually sat on the floor at the edge of the stage. I sat in the back row watching it all. My moment of fame at twenty-four.

My parents sent me a dozen white roses. They made me cry. It wasn't that long ago that my father wasn't speaking to me. They would have come to the show had they not been in Germany at the time.

One thing I learned with the production of my play is that nothing is worth anything if people aren't involved in my life. I had been going to bed at 7 p.m. and waking at 4 a.m. all semester long. I was not participating in relationships with people. All I did was study and write. After the play was performed, I remember standing in the hall outside my dorm room, excited and pumped with adrenaline, wanting to tell someone what an amazing experience I had had. Because I had so isolated myself, there was no one to call. My success was worth very little without having anyone to share it with. I vowed from that day forward that I would give more to my friends other than lunch and dinnertime conversations. I would walk with them, sit with them, go places together like to the mall or the movies or even the grocery store. The best would be watching the sun go down for a place in the grass.

## Aid

The entire time I am at Stephens I go to Twelve Step meetings. I don't know if it's because I'm in a small town in the Midwest, but there are very few young people in attendance at the meetings. Columbia, Missouri, includes the University of Missouri, two art colleges whose names I can't remember, and Stephens. For a college town, I expect more students.

It is snowing. The snow is white sheets laid over the branches of trees. The sun is making its descent like the tire of a Mustang that is driving with caution on the iced streets. Color is a shroud blanketing the sky, falling off the hanger as night introduces itself. This puts me at ease.

In the meetings it is said that all who have a desire to stop drinking are welcome. The front door of the church is over eight feet tall and solid with a single angel carved into its dark wood. I take a seat at a long cafeteria-style table in the church basement. There are no windows; time feels frozen. In walks this woman who is obviously strung out. I place her in her late twenties. She is drooling and bent over. Her jeans are ripped at the knees. Her boots no longer shine. Her eyes look wild and she is shaking. She disrupts the meeting and says she needs help. The word *help* clatters on the tile floor. The old man running the meeting asks her if she is alcoholic. She says she is a drug addict. The old man says she is not welcome. I'm certain I heard wrong until he tells her to leave.

His beard guards his face. He is off limits to criticism. She leaves. I am shocked. I don't know what to do. Should I go after her? I lose my respect for the people in the meeting. I understand the old man was following the traditions that state the only requirement for membership is a desire to stop drinking. Had he given her enough time to think whether or not she was also alcoholic? Maybe the word *alcoholic* would wrap itself around her chest and her heart would pound out *I am an alcoholic*. At this time, there are few meetings for people who only identify as drug addicts.

The arm of the program is not there for her. I feel miserable, but I decide to stay in the meeting and not go after her. I never see her again.

Another time, a drunk is asked to leave the clubhouse. A man with long sobriety told this drunk that he had been coming long enough for doughnuts and coffee without showing any motivation to get sober. The old-timer tells the man he needs to leave. The man is in his forties. I can smell his breath. Cigarettes, beer, and wasted aftershave covet his face. The old-timer tells him he will be welcome when he shows a desire to stop drinking. The drunk leaves. I am shocked again. I said to the old-timer, "I thought all are welcome!"

The old-timer replies, "If you show no effort in stopping drinking, show no desire to do so, you don't belong here."

Amazingly, the man he sends away gets sober at the end of the month and stays sober. He takes a two-year medallion while I am still in Missouri.

* * *

I have attended thousands of meetings and only twice have I seen people turned away. The hand of the Twelve Step program really is always there. I include this with the hope that people will be startled into knowing that aid can be provided and the traditions of the meetings can be upheld at the same time.

## Graduation

I graduated from Stephens College with a bachelor of arts in English and women's studies. Only from this small college could I receive a degree; I was able to design my own field of studies, the classes were small, I had access to my professors.

My parents were at my graduation. We did not discuss my dating life. I was happy to have them there. To have held on to resentment would have affected my relationship with God. My spiritual beliefs at this time were gracefully unfolding like sheets from a hot dryer. I didn't want to wrinkle my connection.

Grandma and Grandpa Morgan also came, as did Grandma Poser. Grandpa Poser stayed in Phoenix, complaining about how much the flight was. Grandma Poser slept in my bed at the dorm and I on the futon. This saved her money. They were all proud of me.

As for mental illness, I struggled. The plague had yet to catch me completely. I thought of it as a Stephen King novel. I knew it was there, I knew something was happening, but in the first 300 pages it had yet to reveal itself. I was on page 150. I still had time before my heart was cut out and my mind completely poisoned.

Annie and I had gotten back together again right after the production of my play. She also sent me a dozen white roses, which melted my heart. We separated at graduation. She had graduated with a degree in philosophy from the University of Missouri and had received a scholarship from another school in their doctorate program. The loss of her didn't leave my heart broken. Today, looking back, I think it was because my mental illness was affecting my ability to grow close enough to anyone to really be hurt by them. Strange, yes. The mind is an amazing instrument. Mine alternated between the low strings of a violin and the hearty blast of a saxophone.

I left Missouri in my van for San Clemente, California, where I would live a short time with my parents.

# Women

## Home

The house in San Clemente is the same house I had left for Stephens. My parents have actually managed to stay in one place for a while. The house is two stories, in a gated community. All the houses looked different because all the houses had different builders. I liked that the houses didn't all look the same. It made it easier to find the right driveway. My parents have a balcony outside their second-floor master bedroom. My mom waves at me as I pull into the driveway at the end of the long drive from Missouri. It has taken me three days. It feels great that my mother is welcoming me back. It is a Friday, so Dad is still at work.

Once inside, Mom comes down the stairs, gives me a hug, and offers to make me a drink. I remind her that I no longer drink.

"Oh, that's right," she says. "How about coffee?"

"That would be great," I say.

Brandy wanders in and bumps into the island in the middle of the kitchen.

"She doesn't see so great any longer," Mom says. "Or hear well."

"Someone told me that as long as the dog is still eating, she isn't suffering," I respond.

"She's certainly still eating. A bag of chow a week," Mom says.

There is a pause. Brandy walks out of the kitchen before I can love on her. Mom pours my coffee and adds creamer and two Sweet'N Low packets. She remembers. I'm touched.

"How is Dad?" I ask after a long sip of coffee.

"Oh, you know, working a lot, spending a lot. Watching a great deal of television when he is home. We're golfing together, though. Even playing a bit of tennis."

There are a couple of tennis courts in the complex.

"And we love going to the golf clubhouse for drinks and dinner." Mom pauses, picks invisible lint from her purple shirt. "It's good to have friends for longer than a year. I finally feel like a part of a community. As far as I know, your dad likes it too."

Now, I knew I was going to be treading water with my next question. It was no longer me whom they settled their stern gaze on. "How are Rose and Hunter?"

"We don't hear from Rose much. I do know that she is still working at Motorola. I think she is relatively happy. And Hunter, well that's another story." Mom lit a cigarette and poured herself a vodka. Brandy wandered in again, and again, hit her head on the island.

"One of your father's associates enjoys peep shows; that's where a person pays to see someone naked in a room, doing whatever the person asks, dancing or whatever—"

"I know, Mom, you don't need to explain any more."

"Well, this associate in Tucson ran into your sister. Well, he kind of ran into your sister. She was the one doing the dancing or whatever. Hunter couldn't see him. Only he could see her. We were going to call you, ask you if you knew anything about it, but we just never got around to it." She taps the ashes of her cigarette into a bowl nearby. "Have you heard from her?"

"No, Mom. The last I knew is that she had been accepted to the University of Arizona and was attending classes there."

"One of her friends describes her as jetting around Tucson in her brand-new baby blue Corvette, spending wads of money dining and wining with people. And they don't think it stops with that. They think Hunter is also doing drugs." She's at the end of her cigarette.

"I'm sorry, Mom. I don't know what to say."

"We have stopped sending her money. Our last conversation with her ended in her hanging up. We, of course, let her know what Paul, your dad's associate, said. She said, 'Well, he must not be of high moral character if he is investing money and time in peep shows.' She has always been good at turning the tables. Do you want more coffee?"

"No thanks, Mom."

She poured herself more vodka. "One of our friends we talked with about her said she must be doing a hell of a lot more in the sex industry if she can afford to buy a new Corvette. The sex industry—do you think she could be involved in that?" This is the first moment Mom looks me in the eyes. She has picked all the lint from her shirt.

"I really don't know anything about Hunter. It has been years since we've spoke. No reason really. We were both just busy with our lives. Last I knew she was swimming with that team in Cincinnati and finishing up high school. I thought she had a chance for the Olympics, but it sounds like she pissed that away."

"Yeah. Before we learned she wasn't going to classes, we learned this from one of her girlfriends who was concerned about her; we thought she was swimming for the U of A."

I had no more response. Maybe her as sexual deviant was tolerated even less than my bisexuality.

"I didn't mean to put a downer on your first hour home. Do you want help unloading your van?"

"Thanks Mom, I can take care of it." I was excited to move into my bedroom and create my own nest.

I left the kitchen, admired the stained glass on the front door—a swan and a young woman draped in burgundy—and stepped onto the drive. I popped open the back end of the van and began with the futon.

Typically, a murmur, the Voices are clear. "You'll never be happy here. They hate you. Hang it up. Go away. You won't be happy here." I tell them to fuck off, and focus harder on the activity at hand. The weight of the futon in my hands does the trick. They return to a murmur.

\* \* \*

Dad arrives just as I am putting my last book on the shelf. He stands in my bedroom doorway and welcomes me.

"Hi, Kris. How was the drive?"

"Good Dad, thanks."

"Mom almost has dinner done. Are you coming down to eat?"

"Absolutely."

There is an awkward pause between us, then he says, "Good. I'll see you downstairs."

He turns, leaves. I have tears in my eyes that he doesn't see. It is so good to have him back in my life. I couldn't have asked for a better homecoming.

## Tony

At this time, 70 percent of the people I date are women, leaving 30 percent men. This would much later reverse itself to where 70 percent of the people I dated were men, and 30 percent women.

I had a crush on Clare and would have gone anywhere with her. She lived in the next city over from San Clemente, Dana Point. I met her in one of the Twelve Step meetings I attended. She had long dark hair, strong hands, and a distinct voice that reminded me of a game show host. She was comfortable in jeans and T-shirts. Her sneakers were immaculate.

Clare had been asked to speak at a meeting in Oceanside. She asked if I would like to accompany her. Yes, yes. She picked me up from my parents' house and we drove to Oceanside.

When we got there, Tony greeted us. He was running the meeting. He had saved two seats up front for us. I informed him that I sat in the back row.

"Oh yeah?" he said.

"Yes," I said.

He grabbed a folding chair from the last row and moved it farther back, all the way to the door. It looked lonesome. We tried to stare each other down. I think he thought I would change my mind and sit up front. Nothing doing. I plopped myself into the chair he had pulled out for me.

And that was that. Clare spoke. Everyone listened. Then we got in the car and drove back. I didn't think any more about Tony until he started showing up at my Tuesday night meeting—the gong show. Even then, I didn't think much of him showing up there, driving all the way from Oceanside to Dana Point to go to a meeting. The distance wasn't unheard of. In fact, he asked me if I would like to go to a meeting he taped in Santa Monica on Fridays.

"Santa Monica," I said. "Isn't that awfully far to go for a meeting?" I was thinking about the distance from San Clemente to Santa Monica, not the distance from Oceanside to Santa Monica, which was considerably more.

"It's a great meeting," he said. "Speaker meeting. Easily a thousand people attend. And the speakers are outstanding."

*What the hell?* I thought. It never occurred to me he was hitting on me. I was being a good little lesbian, thinking everyone knew I was hot for Clare. It really never occurred to me that a man would hit on me. I liked Tony. He was a good man. Maybe at a different time, in a different place, I would have responded to his affections.

## Loaded

It's Friday late afternoon. Tony pulls up to my parents' house in a rickety gold Chevy with two other men. I can see smoke spilling out of the windows. It was a good thing that at this time I still smoked. Three packs a day. Quite the habit.

I settle into the passenger's seat. Tony introduces George and George.

"You're kidding, right?" I say.

"No. Meet George and George. You can call the one with the stiff collar and pressed pants Georgette, if you'd like."

"Stop, Tony," Georgette says. "It's George, I mean, I'm George."

"Hello, George and George," I say.

My mom is standing at the door. She waves us off. Tony backs out of the drive and off we go in a puff of exhaust and cigarette smoke.

It takes us a good two hours to get there. People wrap around the synagogue waiting to get in. I am not looking forward to the wait in line. Tony lets me know I am with him, meaning I get to go to the front of the line and enter the building ahead of the rest. Huge room. Rows of benches. It could easily seat a thousand. And it did.

The speaker is amazing. A dose of humor mixed with serious. I loved the pony story. The speaker, a slight woman with big, red hair, says this—there are two boys standing outside a room of shit. One of the boys says, "Gross, this is just gross." The other little boy is excited, and says, "Far out." The boy who says gross asks the other boy why he is so excited. The other boy says, "With all this shit, there must be a pony in there somewhere!"

The ride back is quiet like we have just eaten lots of banana pancakes with buttery syrup.

We puff up to my house. I thank Tony for inviting me and say goodbye to the Georges.

It's late. After eleven. The house is dark. I thank God for my parents. I thank God for their love. In my bedroom, I undress, throw on a black T-shirt, and fall into bed. The alarm is set for six. I hope to get up to write. I am working on a book. Soon, I will find I am too young to be working on a book. Too young to spend eight hours a day at my desk when there is so much living to do. I do know that some publish really young. I'll call them brilliant. I simply did not have enough brilliance to keep my ass in the chair.

* * *

Tony invites me to do other things. I still don't get that he is attracted to me. I think we are just buddies. Good buddies. I guess he is just shy or waiting for me to make a move. Months go by with Tony and me occasionally meeting up for dinner, or for a movie. We even go bowling once.

One Wednesday, he telephones from Laguna Beach and tells me he saved a seat in the front row next to him, so would I please come to the meeting at the Women's Club in Laguna Beach. I told him I didn't go to meetings on Wednesdays, I go to the movies instead. He told me that Tom is speaking, thinking this would encourage me to come, but instead, it turned me off. I informed him that I especially didn't go to meetings when a supposed guru was speaking. There were supposed to be no gurus in the program. Tony said to me that it is a meeting and I should come. Then he hangs up.

I have no way to call him back. This is before cell phones. So I did what I was taught to do—when someone in the program asks you to do something, you do it. Tony has gotten the last word in and I cannot tell him I'm not coming. I show up.

Tony is thrilled. And Tom is an extraordinary speaker. I especially identified with him when he said that people who were problem drinkers and not alcoholics quit drinking, and their lives got better. Not so with the alcoholic. When the alcoholic stops drinking, all chaos breaks out. This had been my experience.

Years later, Tony asked me if I remembered that night. I said yes. He said that he had a loaded gun and a pint of whiskey in his glove compartment. I was the only one he knew in the area, so he called me. Had he just told me he was bad off, I would have come with no other thought. But he didn't. His pride wouldn't let him. I think of it as a total God thing that I showed up.

## Step One

The Twelve Step program I'm in has Twelve Steps. Jane says we need to start doing these. They will keep me sober and offer me a life beyond the restraints of my own mind. The book that houses these Steps lets me know I will be rocketed into a fourth dimension. I think my head will pop off if this happens, but I am willing to do the Steps anyway.

First Step: I admitted I am powerless over alcohol and my life has become unmanageable. I knew I was powerless over alcohol, I simply did not like knowing this. This meant no more drink. Ever—although program people were into saying "One day at a time." Nowhere in the

Big Book, which is what they called the book that leads us to nirvana, does it say "A day at a time." It says I will recover from "a seemingly hopeless state of mind and body." I will not obsess over drinking, or desire a drink. I thought this impossible and in fact wanted to drink my entire first year of sobriety. The obsession to drink for me did not leave until my first year was over. Then something magical happened and I no longer wanted to drink.

I knew I was powerless over alcohol. Once I put liquor into my body, I had no idea what would happen next, other than the fact that I would crave more. They say in the program that the first drink will get you drunk. I understood this all too well. The people told me that blackouts, which I had frequently, did not happen to the social drinker. A blackout is where the body keeps ticking along without the person being conscious of what is happening. The only way I knew what went on the night before when I was in a blackout was to have people report to me my activities. I was glad I didn't have an affinity for beating people up or trashing someone's home. Mostly, I just made an ass of myself by the things I said: *The temperature is too white tonight and Shirley needs to strip, freeing those melons of hers so that eyes can feast. Deflate the melons and you are the prizewinner of thousands of dollars. And believe me, Shirley is tired of carrying them around. Frank, put a pin to them. Promise her it won't hurt even though we know different. Ha. Ha.* And then I was told that I tried to puncture them with a fork. Maybe I do want to beat people up when drunk.

As for my life being unmanageable, this was a breeze. I had come to the program with no life. Everything prior to sobriety had been taken from me. Swimming, school, people. I had no job. I had no place to be at any particular time other than a Twelve Step meeting.

Today, my life remains unmanageable in the sense that without God there would be no life. I just show up and Management takes care of the rest. I pay Management with my trust. There's not a better deal at any of the local grocers. Not even milk at $1.29.

## Step Two

Have I come to believe that a Power greater than myself can restore me to sanity? Absolutely. I don't include my mental illness when pondering this Step. My mental illness is with me like gum in a two-year-old's hair. Peanut butter can take it out, but she'll be certain to do it again. Fortunately, there is always peanut butter.

The "sanity" in this Step for me is the insanity of the first drink. God has removed the obsession. I have been restored to sanity. As simple as putting a letter into an envelope.

## Step Three

Step Three reads, "Made a decision to turn our will and our lives over to the care of God *as we understood Him*." I do not balk at this Step. Why not, I figure. The best I can do with my life at this point is end up in the intensive care unit of the local hospital. That is my very best. I didn't intend on living past age eighteen. Here I am, well past eighteen, in all my six-foot glory. I can still stand tall. I can invite God in. I made that decision on my knees with my sponsor reciting the Third Step prayer. That decision has not changed with time.

I too am granted a spiritual life everlasting. My God has charm, but also warmth. My God knows where I'm going, but not how I'm getting there. How I'm getting there has a lot to do with my two feet and a desire to move with God's grace. God hands me the flashlight and I provide the batteries. I know how to slide the button to on, and to off when the light's not needed because the day provides the glow. My love for God heats me without making me sweat.

As a schizophrenic, how can I be happy with God? God sees me living. When the sidewalk is littered with weeds as high as my knees, God clears them. Yes, sometimes I am trapped by sickness, but this sickness also gives me compassion for those who don't fare as well as I. Not only do I love God, but I love the people God places in my life. I love the man who beats himself upside his head because he can't hear the world. I can hear the world for him if he allows me to take his hand. And I will take his hand just as I will write about my experience with the hope of reaching those too who find themselves sharing socks with me and not knowing what to do with them when they become damp with sweat. There will always be another pair of socks. I know this because I know God. And the sweet thing is that even if I didn't know God, a pair of socks would still find their way to me.

I turn my will and life over to the care of God on a daily basis. My decision has been made. It remains in place always. I am forever grateful. I owe this decision my life.

## Club Fuck

In the late eighties, early nineties, I am big on clubbing. I dress in all black, wear white makeup, dark eye shadow, and deep red lipstick. It is the middle period between punk rock and goth. I am in the middle period and so are a lot of my friends.

Club Fuck in Los Angeles is our favorite club. We can be as wild as we want. I'm not into the S-M scene, but many at the club are. In one corner there are two women pouring hot wax on themselves and softly whipping each other. Later, they lick wounds. A naked performance-art guy takes the front stage, a piece of string tied around his cock so that it stays limp as he dances and does acrobatics to heavy industrial and alternative rock music.

A row of televisions shows various "wild kingdom" programs. Animals killing animals and eating the flesh, some dragging the meat into dens to feed their children. I was a vegetarian at the time. I understood that kind of meat eating, but I didn't understand how the human population could gorge themselves on hamburgers and overpriced steaks. Later, I was to give up my vegetarianism and find a love in beef, chicken, fish. The idea of slaughterhouses still made me nauseous, though. It was as if I wanted to believe the carnage I ingested really came from the flower and vegetable gardens around town.

I started eating meat again because I came to a point in my life where I was really, really depressed and thought if it were because of my diet, I would have to change it. So I did. The depression didn't lift, but I was certainly enjoying my meat-eating frenzies.

Clubbing didn't take two people. In fact, most people liked to dance with themselves. One night out and there was Marie. She was magnificent in the way she danced to The Cure. Gyrating freely to the music. Floating on the concrete floor. Head down as if in prayer. Dancing was prayer. I knew immediately I wanted her in my life.

I met her in the bathroom. She was intensely telling a story to a woman with blue hair. A young woman with blue hair. Not the blue that elderly woman accidentally get when they try to color their hair white. Translucent white. Marie was recently dumped by some rock model whom she still loved. I leaned toward the mirror and pretended to reapply my already smitten lips.

How to say hello to someone deeply submersed in storytelling? Wink, no. Say excuse me, no. Accidentally bump into them as you reach for a paper towel to dry your hands with, no.

"Wow. You're the woman from the Clairol commercial."

Marie did pause in her storytelling to look at me. Of course, I knew it was a stretch for Marie to be in a shampoo commercial as her hair was cut in a Mohawk.

"You've got the wrong person."

"Kristina. My name is Kristina."

"Marie."

Marie returned to her storytelling and I left the bathroom.

Marie. This was good. I had a name.

## The Horse

I meet Meg in a meeting. She is dazzling. Six feet tall. Long black hair. A true sense of fashion, the glamorous kind. I immediately fall for her. Marie becomes a woman I met years ago and never hooked up with. I ask Meg if I can make dinner for her sometime. She says yes. She doesn't tell me that she is on-again, off-again with a young woman named Kate. This on-again, off-again was to interrupt my becoming Meg's girlfriend.

* * *

Meg pulls up to my parents' house in a gold Camaro. An old gold Camaro that sounded like it should be pushed instead of driven. My parents were out of town. This was good. I didn't have to explain Meg or why I got out the china and crystal. Hunter was home and thought what I was doing was kind of weird, but she went about her own business.

I had spent hours making spinach lasagna, one of my favorite meals. Meg had a bite of it and that was it. She explained to me that she was on a diet as she helped herself to more sourdough bread and butter.

We did the usual get-to-know-each-other kind of talk. Meg had been in recovery from alcoholism and heroin addiction for a couple of years. She was Jewish. She was a manicurist. After telling me she was a manicurist, I looked at my own nails and thought *uh-oh.*

She didn't stay long. Maybe an hour. She said she had a meeting to go to. I simply said great, thinking *what the fuck, couldn't she have told me earlier and then we could have gotten together earlier?* I thanked her for coming.

The Camaro spit fumes, and then moved on down the street.

Meg showed up hand-in-hand with Kate the following evening at a meeting I attended. No more needed to be said. I said hello to both Meg and Kate even though I was disappointed.

Meg and I spent the next ten years in and out of each other's lives. Ultimately, I didn't treat her the way she should have been treated. The last time we were to break up would be due to me. I bailed on her for reasons I can't remember. I do know my brain was really sick at the time. Meg saw me through many overdoses.

Sadly, after our last breakup, Meg returned to heroin. I know that I am powerless over someone else's drug addiction, but I couldn't help but think I was part of the reason she reached for the horse.

## Like Minds

Hunter moved back in with Mom and Dad after crashing her Corvette and dropping out of the University of Arizona. Nothing about her involvement in the sex industry was mentioned. Mom and Dad were simply glad to see her safe.

I knew she was not as safe as Mom and Dad would like. She continued to do drugs. Mostly marijuana. I found things she'd made into pipes, like empty toilet paper rolls.

It's amazing to me how people of like minds always find each other. She met other people who did as many if not more drugs than she did her first month of living in San Clemente. She was driving around in a sporty little red Toyota Fiero that Dad had bought her. Her skirts barely covered her ass. Her breasts barely stayed in her shirts. She wore enough makeup for three people. Despite tackiness, she remained beautiful. Men were the flies and she the spider.

I loved her still at this time. She was my little sister. I hoped that by my example of sobriety, she too would get sober and clean. Meg took her to a meeting of recovering drug addicts. Meg said she was an angel on the way to the meeting and then turned demon on the way back. Hunter did not like the meeting. She thought the people dishonest in their feelings and hated having to listen to what she called one drug story after another. It made her want to light up listening to all the using stories. Hunter was not to go to a meeting again in the next twenty years. Her usage would take her to demoralization, cause her to harm all she once loved, and she wouldn't care. What is it people say—she wouldn't give a rat's ass.

## Jeanette

I moved from San Clemente to Long Beach. Unlike San Clemente, which is a beach town, Long Beach was a real city to me. Cultural diversity. Alleys with trash. On the outskirts, the ocean. On the inskirts, old apartment buildings. And it was gay friendly. Someone told me that the percentage of gays and lesbians in Long Beach was greater than that in San Francisco. I was thrilled to be able to hold my girlfriend's hand as we walked down the street.

My first heavy love was Jeanette. I met her while out clubbing one night at Que Sera in Long Beach. I sat next to her at the bar while I drank one Coke after another. She asked me if I was vegetarian. What a strange question to begin a conversation with, I thought. I told her yes. She said, "But you eat chicken and fish, right?" I said, "No, I don't." (I hadn't yet gone back to eating meat.) "Finally," she says, "I meet a true vegetarian."

Jeanette is Hispanic with a cute bob haircut and bangs that almost hide her eyes. She is curvy, full hips, full breasts, but thin. I am lanky without being curvy. She wears all black including a black men's blazer. Her hands are beautiful, dainty and well manicured. She has painted her nails a deep, blue red.

"I have met you before," she says.

"No way. I would have remembered that."

"Marie introduced us."

"Oh," I said, "that makes sense." I tell her that when I'm dating someone—which Marie and I really weren't doing—I have eyes for only that person. "I definitely don't flirt when I'm seeing someone."

"Are you seeing someone now?" she asks.

"No," I reply.

"So are you flirting with me now?"

"Do you want me to be flirting with you now?"

She writes her phone number down on a napkin. "I have to go. I look forward to hearing from you," she winks and leaves.

I leave shortly after, full of soda and happy.

Upon entering my apartment, I think, *Great, this is great that I can make a phone call and not have anyone around, listening in.* I'd only been in the apartment for a week. This would be the first phone call I made to a woman whom I was interested in since living here.

I have no couch yet. I have one dark wooden barstool that looks lost because there is no table. I have been pulling the barstool up to the pull-out cutting board in the kitchen and eating there. I have white bookshelves that I bought from IKEA and hate. Maybe that is why the four boxes filled with books remain unopened. Why did I buy something I hated? I haven't a clue as to what I was thinking. I don't like white wood, and the wood of these bookshelves is like pre-fab or something. Not sturdy wood. I am certain the shelves will sag in the middle with the weight of the books.

There is a bed in the bedroom. I love the white sheets and cushy white down comforter. There is a burgundy-stained nightstand with three drawers at the left of the bed. On it sits this great old-fashioned-looking telephone—the kind of black phone with the fancy cradle seen in the detective offices in the fifties. I love movies from that time period. There is a large, ornate clock hanging on the wall across from my bed. It says eleven o'clock straight up. I decide to telephone Jeanette. I have no idea if she is a late-night person or an in-bed-by-ten person.

She answers the phone after several rings. "Hello," she says.

"Hi, Jeanette. It's me, Kristina. I met you at Que Sera tonight."

"I know who you are," she says. "May I call you back in, let's say twenty minutes? I'm right in the middle of a shower and have soap in my hair."

"Sure, sure. Twenty minutes. That's good," and we both hang up.

My adrenaline is pumping. I'm not certain what to do with myself for the next twenty minutes. I look at the boxes of books. They seem forlorn. They are not used to not being shelved and in sight. I could test my IKEA conclusion and see if the shelves really will sag. And if they do, I'm out fifty bucks and I may even make some Dumpster diver happy.

*No Kristina. Just breathe. You can do nothing for twenty minutes. The time won't kill you.* I say this to myself.

Exactly twenty minutes later, Jeanette calls. "Do you like M&MS?" she asks.

"Yes," I answer hesitatingly.

"Good," she says. "Which color?"

"Green."

"I'm picking all the green ones out for you so they will be here when you come to see me. How's tomorrow night?"

"Great," I say. "What time?"

"Five. We'll make it early so you can be rested for work on Monday.

You do have a job?" she asks.

At this moment, I have never been happier in my life to have a job. "Yes," I say, trying to sound like *of course I do* rather than *I'm lucky I do*. My employment history is not good.

"Great," she says, and then gives me directions to her apartment. I'm ecstatic.

\* \* \*

Jeanette and I do the move-in-quick thing. A month of seeing each other, and I move in. We make it her apartment because her father owns the rental and, of course, charges Jeanette no rent. I live with her for a couple of years. In that time, I had no real incidents related to mental illness except that I was really depressed and withdrawn.

Jeanette tells me after we've broken up that she envies the person who will walk into my life and pull me out of myself. She says I have a great capacity to love, but have never shaken out the cloak. I get what she means. I get that I don't allow people too close to me, and that as a result of this it appears to the outside world that I don't know how to really love anyone, or anything, for that matter.

Jeanette fell in love with the produce manager at Vons. I knew something was amiss. She had been acting so odd. I would wake up to her staring at me. She said she was trying to get over how beautiful I was so that she could move on. And move on she did.

After she tells me, through my tears, I tell her that I was glad she found a man to love. I tell her that I think it is really hard being gay in the society that we live in, and now she will have more freedom. I really meant what I said despite the fact that I was devastated.

In a short amount of time, she would marry this man at the court-house. I know they had sons because we shared the same hairstylist. I'm happy for them and wish I had remained in touch with Jeanette.

## Hard Eyes

Mom and Dad leave for a weekend vacation. Hunter is left alone. I'm glad Hunter is there so I don't have to run back and forth between my apartment and the house in order to feed Brandy and leave her with plenty of water.

* * *

Jeremy has gone for a morning jog, leaving Hannah to wake up alone from agitated sleep in the hotel room. Her eyes are hard to lift. Tears from the night's sleep of dreams leaves gunk sticking to her mascara; she didn't take time to free herself from cosmetics. Hannah's black eyeliner traces her cheek, ending in a line at her chin.

Mom had dreamt Rose, Hunter, and I had tied her to the carved wooden chair made for her by her father as a wedding gift. We had stitched her eyes open. Mom knew we often complained to Dad that she was unable to recognize sunshine. No one understood what caused Mom to become so distressed. She wore her distress around the house like a dead hat, throwing it in the top drawer of her vanity each time she left the house.

Rose, Hunter, and I had tied her to the chair outside the perimeters of the house. We wanted her to drop all pretense and show her real self in the larger world. Mom said we seemed to think that sticking her with pins would bring on her real self like an acupuncturist announcing chakras.

Mom didn't feel the pins, so we threatened to lay open her skin. Dad walked in before we could remove her clothes and begin tearing open the envelope that was Mom.

"Stop," he insisted. "You may scare your mother into consciousness. She is too tired for that."

We thought Dad was sold on Mom's image and that he had no appreciation for what lived in her mind.

Mom said she woke knowing Rose, Hunter, and I cared to know her deeply. This touched her in a way that diamonds and good sex could not. She felt exposed and alone.

The hotel phone rings, letting Mom know it is 7 a.m. She replaces the receiver back in the cradle with the same automatic motion she has answered it with. What happens when life becomes automated? Does passion skip the moment because we neglect to pause?

Mom doesn't need to tell me it is an effort for her to understand 7 a.m.; at home, she doesn't wake until ten.

She knows Dad would be done with his jog by eight, leaving her an hour to discover her beauty and soak her nerves in crème d' menthe. She vaguely thought of us like a wisp of hair that itched her face. Mom can't remember if she told us she would telephone each morning like a concerned hen.

## Ocean

Jeremy heads east from the hotel. The ocean lies to the west. The surf can be heard as it rolls into the sand, and withdraws.

I know Dad dislikes the ocean. He came on Mom's plea. She loves to spend all afternoon and dusk at the water's edge fully clothed in long sleeves and pants with her wide straw hat and sunglasses. It isn't the tan that draws her to the beach, but rather the tide with its ebb and flow. She identifies with the ebb as the decline of her own life is felt by her briefly, but consistently. A cuckoo appears each hour from the recesses of time and then returns to the wooden box it calls home.

She appreciates the ocean's flow, finding prayer in its smooth continuity and ceaseless motion of change. She prays for Rose's, Hunter's, and my continuous evolution from daughters to young adults to wise women while seated on the beach with the song of the sea licking at her subconscious, finding peace in the powerlessness she experienced at the ocean's edge. She didn't know how to move this peace into her daily life, nor did she think to try, so stricken by the power and dark embrace of alcohol. Alcohol was borrowing her heart, mind, and soul, leaving her with no idea that death is attaching itself slowly to her liver.

## Powerlessness

Dad hates the feeling of powerlessness the ocean easily brings to him. It is different in the city. In the city, Dad feels the power and industriousness of Mankind. Mankind has leveled mountains, pouring concrete onto the earth paving highways that lead from the city to the next and then the next, killing the idea of nowhere-ness in Dad's mind. The mind generates place and the feeling of home. It is debatable as to whether or not home exists without the mind.

Dad lives in somewhere. Where he goes is always driven by his intention. He never wakes up lost.

He loves the feel of his legs pummeling over pavement past the windows of buildings that openly stare at him. He has strong, well-chiseled muscles underneath taut skin. He uses weight lifting as a meditation, a focus of mind and breath. It is not possible to push 400 pounds of metal plates without suspending thought much like one does in prayer.

Dad doesn't consider himself much a man of God. He is too invested in creating his own future to recognize that some things, if not all things, are simply out of his control.

It is good that he and Mom were able to get away for the weekend from the simple distractions of home and work that claim their attention more and more. The groove they have maintained since high school has pinched itself closed.

Dad picks up speed as he thinks of Mom standing farther from him than an arm's length. He misses the presence of her elbow linked with his. He no longer experiences her essence at his side when not in sight of her and even when in the same room, he has moments of missing her.

He confides to me that it is good to have the weekend. He needs to convince himself that Mom still needs him like she had as a teenager. It bothers him that he no longer knows what Mom wants. He knows he can't buy her enough things to make her happy. This thought leaves him feeling crabby. He works twelve- and fifteen-hour days with the intention of making Mom and us as comfortable in the world as possible.

## Deep Cherry

Hannah lines her lips in brick red. Jeremy walks in, sweat hangs in his T-shirt. Hannah adds Deep Cherry. Her lips are done. Perfect. Jeremy falls on the bed, asks her to come, wants her. She thinks of the makeup she just applied. How careful she had been. A hint of rouge. Black liner on both the upper and lower lids of her eyes. A tasteful amount of purple eye shadow. Mascara. A light dusting of powder.

As if reading her mind, Jeremy says, "I won't touch your face."

The morning was beautiful. They were alive inside each other. Afterward, he brushes her hair.

## The Limousine

Mom and Dad arrive home to find the front door of the house open to the wet breeze of dewy morning. Mom and Dad immediately know something is wrong. A locked door does not secure anything, there is always a way in through the mind, but it is discomforting to see your things, your property, available to anyone.

The clock pushes another minute forward.

Mom examines the bong left on the coffee table. Dad tells her it is a pipe for smoking marijuana.

Dad calls out. No one answers. That moment a beer bottle falls over in the sink. *Ring-a-ding-ding.*

The kitchen is littered with vegetables. The stove's burners glow red. Clothes are tossed around the family room. Mom's fingers stumble to light a cigarette, the cigarette louder than a sigh.

Upstairs, Mom finds all the eyes of her stuffed monkeys burned out by cigarettes. In the garage, they find the Mercedes had been driven and Hunter's Fiero, gone.

Their minds leap to storytelling: Miscellaneous boys had convinced Hunter to throw a party. Along with the boys came drugs, theft, kidnapping.

Dad telephones the police. Two detectives come to the house to note the disarray. They were both friends of Dad's. This fact put a gentle edge on what they would tell him.

One of the detectives telephones me at work. At this time, I work in accounts payable at the Ritz-Carlton hotel in Laguna Niguel. The detective asks me when the last time was that I saw my sister, Hunter. I told him that she was supposed to go to a concert with me and friends last night and didn't show. The limousine arrived without her in it. She told the driver to ask me to please excuse her absence.

The detective then puts my dad on the phone and he fills me in. Dad wants to believe that Hunter got kidnapped and the Fiero, stolen. I'd let the detectives pop that one.

## Food

The corner of Fourth and Adams in Laguna Beach is lit by an over-friendly sun whose importance is not lost to the brim of the straw hat I wear. Sweat gropes my breasts, trickling from there to my belly button, then is absorbed into the waist of my pants.

The ice cream parlor is fairly empty of people. I find Hunter in the back booth, hunched over the table, arms crossed to support her head that was still like a melon in a Styrofoam crate not routed anywhere and likely to rot.

"Hunter," I slid into the booth.

Hunter lifts her head, slowly, its weight apparent. It is possible for a head to weigh more than a few pounds on a disenchanted day when even birds stay in the limbs and droop.

"You came. I knew you would," Hunter says to me.

She tells me Thomas had given her a ride to the ice cream parlor. She says that he is on her team, that they were like two detectives working closely together to break open a huge fraud situation in which many people were being taken advantage of financially and otherwise. I think she has finally cracked, all the drugs she had done finally caught up with her.

The next hour spends itself like air being blown into a large balloon that resisted expansion. Hunter stuck mostly to one statement: "Our parents are not who they are and must be arrested for fraud."

Hunter asked me to meet her because she needed me to testify against my parents. She needs me to testify to the fact that they are not the people who people think they are. She said that their names weren't even Hannah and Jeremy. Nor had they ever had kids. Sure, there were many photographs that documented our continued growth. Here we are on the swings together with Dad pushing us. We're all smiling, thinking we're having a good time, but Hunter says we're really not. Hunter says Dad is thinking he wants to bury us in the backyard before we get much older and figure out what is really going on. And we are smiling because we think that is what we're supposed to be doing, but what we really want is to get off the swings so we can go have Popsicles with our real friends.

Hunter doesn't want to die yet and thinks Mom and Dad are going to cause her harm. She wants me to help straighten things out. "I know people often think you're not paying attention, Kristina, but I know you can tell me the exact moment the fly lands on the sandwich, and the person eats it not knowing it is there."

This whole time I keep contact with Hunter's eyes and think of cherries jubilee.

Hunter stands, kisses me on the cheek, and sloshes through the door. I am left, and it seems peculiarly quiet for an ice cream parlor. Hunter, in all her eighteen years, leaves bent over as if in old age.

\* \* \*

Mom is washing dishes when I walk into her kitchen. "Stand up straight, honey. Your back will be glad for it later."

"I can't right now," I tell her. "The wind is caught in my shirt and I don't want to let it out. It smells like Hunter and smelling Hunter would make you miss her more. I don't want to make you miss her more."

Mom turns the water off. Dries her hands. Lifts what is left of her cigarette, takes a drag, and asks me if I'd spoken with Hunter.

"In Technicolor," I say.

"Where?" Mom asks.

"The ice cream parlor in Laguna. The one with the big dog asleep in the corner, the dog whose belly dusts the floor."

"Take a load off, Kristina." This was Mom's way of saying "tell all." I don't like dropping news too often, especially the kind that hurts.

"She's not coming home, Mom." I open the refrigerator door. "Where's the chocolate syrup?"

"If it's not right on the door, Dad must have finished it. What do you mean she's not coming home?" Mom asks.

I respond, "Done. Through. She is through being a daughter and a sister." I shut the refrigerator door and take a seat across the table from Mom. "Her hair was all in knots. It didn't seem to bother her, though. She went right on telling me that it would be better for her to live in the world rather than wait for the world to come to her. Or something like that. I can't tell you all, Mom. I am still her sister."

I can tell Mom doesn't know what to say or do. She doesn't know how to feel about any of this. She strikes a match and lights another cigarette. She watches me watching her. Her hand is shaking. I imagine her thoughts to be that of water. I have no idea why.

"What's she going to eat?" slips out of her mouth. She is crying without meaning to.

## Therapy

I finally seek outside help. My friends are relieved by this. I don't remember how I got the name of Audrey Mitchell, but I did, and this is who I made my appointment with.

The first time I see Audrey, I wear baggy khaki pants that I gather around my waist with a huge and heavy black belt. I wear a white T-shirt, heavy chains around my neck, a wide silver bracelet on my wrist, a long army trench coat, and black combat boots in which I tucked my pant leg. These were my favorite boots, real army-issued combat boots bought at the army surplus store. I wore the boots for years. At the end of their life, I kicked a wall because I was really angry and broke their sole.

Once in Audrey's office, I settle into the middle of the couch. She sits in a La-Z-Boy across from me. I note her Birkenstocks. I am anxious.

I speak first. I inform her that I am in the process of applying to become a police officer and if seeing her is going to fuck up my chances with them, I didn't want to see her.

She smiles. I hadn't expected this. I think the tone more serious. She lets me know she has several clients who are police officers. Knowing this relieves me.

I can't remember what was said for the rest of the session. I do know that I mention nothing about hearing voices. I didn't want to give it up. I thought it was really none of her damn business. So we did like an "I have a mother and father and two sisters" kind of thing. The visit becomes casual and I am able to relax. I make an appointment for the following week.

## Highlander II

This is a place in the book where I jump back and forth in time. I don't want to show all my suicide attempts. Reliving them is painful. To date, it has been at least eleven years since I have attempted to take my own life.

\* \* \*

February 1993. I have just left my gynecologist's office knowing that I will overdose as soon as I'm down the street a ways. The Voices are loud, insistent. My overdosing is not because something bad is happening in my immediate life. I just want the Voices to leave me alone. They say they will if I attempt to reach them. Attempting to reach them means attempting to take my own life.

I am motorcycling down Pacific Coast Highway, traveling from Long Beach, headed for Huntington Beach. I stop midway at a dead gas station. The station looks like it has been closed for decades. Debris collects at the pumps: crumpled paper towels, piles of little rocks, leaves, and twigs. The windows of the booth are dark. A closed sign hangs awkwardly in the front window. The station screams of decay. It is a perfect place to pause and swallow two bottles filled with a mixture of pills. Tylenol is the most dangerous of what I will swallow. An excess amount of Tylenol will kill the liver.

I wash it all down with water so quickly that some of the water dribbles down my chin to my chest. I think, *I will never feel water like this again.*

Back on my motorcycle, I continue on to Huntington Beach. I don't note the day as beautiful, the ride down the coast as stunning. I am on a mission and the mission doesn't include beauty.

At Huntington Beach Pier, I make a left and follow the curve around to a garage. I park my bike and head to the movie theaters. At the booth I buy a ticket for *Highlander II*. I enter the movie theater. The only other people there are two teen girls who sit in the back. I sit up front to the left of the screen. The movie starts. The pills I have taken begin to kick in. My mouth goes dry. My body begins to spasm. I have trouble breathing. I lose consciousness.

I regain consciousness for maybe thirty seconds, long enough to realize I am strapped to a gurney in the lobby of the movie theater. A paramedic leans over me, attempts to speak to me. It is like being a movie star in a silent film. I lose consciousness again.

I come to again in the hospital emergency room. I am curtained off. It is just me. I sit up. A nurse comes in. I attempt to talk to her and instead vomit all over her.

She says, "I saw this coming." She is not mad at me. I don't want anyone to be mad at me.

Meg comes in. She is my girlfriend at this time, again. I learn later that they had found a business card of Audrey's in my back pocket and had called her. She, in turn, called Meg.

Meg saved my life that day. The doctors were thinking I was a drug addict who had a bad trip. Meg told them to test my blood level for Tylenol. They listened to her and ran the test. Meg was right. They immediately gave me the first round of liver cocktail. I was awake to swallow it. It smelled worse than anything I had ever smelled, worse than rotten eggs, and tasted about as bad.

As soon as I was cleared medically, I was taken by ambulance to Charter Hospital in Irvine, California. I was to stay there for a couple of weeks. Again, I spoke of nothing. My silence was too deep for anyone to learn anything about me; a cadaver doesn't whisper. Audrey comes to visit me. After all the months I had spent in therapy, I still hadn't said much of importance. I didn't say much of importance at the hospital, either. I am reminded of the frustration of the psychiatric technicians who worked with me during my first hospitalization when I was eighteen.

## Fear

I spent years not telling the truth in therapy. I so much didn't want to be a schizophrenic, whatever that was, and I didn't want to have to take medication. Somehow I had made schizophrenia synonymous with taking medication. And I was to learn I was right. It does take medication to treat schizophrenia successfully.

My first diagnosis was dissociative identity disorder (DID), the new term for multiple personality disorder. I finally copped to hearing voices, but I did it in a way that the professionals could link my hearing voices to DID. I named my voices and then I played along with the notion that I would actually become each one of my voices. I was terrified. I spent years being too terrified to be honest. I desperately didn't want to have mental illness. I could deal with being labeled with a personality disorder, but not with the fact that with mental illness comes medication.

My dishonesty hurt me. I couldn't receive proper care unless I told the truth, and I almost died behind my deceit.

\* \* \*

Ten or fifteen suicide attempts later, most ending up in intensive care.

Always with me ending up having my stomach pumped. I would eventually move to Phoenix. Meg would tell me that Audrey told her after I had moved, that she was beginning to think I was psychotic rather than anything else. Little did she know, she was right.

## Transmission

I shave my head bald looking for the plate at the base of my skull that will provide me access to the wires in my brain. I am a television with no antenna, just a rigged arch of aluminum foil.

## New Year's

When Meg and I were on, we were on. In the ten years that we were on and off, I don't know that we ever put an entire year together. Today, I believe it wasn't Meg's fault but my own that prevented us from loving each other over years of being together. I was too afraid to give my all. And then I was swallowed up by self-centered behavior that came with mental illness and lack of understanding or a willingness to do anything about it.

One New Year's Eve we were supposed to join friends and go out dancing, and at the last minute, I refused. I didn't tell Meg I was too paranoid to go out, I just told her I wouldn't go and encouraged her to go without me. This was not the first time, not the last, that I would let her down in similar fashion. She returned home before midnight to find me sitting on the bathroom toilet with a pad of paper on my knees, staring at myself in the mirror in an attempt to draw the demon I knew hid behind my eyes.

Had I been her, I would have said, "I'm sick of this shit," and walked away.

Instead she wrapped her arms around me and asked me what she could do to help. I had no idea what to say to this or how to act.

That year we saw the New Year in together and made slow, easy love to the sound of fireworks all around.

## Rings

A different month and year with Meg, and I was excited to give her the ring I had bought as an engagement ring. It was gold with a white pearl. That evening at dinner, at a gay-friendly restaurant, I got down on a knee and asked her to marry me. It caught her by surprise. She carefully put the dinner roll she had reached for down and said, "Yes." I handed her the ring box. She opened it. I could tell right away she didn't like it. I was glad she kept it honest. I wanted her to have something she would like wearing. She said to me that her hands and fingers were too large to wear something so dainty. I understood that.

The next day, we took back the ring I had gotten her and went to a pawnshop. She was convinced we could find rings that we liked for little money. I don't know what little money was to her. We spent $1,000 on each ring. This was not little money to me. I had to really work on being okay with our purchases. The rings were beautiful. She ended up with a wide yellow gold band with a maze of diamonds set into it. And I, with a white gold and diamond antique-ish looking thing that I still have to this day.

Meg and I were to break it off a month or so later. She made it a point of telling me that she had sold her ring to one of her clients. A wave releases itself to make foam on the sand.

## Sally (March 1995)

I bicycle my way around Long Beach. It is raining and I need to go to the specialty store to buy food for my date tonight. It is the first date that Sally and I had been on. At this time, I am working as an administrative assistant to a chiropractor. Sally is the massage therapist. I was shocked when she asked me out; I would have never guessed her as one interested in women.

I wear a yellow rain jacket with a hood and yellow rain pants. The water slides off me and puddles on the floor in the store. The owners are not happy with me. I attempt to say I'm sorry by purchasing more than I had come for. Tomatoes, feta, Greek olives, a long stick of bread, olive oil, pasta, and two slices of chocolate cake. All will easily fit in the canvas bags that hang on both sides of my bike. The bread I would bend in half.

Sharon, my roommate of a few months, is gone tonight, so Sally and I have the apartment to ourselves. The apartment we live in is a duplex.

Sharon and I have the upstairs. There is a large living room with wood floors and a fireplace. The kitchen is like a long hall to the right of the front door. Sharon has tiled the kitchen in black and white squares. The cubbyhole of a room off the kitchen contains Sharon's desk and my drawing board, along with a large mirror I can see myself in so I have a body to refer to as I draw. I draw dark things—monsters and gargoyles, little kids getting beat up and wicked men and women. My wicked men and women always wear hats and long coats with no buttons. My bedroom, containing only a bed, is off this room, while Sharon's bedroom is off the living room.

Sally shows up in a sequined blue dress that is sheer enough for me to see her bra. I am hoping the dress doesn't mean sex. I am wearing black pants with a black wool turtleneck. I never have sex on a first date.

And then over dinner, I was to learn that Sally has never dated a woman. She is late thirties at this point. At least late thirties. Jokingly I ask her what has taken her so long. "A husband," she answers.

"Oh," I say. "Do you still have the husband?"

"No," she says.

"Children?"

"Yes, one. Age eight."

"Good age," I say.

Dinner is nice. Good conversation. She likes chocolate cake. I make coffee.

After coffee and cake, we move to the couch. She sits at one end, I at the other. She moves closer. I force myself into the crease of the couch. There is no more room for me to move.

"Do you want it?" she asks.

"Want what?" I try to sound innocent.

"Sex," she responds.

"Not tonight. First date and all, you know."

"What about kissing?"

I can smell her breath. Mint mixed with coffee.

"I'd rather not," I say. "First date rule—no hanky-panky of any sort."

"Too bad," she says and moves back down the couch. "Why do you have that rule?" she asks.

"I just do," I say, not wanting to tell her that I am an emotional wreck and don't want to drag anyone close enough to me to get hurt. I was tired of hurting people the way bacon got too crisp. Bacon would always get too crisp if left on the grill too long.

"Should we call it the night?" I ask.

"Sure," she says.

I hope she doesn't hear my sigh.

I lead her to the door, open it, and move to the side, allowing her to leave.

"Thanks for dinner," she says.

"My pleasure," I say and shut the door behind her.

She comes with a kid. *Not a good idea,* I think as I start clearing the table to wash dishes.

The rain has stopped. I am able to hear crickets once again.

## Vehicles

I sell my Ford Probe and buy a Trek bicycle. The car had become too tiresome. A machine with thirst for gasoline. My body is strong. The longest ride I have each week is from Long Beach to Huntington Beach for therapy. It takes an hour each way, to and from. The ride is beautiful. Down the coast on the bike path in the sand. Magnificent sunsets. God with a paintbrush. Rothko canvases. Did Rothko have God? If he did, would he still have slit his wrists?

Later, I will need to travel farther. From Long Beach to West Hollywood for meetings. My sponsor in the Twelve Step program is Maud, and she is lovely and sure-footed and lives in West Hollywood. I could figuratively feel her foot on my backside when I had done stupid.

I sign up to take motorcycle safety training classes. Typically, I do things ass backward in true alcoholic fashion; I buy a motorcycle before I can ride it. I recall the time I bought Rollerblades. Jack had suggested to me to rent a pair of blades before buying to make certain I could indeed blade. I didn't listen, once again thinking I know best. I bought a pair of Rollerblades for $350. And what do I know? I know I tried to blade and repeatedly fell down. I learned I couldn't do it, and the $350 got lost in my trunk. Years later, I would give the blades away.

So now I own a motorcycle I can't ride. Fortunately, I was a natural. The man who taught the motorcycle safety training class was surprised I had never ridden before.

In one exercise, I watch this woman rocket from her seat over her handlebars, into the shrubs. It was like watching a cartoon in slow motion. I laugh hard. This is not a nice thing to do. She is automatically eliminated from riding any longer. She leaves with her husband.

Motorcycling is fabulous. The original bike I bought for a couple hundred dollars proves to be a dud. I get rid of it and purchase a Honda I name Gertrude after Gertrude Stein. Both the bike and Gertrude are sexy in their own ways. The wide girth of the tank reminds me of the wide girth of Gertrude.

The worst thing about wearing a helmet is sneezing. The best thing is the day I crashed, it saved my life. I had been riding for a good three years before I bit it. The choice was hit the dog that ran out into the middle of the road, or hit the truck. I chose the truck.

The day it happened, I was wearing high heels instead of boots. The pavement took a large chunk of flesh near my ankle. Other than that, I bruised my shin badly. That was it. Grandma Morgan was glad I crashed without really getting hurt. My bike was totaled, and she was thrilled I didn't ride after that. Riding was freeing. Being in a car again was initially claustrophobic. I adjusted.

## Still Life

Things got bizarre. Looking back, I know I did bizarre things, but at the time that I was doing them, I didn't consider them bizarre. After the administrative position with the chiropractor, I got a job at the public library as a clerk. Sally and I remained friends; she started dating a guy and I started seeing Meg again.

Working for the library was a great job; I loved the work, I loved the people. It made no sense that I would put my job in jeopardy, but I did. I began leaving the apartment for work at the library, and instead of going there, I would wind up in Santa Barbara, a couple hours away down the coast. I was convinced people were watching me, paying me uninvited attention.

The times I ended up in Santa Barbara, I would park my motorcycle and lug myself and my helmet to the library. People were watching me. People thought I was a homeless person. People thought I would steal books. People thought I hadn't showered this month. People thought, people thought, people thought.

My Santa Barbara trips would end by me telephoning Meg, letting her know I was in Santa Barbara and that I needed help getting home to Long Beach. She always came. I followed her home.

At times of travel, Gabby, the librarian in charge of the library branch I worked at, would cover for me. She would count it as a called-in absence due to illness. Her kindnesses at this time in my life were amazing. She didn't write me off as a bad employee. She cared what happened to me. She cared about what was going on in my life. I didn't know how to tell her or anyone what was going on in my life because I didn't know what was happening. Somehow, I thought the Voices I heard were heard by everyone, and everyone wasn't talking about them.

Once at the library the Voices got so bad that I excused myself to the restroom. In the restroom, I slid into the corner between the wall and the toilet. Next, sweet nothing.

One of the employees found me in the bathroom, in the corner, completely still and unresponsive. Gabby called the paramedics. They came. It took time for me to come out of the catatonia. One fireman kept talking to me in an even and calm voice, attempting to coax me into alertness so that I could leave my position on the bathroom floor.

I eventually got up. I don't really remember walking from the bathroom to the break room table. The paramedics left after checking my heart rate and pulse. I guess they always check heart rates and pulses.

I left my motorcycle in the parking lot and caught a ride home from Hong, one of the pages at the library.

I was still out of it when I got home. At the time, I was renting a room from Alice, another librarian. Sharon had moved in with her girlfriend, and I didn't have the funds to be the only one paying the rent. Alice had seen me through some bad times. Too many bad times.

She let me know that evening that I needed to move. She couldn't handle it any longer. *What was the "it"?* I thought. The big "IT."

I understood why she wanted me out. It still hurt, though. Another window is locked in place and the mini blinds drawn.


## 100 Cents

Who knows what acts as the final finger that snaps the rubber band off the Sunday paper allowing current affairs to spill onto a cracked breakfast table with an oil slick from last night's salad dressing?

I find myself in the weight of bluish dusk as the common reality blinks to a close and the second reality takes me in a hug. I remember entering my bedroom on two feet and laying myself down into the folds of an unmade bed like a bookmark.

Armed with this memory, my mind relaxes knowing that my body is out of harm's way, unlike the time I laid in the dirt at the park and a big dog used me like a blanket, practically smothering me with his left paw.

I still have to learn whether or not my migration is something I can control through strong will or whether it is inevitable when off medication and slapped with stress. I have been experiencing the strain of the common reality. Emotion plays no role in the second reality. I am free to float like a plastic fork in a sink filled with water. However, unlike the fork, I can listen and I can think.

The Voices of the second reality resonate so near my spirit ear, or what I think of as my spirit ear, that I can't hear what is said from the common reality. I do not really know how to refer to my bodiless form. Perhaps, I am just an energy mass that thickens a small portion of air like white mist without the dampness.

*Stay with us. Be with us. Watch with us. Die with us.* Nothing they say is more complicated than this. Mostly, I experience them as a hum, fireworks that sting the sky without a final burst. I thought I would experience fear in this state of limbo, but then again, I was stripped of the freedom to feel.

It does occur to me that I am alone and lost. I try to panic within myself in order to return to my life-breathing body. I imagine eating a peeled orange, imagine salivating, but without glands this is not possible.

Time, I know, pulses around me at sixty minutes per hour. The sun will have necessarily changed positions with the moon, and the sky may be littered with stars. Clouds may have curtsied and left.

One time my parents sat my body against the back board of my bed, placing my cat in my lap, thinking that the love of the animal would draw me back, and it did after an hour of purring, kneading claw marks into my thigh.

I do not intend to bring hardship to my parents by swimming away from the core of my body into my mind and then into a state of suspension. Nor do I enjoy bringing hardship to myself. Doctors explain to me that the chemistry in my brain causes me to experience impaired thinking. Medicine remains a practice, so through the practice of medicine, they prescribe drugs that will assist my mind in thinking appropriately.

I flirt with the idea that the government picked my name from a large glass bowl containing the names of all Americans born in March of 1964. Before I can remember anything, agents placed a dial in my brain, wiring it to my God-given will, causing me to march to three different drummers: God's will, self-will, and the government's will.

I can explain why God wills me to do things. I can explain why I will me to do things. But I cannot explain why the government wills me to do things unless I have some unseen power that helps them to prosper. Maybe my dollar is worth 100 cents and my step forward or backward has a ripple effect on the rest of the community.

Certainly, if I am powerful enough to make history, my deeds will influence change. But thus far, I am locked into a family portrait that hangs on the wall in the hall. The Voices I hear over the regular traffic of my life insist that evil is heavier than kindnesses. Evil goes noted as smiles fall to the ground with a ping, evaporating into silence. I hope evil falls under the same laws as vampires and needs to be invited in. This gives me hope, as I know I lack the social incentive to invite anyone in.

## A Trip

The study invites me to sit and gather my senses. I take off my shoes so my feet can think better. I heard the expression *thinking on your feet* and thought it meant good to do this, to lose the shoes.

My favorite book contains God. I believe all books contain God. God and I build things together with a hard hammer that never misses its mark. The largest thing we have built is a staircase with no last step. At first, it wearied and frightened me to think of journeying up steps with no end. Coming to an end included rest and the reversal of misfortune. I would travel far only to find myself once again. Complete.

On all the trips to date, nothing significant has happened to steal my last breath even though my mind fainted a few times at heights exceeding my imagination.

As I said early on, when I learned I had mental illness, I thought at first the doctor was lying. I thought he was interested in my doing things that others did, like wearing matching clothes, and showering after sweating. Because I did not do these things, I thought the doctor was passing judgment, telling me that I was strange.

Paranoid schizophrenic. After the doctor said this, a revelation followed. I realized that I had known this and that my obsession with suicide was larger than I cared to admit. I was no longer terrified to accept the fact that I didn't have a personality disorder and that I would indeed need drugs to treat what I had.

I was tired of fighting for my bit of earth crammed between the roof of my house and the closest star. The fight left me blind to what was really in front of me. I couldn't imagine how I was going to outgrow illness like one outgrows the need to always appear right.

## Crows (1997)

I am renting a room from Hank the morning my mom calls and asks me to drive to Bel Air to see my father. Dad had been commuting from there to the home in San Clemente for several months. He urged my mother to move, but she was done giving up everything for him at a moment's notice. She wanted to keep her set of friends, wanted to play golf on the course she liked. It had taken years, but she had finally settled into life in San Clemente after having moved from Dayton, Ohio.

She calls me and asks this of me. I ask her what's up. It was unusual for her to telephone me, and then to ask me to go visit my father, even more unusual.

"Mom, what's really going on? I'm just not going to shake off sleep and jump on my motorcycle to go say hello when all I have to do is pick up the telephone to do that."

"I think your father is cheating on me."

"Really?"

"Really. Please, will you go catch him?"

The thought of "catching" my father doing anything was not pleasant. "No Mom, I won't do that. I'm really sorry this is happening to you."

She was infuriated with me. "Can't you just do this, just this one thing?"

"No."

"Fine," and she hangs up on me.

It doesn't surprise me that my father is having an affair. They had both been unhappy with each other for a long time. At least that was my take on the relationship.

"Kristina," Hank called from the kitchen. I walked in. "Check this out, there are four cabinet doors opened and one drawer."

Ha. I had done it again. Left all that open. It drove Hank crazy when

I did this. I couldn't explain why I had a problem shutting the doors and drawers.

"Sorry," and I shut them. I turned to Hank and said, "If your mother asked you to go catch your father having an affair, would you do it?"

"No. Not any of my business."

"That's my thought on it too. I'm going back to bed. Maybe I'll see you at noon."

And I did. I went back to bed and slept with no problem. This made me feel like a horrible daughter.

When I wake, I call Mom. She answers the phone.

"Hi, Mom."

"Hi." I immediately could tell she'd been crying.

"I'm so sorry this is happening to you."

"I drove up to see your father and the bitch answered the door." She was having trouble talking. Crying took great breaths of air and stole her speech, or at least slowed her speech. "I punched her in the stomach and then ran into the condo. I grabbed her purse sitting on the kitchen table. This ugly purple thing. Before she or your dad could react, I pulled out her wallet and took out her driver's license. I wanted the bitch's name. She came toward me so I punched her again. She went after me and, and—"

"It's okay, Mom, just breathe."

"—and I thought your father was going to protect me from her, but instead he stepped between us, protecting her, and told me to leave. I left. I didn't know what else to do. I still have her driver's license. She's not getting it back from me."

"Oh, Mom." I was at a loss for words. I really felt for her. In her fifty years, she had never been alone. "What next?"

"I don't know. I just don't know. I guess I put the house on the market. I guess I move." She was sobbing. "I gotta go."

"Okay, Mom. I love you, Mom," and she hangs up.

I stare a long time out the window of my bedroom. Long enough to see a crow fly into the tree outside and leave. And then come back. Or was it a different crow than the first?

## Colon Cancer

I was at work at the library when I got the news. Rose called and said Grandpa Poser had died. He had had colon cancer for a while, so death wasn't too unexpected. I always thought him having colon cancer was ironic, as he was the one who was convinced you never leave the house in the morning until you've had a bowel movement. And having tomatoes and onions with breakfast would keep a person regular. His death was still devastating, though. And it hit Mom hard, and Grandma Poser even harder.

Mom and I met at the Long Beach Airport, flying to Phoenix together. I don't remember Grandpa's service at all. I stayed in Phoenix for a week. The entire week, I slept with my grandmother in her bed. Mom slept in the room she had grown up in.

I remember everyone telling my grandmother she was now free to do all those things she couldn't do when Grandpa was alive. My uncle was pushing for my grandmother to sell the house, buy a condo, and play golf as often as she wanted. None of this registered with her. All she knew is that the man she had loved for the past fifty-five years was dead. She moved around as if in a sandstorm, feet dragging and breeze blowing her backward. She was blinded to all forward motion. I stroked her hair at night.

## Water

The first day back at work after having left Phoenix, I got another telephone call from Rose. Grandma Poser was dead. This hit me even harder. I couldn't imagine how my mom must feel with both her parents suddenly gone. The only explanation for Grandma's death was a broken heart. A heart attack. They didn't perform an autopsy, so no one was ever to know that her death was anything but a broken heart.

Mom had woken to hear water running in the bathroom. She got up to check on it. She found Grandma curled on the floor as if she had just suddenly gotten tired and wanted to sleep for a moment.

I flew back to Phoenix. On the plane, I wrote down what I would say at her service. I have misplaced it and have no memory of what I said. I do know that I believed my grandmother to be happy dying as she did. I could only hope that she and my grandfather were indeed together again.

Mom was to fly back to San Clemente, pack the house, and return to her childhood home.

## Forever

Hannah emptied the home she and Jeremy had shared in San Clemente of everything to include the lawnmower and tools, except for one thing. She left the bronze statue of Don Quixote sitting on his horse without Sancho at his side. It was at that moment that Hannah claimed to be the voice of reason in her relationship with Jeremy. Jeremy was the one to attack windmills while she fed her daughters and knotted their shoes. It was only at Hannah's insistence that Jeremy became responsible.

Hannah had tied Jeremy to responsibility with thread as strong as dental floss. First the ring, then the wedding, then a home with a mortgage and an electric bill, furniture and children, a dog, and a car. The list was stapled to Jeremy's skin in the same way that lotion is absorbed, quietly and without strain.

Life opened to them. A perfumed letter pulled from an envelope. They both enjoyed the scent for a long stretch of time until Tuesday came and Hannah burnt the salmon. Hannah was the first to learn the scent of the relationship had darkened and changed. I would be the next to learn, and then Rose and Hunter. Grandma and Grandpa Poser would never learn that the time for divorce had come. They would die with Mom never having told them.

Hannah reasoned that everything in the house belonged to her. She was the one to dust it, wash it, air it out, sweep it, and cling to it like a raccoon with a gold coin held in his fist inside of a bottle, and the bottleneck making it impossible to remove the coin without opening his fist. Hannah had to let go. She had to open her fist.

The movers did as she asked, moved it all into a home already filled with furniture and scorpions that hid beneath wood and fabric. The spiders were just waiting for Monday to lay eggs.

Jeremy's new woman, Betty, called Hannah a thief after she learned Jeremy couldn't find a tie. Jeremy had broken into the house through a second-story window in need of ties, only to find them gone. Upon learning this, Hannah took the box that contained the ties to Salvation Army as a donation, although it was hard to walk away from ties that failed after having the hope that forever is as strong and permanent as a falling day.

## Mama

Rose didn't trip at the door like so many people do. The concrete is cracked there, and ladies in high heels usually lose their shoe.

Paul liked the way Rose moved, cocky, like she was the best thing that ever walked into Harold's Bar. She threw her head back slightly as she drew smoke from her cigarette. She was wearing a short mini-skirt, hot pink and proud. Paul wanted to leave the stage, but instead drummed harder.

Rose sat right in front. When her eyes settled on Paul, Paul didn't look away. No way. Paul wanted this one. His mama said to always leave the ones alone who seemed to cast spells; don't let your heart leap on a first glance. This kind of woman will eat you up. Paul thinks, *What does Mama know? She jumped in front of a bus two years ago.* Paul didn't make this up. Mama's as dead as the goose that came to Christmas.

## Applause (November 1997)

Paul shaves his head to hide his age from Rose, from the other women he may meet, from Hannah, who would not approve of the twenty-year age difference between him and her daughter.

A steady breeze of smoke had carried Rose to a small table in front of the stage, a leaf carved into the top. Rose put her cigarette out on its vein.

Rose was close enough to Paul to smell his sweat, an odd mixture of alcohol and mint. Paul winked and drummed charm. Rose vibrated from his gaze. Later they would make love in the alley, Rose's small size thrown up against graffiti, her slender legs easily wrapped around Paul. Their baby, Frankie, would be conceived here.

Paul had drummed with the best in his youth. His gentle spirit and large hands beat sweet cream into rhythm that buried itself into the souls of audiences. He was sought after and he sought the high applause given him. When this high was not enough, he moved on to find laughter and contentment in a bottle of whiskey.

He told me that drinking toward drunkenness was like having a million women gently stroke his face, tickle his face, love his face.

## Lost

Hunter is missing in action. The last place she was seen was Grandma Poser's service. She looked worn, her clothes dirty. Too many drugs were catching up to her. And whiskey wasn't helping. After the service, at the reception, she got drunk. I didn't know the man she started flirting with. He brushed her off the arm of his jacket and walked away. I had never seen Hunter look so lost.

She started flirting with another man, an older man. She had better luck this time. The two of them were laughing at the same jokes. They left together. I'm certain Hunter was impressed with his Mercedes. I have never known what happened to the baby blue Corvette she bought in Tucson years before.

## Dead Time

Hannah emptied the many photo albums, pinned all the pictures to the walls, brought the feeling of a mausoleum to her new home, the home she had grown up in. It took her hours, and three black markers, to free the photos from Jeremy.

Paul asked Hannah why she left dead time hanging on the walls. Paul didn't own a photo and lived without sentiment. Apparently he had no ties and was left to borrow one each time he attended a funeral.

Her only response to Paul was to drag on her cigarette and lock eyes with him. Paul was the first to look away, muttering something about smoking and the need to go pull tomatoes from the garden.

Hannah allowed dust to settle and build on the surface of the furniture. Meanwhile, the weight of the air kept a fresh breeze from blowing inward, past the front door of the house.

## Stand Up

Paul lost his drum set to cocaine. No drum set, no work. No work, no money. No money, and desperation settles into his toes. Not even socks can hide the fact that he steals anything worth a dime from Hannah. He depends on her to be drunk enough so as not to notice the missing microwave or television set, or crystal doorknobs. All gone.

He snorts cocaine behind the pea vines in a chair he moved from the family room to the mud outside the garden. He snorts cocaine and feels his face dissolve, leaving his skull exposed. Flies enter his eye sockets and he doesn't care that there is no sound other than their buzzing. He tells me his mind separates from his body, a bullet being released from its chamber. The skull he becomes leaves him with no expression although inside he feels he is bursting and all drives are heightened. He wants to do things that he is incapable of doing, like jumping off the Bank of America, migrating with the birds heading north for a place of safety.

He wishes to separate from the rest of the world while fueling his desire to be one with everything. He dreams of walking away from the mirror and becoming millions of people other than himself, and then he thinks to drum his way back into his body. He listens for applause while crawling on his knees through a park toward home. Sometime today he will see Frankie. He wants to be standing for that.

## Marigolds

Hannah says my shaved head drives her to drink. I tell her it is the bent sunflowers. She makes me rub dish soap on my gums. Close my mouth for five minutes. God still continues to talk to me. As did the Suits. Ignore the evil in your life by not looking up. Blindness as a powerful thing. It never occurs to Hannah to say I love you back. The marigolds need planting.

### The Fedora (November 1997)

Jeremy's girlfriend, Betty, is a small, blond woman who likes to wear hats and who still looks good in jeans. She is the same age as my father, fifty-three. She is a Hollywood woman, meaning she has hung around all types of people, including gays and lesbians, with no judgment. She also is working in Hollywood, trying to sell the television script she is writing.

She takes an interest in me. *Of course,* I think. I am one of my father's daughters. Common sense says she would take an interest in me. My father has told her that I too am a writer. He has also told her I date women.

It is a brisk evening in November, requiring coats. I have on a long black coat that resembles a navy peacoat, only longer. Meg has on a long leopard coat, and my friend Hank is in leather. The three of us head to my father's in Bel Air. We have been invited to dinner and to the Comedy Palace by Betty. Hank drives, Meg sits in the passenger seat, and I in the back. This is the first time I have been invited to my father's apartment. I wonder what his definition of a bachelor pad is. I will soon see.

We arrive. There is plenty of parking space. The apartment building reminds me of something out of the Lonely Planet *Greece* book I have shelved dozens of times at the library. It is a pasty white stucco with something akin to a steeple on the top. We enter the lobby—granite floors and brushed soft yellow walls. It breathes wealth. The elevator is right there. Dad is on the fifth floor, his door to the left.

Betty answers the door wearing a black velvet fedora. I love it. Dad is the one who told me that Betty is always wearing hats. She invites us in. We step right into the living room. There is a bar with a mirrored wall behind it. Light reflects off the crystal glasses and bottles of liquor. The couch is a warm brown leather. There is a matching chair with an ottoman. A counter separates the kitchen from the living room. The kitchen is modern and so large, it looks like it belongs in a three-thousand-square-foot house. My father is a fabulous cook and enjoys serving people; it makes sense that he would have an amazing kitchen, granite counters with a built-in chopping block, stainless-steel appliances, gas burners, fancy water fixtures, and room, plenty of room.

Betty asks us what we would like to drink. We say water in unison. She pours water from a pitcher in the refrigerator into crystal glasses retrieved from the bar.

"Cheap guests," she jokes.

"They don't drink," my father says. I am glad he remembers this. We never really talk about my sobriety. We never really talk. I am certain that Betty orchestrated this entire evening. It is the first time my father has met my girlfriend. He is a gracious host. It is not apparent that he dislikes gay people.

Betty boasts that she spent all day making lasagna for us. She serves it out of an aluminum container. Hank will joke later that she bought it from Costco.

## Time (December 1997)

I break up with Meg for the last time. I don't recall why. There doesn't even have to be a why. I get it in my head that I need to be alone. The Voices back me up—*be with us, see with us, hear with us, live with us*—everything *with us.*

I move from the condo we had shared for the last year into Ursula's home. Ursula is a seventy-year-old woman on a walker who needed someone to buy groceries for her, do her laundry, fix meals, take her to get her hair washed, and an assortment of other small tasks. I learned about her from one of the patrons at the library.

Again, I found myself too self-centered to make a good roommate for Ursula. She would have liked me to hang out and watch television with her in the evenings and other times I wasn't at work. I didn't do this. I hibernated in my room. It was as if I allowed myself to be sick when I wasn't at work or doing chores for Ursula. And I was sick, too sick to really know I was sick, but sick enough to know something was terribly wrong. It amazed me that life went on and I suffered through it. I hadn't seen my therapist Audrey in years. I did have a doctor who prescribed me meds, but I was not the best at taking them as ordered. And when I was med compliant, I was still having tremendous difficulties. I didn't know then that it would be years before my meds were right. It's a good thing I didn't know this because I may have shot myself if I had.

# Transitions

## Richard

I met Richard as a nine-year-old. He was fifteen. His family was close to Grandma and Grandpa Poser. Richard and his older brother, Brett, would come to our house to swim, hang out, and drink beer. They were great fun. They would play sea monsters and dibble dabble. Dibble dabble is a game involving a wooden matchstick. Someone takes the matchstick to the bottom of the deep end of the pool. Slowly, the match rises to the top. All of us stand at the edge of the pool deck, waiting to catch first glimpse. Whoever jumps in and retrieves the matchstick yells dibble dabble and earns a point.

So all growing up, there was Richard and Brett. When I entered my teens, I became convinced Richard had a crush on me. He continually asked me to go places. I always declined. I didn't want to encourage him. I knew I wasn't interested.

It was after Grandmother Poser's service, some time in 1998. Grandma and Grandpa Morgan invited Richard to their cabin in Pinetop, Arizona. The cabin was on the eighth hole of a golf course. Richard could play all the golf he liked for free. Seeing as Richard had become a golf pro, he liked to play a great deal of golf. Richard took my hand in his and begged me to go with him, promising a really good time. I was in town for only a few days. I did not need to tell Richard that I had a girlfriend waiting for me in California.

That was the last of Richard until I telephoned him ten years later.

## Even Now

I telephone Richard not considering the time. It is late—eleven. I haven't spoken with him for ten years. It was easy to find his phone number. He was listed in the phone book. I'm not certain why I call him. Maybe it is because he was always so stable, and my life currently is nothing but chaos. I am still managing to make it to work. I am still living with Ursula.

Richard answers.

"Richard. This is Kristina Morgan. Do you remember me?"

"Sure I do," his voice is not sleepy. This is good; I didn't wake him. "Wow. Where did you come from all of a sudden?" he asks.

"Long Beach. I live in Long Beach, California." I know he means something else. I just don't know the answer.

"How've you been?" he asks.

"Okay," I lie. I don't want him to know how fucked up I am. "How've you been?" I ask.

"Great," he answers. "Even better now."

*Excellent.* I think. He still likes me.

We are on the phone for an hour. And then I call him the next night and the next. Thus begins our relationship over the phone.

I fly to Phoenix to spend the weekend with Richard. His mother has sent a gift to our hotel room. It is for the "love birds." It is a basket that contains fruit and bottled water. She knows I don't drink.

Richard and I have a great time. I think I am falling in love. I know he loves me.

## Corners

I moved from Long Beach to Phoenix with the thought of marrying Richard. I moved into the home he shared with his mother. Before this move, I had told him what it looked like when I got sick. Not pretty. I tell him that I hear voices and think the government is looking for me. I tell him I see people wearing suits stalking me. I tell him I can barely leave my bed. I tell him I attempt to die. He says he will love me so much that I will never get sick again. Nice thought. I should have been alarmed by this. I should have thought that he is not really getting the gist of mental illness. Instead, I live in the idyllic future of two people in love, ready to commit formally.

Richard has an amazing family, and sometimes I wonder if it is his family I fall in love with. All the brothers and sisters and the in-laws, nieces, nephews, cousins, grandparents, get together and celebrate every holiday and birthday together. No one in their family is a drunk. No one in the family does drugs. They don't fight. There is no conflict, just a true sense of everybody wanting the best for everybody, which is all reflected in the actions they take of loving one another. They readily extend their love to me.

I have a job awaiting me when I arrive in Phoenix as a surveillance officer for the state's juvenile offenders. I work in conjunction with the parole department. I don't think the ramifications of this job all the way through. I simply think about the kids I will be able to help get on with their lives free of crime. I don't think about the fact that I will be spending most of my time driving around the valley, alone in a car, alone with my mind and no distractions. Driving from home to home to meet with the juveniles is not enough to keep me focused.

\* \* \*

I have a therapy appointment. I sit in the breeze of a doorway. The vase beside me holds dead daffodils that wave at nothing like the collar of a man alone in the desert, grit gathering in the crest of exposed rib, the vultures are not cruel.

The man beside me flinches at the sound of a window being closed.

Before too long, before my need to urinate, I am called to the back room. My baseball cap hides the rat's nest in my hair.

*Have a seat.*

The vinyl sighs as I sit. There is a young palm in the corner with fresh fronds. It is me and this woman squeezed by a bit of tropic. I think light. Her first question pinches my flame; she wants to know if I hoped to die. I tell this woman what it feels like to be awake—the taste of spice with every sliver of pie, death a thicket away.

* * *

One of the best things my therapist, Claudia, did for me was to suggest that I apply for the psychiatric benefits offered through the state. This I did not knowing how much help I was really going to need.

Thursday afternoon. I am with Claudia in her office. I end up sitting in the corner on the floor of her office, catatonic for hours. I know it is for hours because the next time I actually speak with Claudia, she asks me for money for the three hours she had to turn clients away while I was being tended to by a psychiatric team.

When I snap out of the catatonia enough to walk to the ambulance that awaits me, I am taken to Banner Behavioral Health Hospital on Earll and Miller in Scottsdale. The psychiatric team that is helping me is relieved that I finally said I would go voluntarily. This meant that they could take me to a hospital they preferred rather than involuntarily committing me and taking me to the county hospital.

Psychosis has deeply embedded me once again. I am overtaken by the differing realities vying for my attention. Once at the hospital, they walk me to the isolation room, where I proceed to crawl on the floor, desperately in search of a corner to tuck myself into again.

Typically, when being admitted to a psychiatric hospital, you meet with an intake person in the front office who evaluates whether or not you need to be admitted, and if yes, you are then walked onto the unit. This time, the evaluation team had to come to me with their many questions. I remember struggling to hear them over the Voices from the other realities: *Do you dare disturb the universe, kill me, kiss me, do with me, die with me.* I remember one of the nurses being really kind, telling me that I am doing a great job. "Just stay with me," she keeps repeating.

After the questions, they jack me up with Haldol, an antipsychotic medication that works almost immediately. They left me on the bed in the isolation room. I don't remember falling asleep. I have no idea how I got from my street clothes into a hospital gown.

Richard, his mother, and one of his sisters come to visit me that night. I am escorted from the isolation room to the couch across from the nurse's station. I am so drugged that I slide down off the couch, onto the floor. Richard keeps lifting me back up. I am so medicated that I am drooling and can't focus on what they are saying. It is like being in a cartoon with the volume off, and mouths just opening and shutting at will. I have no idea how long they stay with me. Time lost its place in the world. I do know that it was a mistake for them to come this first day. I scare them. Richard is the only one to visit me again after many days of my being there.

This all happened on a Thursday. The psychiatrist assigned to me had twenty-four hours in which to see me. My psychiatrist didn't come that night. That night, my first night on the ward, they push my bed out in front of the nurse's station so they can keep an eye on me. I have no idea what they thought I might do in the drugged state I was in. I lost all sense of myself as a person; it was not embarrassing at all to have patients and staff alike watch me sleep.

## Another Break

A case manager wakes me the next morning wanting to talk with me. I tell her to fuck off and let me sleep. She is taken aback. I think she is used to patients wanting to talk with her. On the ward, it is a high point for the patient to actually talk to staff. It is a relief from pacing the halls or standing alert but silent, inactive, a sentient being with nothing to focus on.

She does leave me alone. I do fall back into drugged sleep.

I finally wake up crazed with a filthy mouth. I don't really understand where I am or how I got here. At the moment, all I know is that I am desperate for a cup of coffee. Strong. French roast. Okay, I would settle for Maxwell House.

No coffee on the unit. This year they considered it bad for mental patients.

There are telephones the patients can use. Patient. I thought, *Be patient, not a patient.* I tried to calm myself. It doesn't work. I am still wild with the word *fuck*. I had yet to see a doctor. They could offer me no help with medication without her consent. Dr. Jill Pool was the name of the doctor I would be seeing.

I did remember my grandparents' telephone number. I can't remember if my telling them where I was was the first they heard about it, or if Richard called them and let them know. I ask them to please bring me caffeine. Coffee and soda both. There were other things I needed, like soap. That would come later.

I get off the phone hoping they aren't disgusted with me for falling apart again. I finally realize that I had fallen apart and was indeed in a psychiatric hospital. I inform the staff I am fine now and need my shoes so I can leave. Never mind actual clothes. I have seen people on the streets in hospital garb. Of course, these people usually had few options and I actually did own a shirt. Even a hat. That's it, I needed a hat to keep my mind warm and humming properly along.

I am stuck on the unit all day waiting for Dr. Pool. At 5 p.m., in walks this woman through the locked doors. I instinctually know it is her and bum rush her.

"Where the fuck have you been?" I say to her.

She too was intuitive and knew that I must be Kristina, the patient she was to see on the eleventh hour.

"Into this room," she points toward a small room that contains only a desk and two chairs. Nothing on the walls.

We sit. "I want out now," I say.

"Fine," she surprises me by saying this. "It's late on Friday. I've had a whole week of patients and, quite frankly, I'm tired. You had a psychotic break, may still even be in psychosis, but you want out, and I'm not going to fight with you. So fine, I'll sign you out." All this is said brusquely and with heat.

My story changes. "No. Don't sign me out. I'll stay. It will be good for me to stay."

I have no idea what I dribbled on about after that. She leaves and I said *fuck it* to no one but the bare walls.

* * *

Richard comes the next day with clothes and soap, shampoo, tooth-brush, a blow dryer, comb, brush, basic stuff.

Now I have the means with which to get cleaned up and in fresh clothes, but not the desire. Everything seems difficult. I am so amazingly tired and defeated. I think back to the doctor of my youth, the doctor who saw me in the first psych hospital I was ever in when I was eighteen. My father was to tell me that the doctor told him I would be in and out of hospitals for the rest of my life. I don't know why that doctor said that. I remember it infuriated my father. I also don't know why my father would want me to know something like that.

* * *

Upon release from the hospital, Richard comes to get me to take me to his home. I say *his home* because he let me know on the way there that I needed to move. He said he was not strong enough to handle me. I was so doped on meds that I had very little to say. In fact, I think I just said okay.

I moved from Richard's into my grandparents' home. I did return the engagement ring to Richard and wished him well. We had no contact after the move. The no contact I think was mostly because I was too exhausted to lift the telephone and talk. My depression swallows me and will not spit me out for some time.

## Sun

Rose tans on a towel in the driveway. She doesn't want bugs to bother her. She thought if she stayed off the lawn in the backyard, they wouldn't.

Hannah's home is located on a main street with no dead end. Rose has been living with Mom for some time now.

Jonathan drives past and then turns around. He notices Rose and remembers her from high school.

"Well, if it isn't Johnny boy in a big black truck." Rose lights a cigarette and puts the match out in a pool of perspiration that has puddled on her stomach.

"You remember me?" he asks.

"Behind the bleachers at halftime. You gave me a note."

"And I walked away." He pauses and continues, "It said Michael loves Rose."

"He did love me, for a while," Rose says.

"Have dinner with me tonight." Jonathan said it more like a statement than a question, a note written in the air that hung with no doubt and could not be retrieved. Its immediacy caused Rose to smile.

## Fury

That night Jonathan picked Rose up and they went out to dinner. Rose wore a sheer blouse with a black bra and a leopard miniskirt.

Jonathan must have liked what he saw.

They were living together within the month even though Jonathan had divorced his wife because she wanted to have kids and he didn't. He would come to love Rose's daughter, Frankie, over the next few years. It was out of love that Jonathan would turn Frankie over to his friends down the street temporarily, the religious couple who didn't care about shoes, when Rose's complaints and bizarre behavior became too great, leaving her like a split lemon at the front door.

Rose believed she was just tired because Frankie was a constant whirlwind of activity on a desert floor. Without Frankie, it was Jonathan's hope that Rose would be forced to recognize why the doctor wanted her on lithium. Even without Frankie, Rose will not be able to slow down but will be the puppet whose demon will continue to pull strings rapidly against the wind.

It may be said that she is tired. She cleans house all day long beginning at one in the morning. She irons sheets and lines up the green beans in column three on the pantry shelf. The rice will go in the fifth column on the second shelf, beside the tortilla chips.

Rose made a series of telephone calls to me just before Frankie was sent away. "He divorced Mom. How could he have divorced Mom? How could he possibly do what he said he would never do?"

Rose spoke of the yesterday that came and went twelve years ago. Rose holds our father to the notion that staying loyal and loving one person in a lifetime is like handing God a flower. "God doesn't care for the flower Dad handed him."

Rose confuses who she blames, God or Dad. "If there is a God who plans people's lives, why didn't he take better care of our mother? Mother gets dropped like a penny in a pond of wishful thinking. Mud and more mud just sucked the life right out of her."

Rose always makes Hannah the victim.

Rose remains furious with Father. It has been twelve years. Her thinking sinks to the bottom of her coffee cup and cools.

Rose's heart had to harden against Father in order to keep her fury blowing east against the side of the house, pounding on the outside wall of the bathroom, giving him reason to look in the mirror each morning and know why she is angry.

Her fury toward Father for divorcing Mother remains attached to the buttons of her shirt. The wishbone is left sitting on the kitchen counter hyperventilating with the African Daisies.


## Quiet

Rose met Jonathan on a warm September day. Rose told me that she asked him to take her someplace still. Jonathan picked a place where the trees were loving and isolated from the city buildings and car exhaust. Their leaves were thick and green and allowed for patches of light to bounce off them and slide down their trunks, hitting the ground with spectacle.

It was one of those spots that they threw the blanket to the ground. Rose grabbed two corners while Jonathan grabbed the other two, making a smooth patch of red wool in the dirt. Rose marked each corner with a stone, weighting the blanket in place.

"It's lovely here. I haven't been someplace so quiet in a long time."

Rose made a tunnel of her mouth with both hands. "Aho, aho, aho. Hello. Good-bye. Feed me." Nothing echoed back. "You would think something would echo back," Rose said.

"Not in the trees," Jonathan responded. "There needs to be a mountain wall to catch what you are saying, or you need to be in some sort of cavern."

"It's still lovely even without the echo." Rose wore brown shorts, long to the knees with ample pockets, and hiking boots. Her midriff showed with her white T-shirt, sporting the logo of *Move On* in yellow lettering across her chest.

Jonathan threw her softly to the ground, his arm around her, landing on top of her. "I thought your shirt said *Come Close,* so I thought I would."

"For you, baby, it does. It says *Come Close.*"

Rose's hair spread out, framing her tanned face, looking much like the masks seen at craft shows that are made out of clay with hair and feathers added to their outer edges. Jonathan ran his fingers from her eye to her chin, his fingers pausing at the dip in her throat, the weight of a fossilized bee, and then settled his mouth on hers. Rose allowed all this to happen. Rose said she could live with this weight forever, with the knowledge that he was there, heavy enough to be felt but not so heavy that it cut her voice from her like a similar weight had Hannah.

Jonathan rolled off her, resting his weight on one elbow with one leg casually tossed over hers. His free hand roamed the cotton of her shirt, pausing at her breasts, pausing at her heart, letting his hand hear her steady beat.

"My heart is talking to you," she said.

"What's it saying?"

"That I could really grow to like this. That I could really grow to like having you to myself."

"You have me, Rose."

"And how do I have you?" replied Rose. "Like a having you between work and dinner kind of thing?"

"Do you want more, Rose? Are you telling me that you don't want to run away with that mouth of yours?"

"It's a good thing you don't talk much," Rose said. "I don't have to choke silence into you. A man of few words, that would be you, and a woman with a nonstop tongue, that would be me. I don't expect you to listen to all my ravings, just most of it," and she laughed.

Jonathan had now settled on her sex. She moved her right hand, placing it on top of his, encouraging him to continue, pressing, stroking. The trees heard her sigh.

Jonathan liked to think he was loving her into a silence she felt to her core, speechlessness as life-changing. He thought she could get used to this silence as long as she was wrapped in his arms. It beat smoking marijuana to get her mind to slow to a pace others could tolerate. He did care for her. This understanding settled her like a letter B stenciled alongside an A in black ink. The alphabet expanding. He slowly unzipped her shorts. A lizard walked through her hair. The leaves shimmered in a soft C. Sun surrounded them on all edges of the blanket.

"I haven't felt this warm since Frankie's birth," she said.

Jonathan thought Rose was one of the prettiest women he had seen. He loved how he was around her. Protective, caring, wanting to help. Rose's need for help did not scare him off. It made him want her even more.

He knew not to fool himself; with Rose came Frankie. It is true that he'd never wanted children. And then there was Frankie. Frankie with her dark skin and crazy, ratty, stand-up hair. Frankie liked to call him Brother John. She would smile with deep dimples that answered her eyes when she called him this. He loved watching her play with Barbies in the yard as dog. Frankie was dog. She would walk on all fours, swish her back end back and forth, and charge at the dolls. Fiercely, she ate the heads off the dolls and then spit them out onto a plate with the rest of the heads. After playing dog, she would play doctor and repair the Barbies' heads by attaching them to their bodies, again.

Jonathan made slow, easy love to Rose. The stones worked hard to hold the red blanket in place. The blanket stayed and they loved. Rose remained silent except for the dragon breath she released at orgasm. Their bodies shuddered in time to each other. A lizard turned around, heading back to the shadow of the tree it had left.

They dressed each other before sunset. Jonathan tugged Rose's shirt over her head and pulled her arms through. Rose pulled one leg of Jonathan's shorts over his ankle and then the next as he heaved half of his weight onto her for the sake of stability.

Together they shook the stones from the blanket and folded it into a square that they tossed into the back of the truck.

Rose seated herself in the passenger's seat and Jonathan took the seat behind the steering wheel. The back tire hit a bump. Only Jonathan felt it. Rose was too busy talking.

"And we'll pick up Frankie and take her to a pizza parlor and then maybe out for some ice cream. Can we stop at the bank first? I have a check I need to deposit."

"Sure," Jonathan replied.

"Oh and look, Jonathan. There's a cat. It doesn't belong out here. Stop. We need to pick it up. Oh no, now you're too far away. We'll never catch him now. And he'll starve and get squashed by people who don't care. We don't squash living things, Jonathan. You and I. We don't, but—"

"Rose, slow down. The cat will be okay. Now where are we going? Which bank?"

"Let's do the bank after we pick up Frankie. Okay?" Rose asked.

"So how do I get Frankie? Is it the same house I pulled up to last week?"

"Yes, the farm. We call it that because the corral is now used to grow groceries in."

"Groceries?" Jonathan asked.

"Yes. Cantaloupe, strawberries, lettuce, cucumbers. The entire produce section at Safeway's grocer. Well no. Maybe not quite that much."

They pulled before the house. Rose jumped out before Jonathan had the truck in park.

"Stay put, Jonathan. I'll get Frankie."

"I'd like to see the house."

"No, you have to trust me on that. Okay?" and Rose smiled. Jonathan blushed. He could feel himself rise to her smile.

Jonathan looked around the yard, noting the broken-down truck, the broken-down car, lumber, pesticides, large pots, rotting newspapers.

He thought the inside couldn't be as bad as the outside. But he stayed in the truck anyway, respecting Rose's wishes.

Hannah came out before Rose returned. She wore a tight T-shirt with no bra. Her T-shirt just made it to the top of her shorts. She wore flip-flops. Though Jonathan was certain she must have washed her clothes, her toenails with their deep red polish seemed to be the part of her that was most taken care of.

"You could come in, you know," Hannah said as she lit a cigarette. "She told you to stay out here, didn't she?"

"Yes, ma'am, she did. I'm Jonathan."

"Yes. I know. And I am Hannah, but I figure you knew that already. My daughter's beautiful, isn't she?"

"Yes. Yes, she is."

Hannah's cigarette dragged through the air making it heavy.

Jonathan felt the weight of Hannah's presence like an iron ball settling on the roof of the truck. He started drumming his fingers on the steering wheel, wishing that Rose and Frankie would appear and break the intensity of Hannah's stare, crossing out the question that lay between them.

Something softened in Hannah's face. "Take care of her, will you?" Hannah ran her hand down her cheek, a brief loving moment of self-care, and then turned to walk back into the house. The house seemed to move toward her as she did this, swallowing her through the open door. The screen door banged behind her after she entered. Jonathan shuddered. He had never seen such resignation in a person. Even the porch seemed disconsolate.

Just for a second, Jonathan thought to drive away. Something he could not explain pushed him to stay. The car clock skipped another minute. Rose and Frankie walked through the door, banging the screen door open. The bang pushed him out of his thoughts quick enough for him to catch the smiles of Rose and Frankie.

## Yellow Elephants

Samantha is a tall woman with a Ph.D. in psychology who believes hurt can heal and joy can be found. Her plaque on the wall reads Licensed Therapist. I am reminded of Lucy in her lemonade stand. Mom calls Samantha a symphony. I think of God orchestrating the sounds that resonate in the forest and collect on the first steps of city hall.

Mom came to Samantha's office in June of 2001, feeling that she missed something in her life because of being too close to her name to fully stand on top of it and see clearly. Love. Mom ultimately wanted her family to understand the power of love regardless of mistakes made along the way. Regardless of the harm they may have caused each other like a hot wax candle tipped onto a wood floor. It is impossible to remove all the wax. Mom knows this but doesn't want to believe it.

Mom entered Samantha's office a sad woman in brightly colored clothes. Yellow elephants marched across the chest of her deep pink T-shirt, their trunks quivering in tandem to her breath. Neon green shorts hung loosely from her waist to mid-thigh, the color of lime Jell-O. She wore doctor-issued white stockings to help with circulation, and white Keds laced and tied in a double knotted bow. Her hair was uplifted by a pick and hair spray. Gold pineapples hung from her ears. Her fingers were stained by nicotine.

I had come to Mom's session with her at her request. Samantha welcomed me.

Samantha and I could see Mom's hand shake as she brought it to the dip in her throat each time she spoke, as if she needed to either soothe herself into speaking, or restrain herself from telling all that she wanted to tell. It was probably a bit of both.

The colors and designs of the room made it warm. It was carpeted in deep blue with walls painted red-clay brown. There was a stained glass window, a large print of Van Gogh's *Starry Night,* and an abstract of Rothko's done in desert colors.

Samantha didn't sit behind her desk when speaking with clients. She moved to the fat leather couch. Mother chose to sit across from her in the winged chair. A coffee table rested between them on which sat flowers and porcelain cups of tea, butter cookies, slices of orange, and Bosc pears. I sat at the farthest end of the couch, as far away as I could sit from Samantha.

Time was turned from us. Samantha likes clients to intuit time during their first session, taking as much time as they needed, even as late as the newspaper arriving at night.

I have been to many therapists. Never once did they serve me tea.

"Kristina, would you like some tea?" Samantha asks, her voice the sound of stones skipping across water—steady alluring.

"Yes," I say. Mother has already said no to tea.

"I am quite chilled most of the time," Mom says, "even in the sun. But I can't bring myself to wear a coat in Phoenix." She rocked forward in her chair. "People would think me odd."

Samantha lets the word *odd* sit between them like ash on the end of a cigarette. Eventually it falls to the ground and disappears.

I shift my weight. Samantha will accept my line of thought like blue hair on old women. I swallow my tea in one gulp. The teacup is set gracefully down on its saucer. Glass to glass. There is no ping.

"Many things are a demonstration of contradiction," I say to Samantha. I think of Mother's bright dress. I think how wind flies without moving while looking out a window to a cloudless sky.

I turn my stare to Mom. She doesn't talk about the weather. I feel the storm settling in her chest. She loves Bosc pears. Picks one up. Its weight is magnificent. Pears will always weigh just that much.

"Hannah, are you afraid to talk in front of Kristina?" Samantha asks.

Mom says no, but doesn't continue talking. I know she is tired to the bone and dying. I don't know if she wants to stop this dying. Her wishbone has been tugged from tendons and fat and cleaned. It dries on the kitchen counter, the blinds raised. The cat leaves it alone.

I put five butter cookies in my mouth. My cheeks swell with my effort to chew them with my mouth closed. When I'm done swallowing, I say, "I like a full mouth. It allows me to taste the emptiness afterward. To know that I can be without God and then marvel at my ability to invite him in again. He always comes. Heavy foot and all, but with a light heart and a generous smile."

Mom bit into her pear.

There is supposed to be a sliver of moon tonight.

\* \* \*

I sigh and place my writing pad and pen beneath the blanket on the side of the bed left open. I sleep beside my family history I am writing. I hold hands with each of them as I dream of stones the color of jewels being dug up after years of leisure in the mud.

## One Thought

I had just finished another stay at Banner Scottsdale. I was there for two months, mostly because my doctor would not release me until I found a twenty-four-hour care facility at which to live. Via Agave on Baseline and Seventh Street was to become my new home. I spent days lying in bed with black sheets, drowning in dulled light. What is not simple—to wake from drowning.

I shared an apartment with Stormy. There were ten apartments, all two-bedroom, so when filled to capacity, there were twenty of us total.

One of the most important things staff did was dole out our medication three times per day. I hated having to wait in line for meds because I hated being outside, away from my bed or away from the porch. All I did was sleep and sit on the porch. I spent hours sitting on the porch, alone except for a pigeon, watching people enter the super-market across the street and come out fat with groceries.

I waved at cars that didn't know me, counting Mustangs as they sped by.

I would speak incoherently to my roommate, telling her I was not from this reality. My body was doomed to be here, trapping me.

My roommate was young, twenty-two. She shaved stripes into her eyebrows and wore a boot on her left foot, a sandal on her right. The bottom of her never matched the top of her. Jeanette was always giving her a hard time, saying that she dressed like a crazy person. Jeanette didn't like to attract attention to herself, so on our required Sunday field trips, Jeanette would not walk near Stormy at the mall. Our field trips were always to the mall. None of us had any money. I wondered if they were trying to make thieves of us.

I hung a single thought on the moon and slept the erratic sleep of people tired by inactivity with no motion eclipsed by work or purpose.

## Kindnesses (1999)

I didn't work while at Via Agave. I thought that one day the cars I waved at would recognize me. Would recognize that I needed to get off the porch. One of the Mustangs would stop and carry me to a city building where I too could punch in at eight, drink coffee at ten, eat roast beef from the lunch truck at noon, and leave weary at five.

My desires were not much: combed hair, clothes that smelled of Tide, shoelaces, and a boss who expected me to be present every day, able to sign my name and spend money on the second Friday of every month.

Instead of work, my mind took my attention away from the day and traveled with cars to constellations printed on the sky at night. I usually parked at the Big Dipper. My understanding of astrology was limited to this. I thought the Big Dipper was useless because the pail of water to fill it was left by a river two blocks away.

The blisters on my mind were slowly healing. I can tell a person how in a diagram that has God meeting Modern Medicine, and my desire moving beyond Suzette and William of Portugal.

As my mind healed, I wanted less and less to be at Via Agave, drooling into my shirt pocket while sitting on the porch. I was depressed about my circumstances. Don't get me wrong, Via Agave had my best intentions in mind. I was simply unmotivated to do anything while there, and aside from medication time and field trips, there was no structure and nothing to do. At that time in my life, having nothing to do was keeping me very sick.

My solution to all of it was to ask my grandmother and grandfather if I could move back in with them. "Absolutely," was their response.

They came to gather me on a Thursday afternoon. I was surprised to see my grandfather in the passenger seat. Obviously, he wanted to get out of the house and take a ride. He was mostly confined to the house because of his broken neck. He wore a metal halo screwed into his skull. He broke his neck when he got up to go to the bathroom in the middle of the night and fell. This happened at their cabin in Pinetop. They drove home thinking nothing much of his fall because he seemed to be all right. My grandfather was never one to complain, so when home one night at dinner he said he had a raging headache, Grandmother knew to take him to the doctor. And the doctor discovered his broken neck through a series of X-rays. Of course, he was immediately hospitalized.

I felt bad that I felt bad with nothing physically wrong with me. My grandfather never judged me. He never said anything to the effect of, "Look at me, you think you've got problems, well let me tell you."

I packed my few belongings into the car, thanked the staff, and left. A couple of hours after being at my grandparents' home, I panicked, thinking *what have I done?* If nothing else, Via Agave was a safe place to be. I called Via Agave and asked to come back. They said no, I had to go on the waiting list again, and there were many waiting.

I didn't want my grandparents to see me so sick. My attempts at acting not sick were not very successful. I stayed in bed around the clock, leaving my room only for cheese Danish and glasses of milk. Meanwhile, my grandmother had her hands full with my grandfather. It hurt me that I wasn't of any real help to my grandparents, and I thought about how far I had come from the young punk eighteen-year-old who didn't give a damn about anything.

My grandfather never recovered from his broken neck. It was one complication after another. He was given a tracheotomy and a feeding tube. He kept getting pneumonia. He was limited to a wheelchair for quite a while. My grandmother made one of the hardest decisions of her life; she decided to place Grandfather in hospice. Their three sons, one of whom was my father, flew in to see him. Grandpa was happy to see them, as always, and had a typically loving conversation with them. I don't think my grandfather ever realized he was dying.

My grandmother visited the hospital all day every day, usually leaving around five. This particular night, actually my birthday, March 27, she decided to stay later. My grandfather died that night by nine, and my grandmother got to be with him right up until the end. I didn't know until years later that my grandma questioned her decision to place my grandfather in hospice on a daily basis. She continued to live her life with regret. And grief. However, neither of those two things kept her from loving whom she loved and being kind to everyone she came across.

## The Wig (April 2000)

The shuffle of my grandmother's feet down the hall outside my bedroom door was as loud to me as the bass of a speaker turned all the way up playing Mötley Crüe. I wanted to scream at her to walk more quietly. Pick her feet up and put them down as if she were avoiding land mines or deadly wires.

It was 10 a.m. again. Again, another day, and I had woken up. I prayed to not wake up. Let the Voices reach me only in my dreams. They never visited my dreams. They only wanted to snag me when I was awake.

At this time, I was a client of Maricopa County's Psychiatric Care. I had had an interview with them just prior to going to the hospital this last time. They approved me while I was in the hospital. I had been assigned a site to go to, a case manager, and a psychiatrist to see.

I was on medication. It was not the right medication. It was not helping me. Looking back, I know this. But it is very difficult to come up with the right kind of pharmaceutical cocktail. It comes down to trial and error. Yes, the psychiatrist has the experience of prescribing this medication for these kinds of symptoms, but again, it is the practice of medicine.

Also, I had to learn that even if the medication was right, medication is probably 70 percent of me being well, with the other 30 percent of me taking action. I would not get well as long as I made the decision to slowly die in my bed. But then again, that was the thing. I wanted to die—but at age thirty-six, it was unlikely that natural causes would take me. There was no one lingering in my closet with a pillow waiting for the right time to suffocate me. I thought of trying to find someone to pay to murder me, but I had no cash and no idea of where to look for someone to do this. Plus, I was still not leaving the house for anything other than medical appointments.

My grandmother was astonishingly patient with me. She was not insisting that I do anything. However, Elizabeth, my case manager, wanted me out of the house. Elizabeth said my depression was never going to get any better if I didn't start moving. I knew she was right. She signed me up to go to Tri-City, a day program for people with serious mental illness. SMI is the acronym for people like me.

The only way I knew of having any chance of being ready for the van to pick me up in the morning was for me to sleep in my clothes and my boots. That way, when the driver honked the horn, I could just roll out of bed and get on the van.

The Voices hated motion. They preferred to have me in bed, staring at the ceiling, practically catatonic on a regular basis.

At this time, I was wearing a Cleopatra wig. I was tired of people thinking I was a guy because my hair was so short and I was so tall. The Tri-City staff clapped the day I showed up without my wig. They thought it was a sign of me being more comfortable with me. *How ridiculous,* I thought. I forget the reason why I stopped wearing it.

Exercise class at Tri-City was all of us (there were about fifteen of us) sitting in a circle, tossing a beach ball back and forth to one another. And the rest of the groups didn't get much better than this.

What Tri-City did for me was get me out of the house. Put me in motion despite the Voices. Give me the possibility of engaging people outside my own reality.

Tri-City closed after about a month of me attending. Death came blowing through the window. I overdosed again. Grandmother called 911. The paramedics came.

While I was in the ICU, my grandmother sat with me eight hours a day. I was there for three days and was to be sent home with no additional hospitalization. I was glad for this.

## Moths

It has been two years since I stepped into life other than Tri-City. For two years, I lived with psychosis and depression in a room in grandmother's house hoping to die. Before dying, I thought I would take a few classes at the community college.

I dress in a black suit and apply lipstick, treating registration as a formal event, and hiding any signs of my illness.

The other people registering wore shorts and flip-flops and were considerably younger than myself.

My grandmother sat in a chair, her purse clutched to her lap. She had driven me to the school and had come to support my applying.

I flipped through the schedule of classes not intending to pause at English. I paused at English and fingered the prefixes of the various courses, stopping at creative writing. Ten years prior, I had intended on becoming a writer. It had been ten years since I had written a word much past *dear* on a card.

I was too exhausted to carry on a conversation over the telephone, so I was certainly too exhausted to write. I pushed peas on china at dinnertime instead, and poked at ice cubes in the water glass.

Still, for some unknown reason, I was motivated to try. I signed up for creative writing. Little did I know how much this one thing would change my life. A moth flutters around the hat of a lamp. The lightbulb burns out, and the moth seeks another source of light. My flutter carried me to Sandra Desjardins, the instructor of the creative writing course. She is magic. Regardless of whether or not I wrote one word in class, I knew I needed to be around this woman. Her energy brightens rooms, encourages me to see the little girl with the red cape ride her bicycle as if the day depended on her making it to the park and then back home again before dark.

To this day, Sandy is always just an e-mail or phone call away. I became a poet in her class, something I would never have thought I would become.

## Gifts

I met Bob in Sandy's class, and then later, Bob's wife, Marty. Ten years, and we are still in each other's life. Bob is in his late seventies, and Marty, in her early eighties. I can only hope to be as active and sharp as they are at their age.

They are spiritual people and their religion and sense of God have empowered my own beliefs. They have never pushed their beliefs on me. One night at dinner, they gave me a gift of a small gold cross. In giving me this gift, they said they would understand should I decide not to wear it. I did decide not to wear it, but I still have it. I can touch it and look at it all I want, along with other things that are precious to me. This is far from the days of lying in bed wanting to die, trying to believe that nothing was precious and that I cared very little. Bob and Marty are two of the people who helped me move away from that time. They include me in their prayers and I believe their prayers are heard. When I can't seem to do life on my own, I think about Bob and Marty and some of my other friends and I do it for them, and I do it for God.

Bob sent me a copy of his latest book, *Like Father . . . Like Son*. On the inside page he wrote "To Kristina, a dear friend and the daughter we never had." Things don't get better than this.

## Liver

Hannah had not been able to abide by city law. For years, the fire department had been after her to clean up the yard, warning her that if she chose to ignore their orders, she would lose her home.

She lost her home.

Hannah left her home sad and drunk. She drove to a room inside the home of a friend ten miles away. The room was ten by ten with one closet, dirty carpeting, gray walls, and a bed whose mattress sank deep in the middle.

Hannah envisioned herself laying down and allowing the mattress to swallow her. She laid down, sunk into the bed, closed her eyes, and imagined death.

* * *

It is Thursday when Mom's roommate telephones at three in the morning. He says that Mom is shouting strange things as she paces the kitchen floor. He can't get her to sit down and calm down, or even to put some pants on.

I give him the number to the crisis line and tell him they will send out a team of counselors to help her.

He did and they came and drove Mom to the nearest psychiatric urgent care center. From there, they telephoned me.

"We have your mother here. She insists she speak with you. She's in a pretty bad state of mind, and we thought that your speaking with her might calm her down."

"Okay. Put her on."

"Kristina?" Mom said once she was handed the telephone.

"Mom."

"Run. You have to run to the right religion. I got it all wrong and trusted all the wrong people."

"Mom, slow down. How can I help you?"

"I'm not scared, Kristina. I'm not scared. I think I'm going on a long trip and just wanted to let you know that my telephone will be disconnected for some time. But we'll see each other soon. I promise, baby."

The psych nurse came on at that point. "Hello, Kristina?"

"Yes."

"We're going to send your mother to a medical facility. She's not looking well. That's as much as I can tell you. She'll be going to Boswell in Sun City. You can call her there."

"Thank you for your help, and for keeping me informed."

"Sure. Good luck to you."

The line goes dead. It is three in the morning. I don't know what to do. I softly return the phone to its cradle and turn on the television. Mom will be in a coma and placed on life support within the hour. Her liver quit working. Everything quit working.

## Daughter, Mother

The nurses tell me she is in a coma. I don't expect to be talking with her. I'm standing beside her bed and she opens her eyes. Attempts to sit up. Gets halfway there, and then falls back. Before her eyes close again, I say to her, "Mom, I know you loved us." She closes her eyes again. I am certain she heard me. At least I need to believe that she had.

\* \* \*

My next visit to her, I sit at the end of her bed for hours, writing. She is the dead weight of a semicolon. I note that her toenails are neatly painted crimson red. Her toenails were always neatly painted.

A nurse comes in and asks me if I'm ready. I say yes. Mom had been removed from the breathing machine hours ago, but they had placed a breathing mask over her mouth and nose. This little bit of air was keeping her alive. Mom was officially dead within a minute of it being removed.

The room felt obscenely bright. I bent to kiss her forehead and that was it. No string instruments playing a concerto. The air didn't ruffle as her spirit flew away, if that is indeed what happens at the end. I had never stopped loving this woman. I thought her death tragic. I thought her death just. Her suffering ended here. I would learn to live with my regret. I had not been a good daughter over the past few years. I didn't push my illness aside often enough to spend time with her. I would not learn how to push my illness aside until years after her death.

## Grief

Rose, Frankie, and occasionally Frankie's dad, Paul, lived with Hannah up to her death. Hunter stopped in on occasion, also, always when she was otherwise homeless.

Life doesn't propel Rose further like a calendar with torn pages at the end of the month. Grief and anger at the people she believes contributed to Mom's death feed on her every day. She feels she two-steps with vultures waiting to pick out her eyes. She tells me that Mom is strapped to her back like a knapsack stocked for a long hike. Mom haunts her. Rose carries her to the shower, to breakfast, to play with Frankie, to dinner, and finally to bed, where sleep overtakes her as she curls her thin body around the pillow of Mom. Peace finds her. An uncovered root digs for water in the moist earth and drinks in the shadow of a bare oak. Leaves shake off in preparation of death.

Rose knows that Mom tucked the love she had for her in the pleats of an open drape lining a window she had cleaned for the first time in five months. Rose pulls the drapes across the window when she leaves the house for the last time. She believes Mom's love attaches itself to a strand of her hair. The bulldozer will come Monday and flatten the house and garden that sits on the east corner of the acre lot.

Rose tells me she will always think of the house and garden as beautiful, without its visible litter of broken Chevy trucks, planks of wood, rotted tires, and kitchen sinks. The smaller trash is overshadowed by the larger items, going unnoticed like pins would in a sea of nails.

Rose reminisces about mornings spent watering the garden and pushing Frankie on the tire swing. She recalls tomatoes from the garden with feta cheese on sourdough toast. She remains adamant that Mom didn't have to die, although she is left with the image of Mother standing in a dulled bedroom, wearing a soiled T-shirt, pants ripped high near the crotch, and rubber flip-flops, guzzling vodka from its liter bottle at six-thirty in the morning.

Rose tells me that Mom died from a broken dream that could have been repaired if people had just loved her enough and in the right way.

"How do you know when you're loving someone in the right way?" I asked Rose, with a heavy pain in my mind as I thought of all the weekends I did not take Mom to the movies.

Rose replies, "The person will feel better for having been in your company."

Rose feels like she was the only one, aside from Frankie's kid-love for Grandmamma, who carried Mom through her dark nights. Paul was also there. Watching. Watching Mom's slow suicide, but he could not keep from stealing from her long enough to say, "How are you doing?" and "Can I help?" They both befriended the demon that would kill them, stripping color from their lives like a turpentine wash.

## Stuffed Giraffes

Frankie paints and plays. She paints furniture and walls, faces and dogs. She once painted a grilled cheese sandwich blue because she hated wheat. Take the color of wheat out of bread and have blue. "It's like eating the sky," she tells me.

Frankie draws in my study. She draws a white woman with long turned-up hair and no arms, standing in front of green hills. I think the picture is not of Rose—Rose's hands are always singing shrill notes in the air as she talks—yet Frankie says it is. She says it is her mommy after she has her nails done. It is her mommy quiet.

The thing Frankie and Rose most have in common is talking. Frankie breathes in between stories as Rose pushes everything into the same sentence, all in the same breath, with no periods and no place for the weight of a comma.

Frankie tells stories about making girlfriends while playing with Cootie bugs and discovering that Lucky Charms has colored marshmallows that dissolve in milk that sours from sitting still for two weeks in the heat. Heat is not good for luck or charms. Heat is honest.

Frankie does not talk about a father who has no home and never bathes. She does not talk about her grandmother locking herself in the bedroom, crying loud enough to be heard from the hall, not letting Frankie in so they can play soldiers.

Frankie is good about playing alone with her dolls and stuffed giraffes, so life moves on.

## Cards

Grieving loss of love is like lying beneath lava with a cocktail straw in my mouth, sucking in sky that no longer provides me with shelter. I slip into sorrow while my niece pulls the old maid from my hand. She doesn't understand that old maids no longer exist. The world moves on, or so I like to believe. Aging single women can push that word *spinster* into the hole men dug for them to get lost forever with chipped pieces of brick and earth.

## Marijuana

Rose tells me I should smoke some marijuana. I tell her I had tried one time and all that happened was that I ended up seated in the corner of a room, rocking and paranoid. And then of course I experienced a dry mouth and a huge hunger for corn. Rose tries to explain to me that I just smoked it wrong. She says she could teach me to smoke it right. I don't believe her. I say to smoke is to smoke is to smoke.

## Black Clothes

I was the one to make Mom's funeral arrangements. Rose couldn't find the heart to help. Mom was alive for her the second day she was gone, just as she was the Tuesday before her death. Rose told me that she and Mom didn't have to have daily contact, they always knew that if their clothes were ripped from them, if they were left vulnerable to the mood of the day, they would be there for each other. Mom felt she had much to make up for because of her constant hand in Rose's hair when she was young, pulling on her even when she did no wrong.

Although Mom allowed for God like Frankie allowed for Santa Claus and the Tooth Fairy, she didn't attend church. This left me the task of picking a place to hold the service. It was November 2003. Mom had died a week earlier.

I flipped a coin. Heads, go right from the house. Tails, go left. I went left at the end of the street Grandma and I lived on. I ate one doughnut in little bites as I drove from home to the nearest chapel.

The chapel sat on a corner lot at the intersection of busy streets. It was the size of a large three-bedroom house, brown with a green roof and a large dirt parking lot. No one old enough to ride a bike could miss it. It was not tucked between a dry cleaner and a dog-grooming place, but was surrounded by empty lots on both sides. A cobblestone walkway ran from the front door to the lip of the gutter on the street. I thought Paradise Hill was a strange name, but parked anyway.

He was just getting out of his Cadillac when I pulled up in my beat up Ford Escort. He was a young guy, maybe forty, with a full head of hair that matched the brown of his eyebrows. His name was Fred. I thought his name went well with his plaid shirt and blue tie. He seemed surprised when I smiled as if people in black clothes can't be friendly. Priests, Johnny Cash, Georgia O'Keeffe—they wore black. Georgia said her life was filled with color so she found no reason to wear it on her body. Suits me just fine.

My smile shook loose Fred's smile. I felt his handshake in my toes.

Fred's office had plush maroon carpeting, beige-painted walls with posters of waterfalls and forests. Fred pulled a legal pad from his desk drawer. The absence of a computer was comforting to me. It made death feel really old.

Hannah Morgan. He wrote Mom's name at the top of the pad. At that moment, her death became finalized with me. Up until then, tucked in the back of my mind, I still thought I could drive to her house and share a bowl of Cheerios with bits of banana in it. Frankie stamps her foot on the ground insisting that Grandma is just hiding. I don't have the heart to tell her yet that Grandma will never open the door again.

At the end of Hannah's life, she would telephone friends sloppy drunk at two in the morning. She thought her blue house a bad omen because the sun hated it. She thought that tap water was poison, and if she ate more potatoes her lungs would work better. She drove friends away. Death was a passenger with her on countless nights.

Fred asked me how Mother had died. I said she died of a broken heart. He accepted this answer by moving on to the business at hand. He did not allow for sentimentality. He just forged on with his questions, wanting her service to be exactly like I wanted it. I stayed on track. We finished the finale of Mother's death within an hour.

After I told her how much the funeral arrangements cost, Rose said I should have snarled. Maybe then I would have gotten a better deal. Fred might have thought I would throw sugar in his gas tank and key his car if he didn't offer me something reasonable. That is more Rose's style than mine, and Rose is the one to wear the bright clothing. She has shirts with stars on the shoulders and skirts with rings of roses around the hem. Her clothing speaks more to the sweet person she wishes to be rather than to the bitter, sarcastic-with-a-flare-of-heat person that she claims to be. I wear black mostly because it is convenient, and loads of laundry don't have to be separated into piles of light, dark, and color.

Rose told me that she bet after the smile I gave Fred, that he thought I would be an easy sell. She says my smile is genuine and large and could cause people to manipulate me because of thinking I'm a pushover. She says I don't understand that people are looking to take rather than to give. Rose gets upset when I leave my purse in the car. She says I am begging someone to break the car window and steal it. I smile at Rose as she says all of this. She asks me if I heard a word of what she said and I always tell her I heard "the" word.

## Alcohol

It was a Phoenix day in winter not requiring coats. November 17, 2001. Knee-high socks go on sale, for a fashion trend of short skirts and knee-high socks. This fashion was not the fashion of funerals. It was as if funerals counted on everyone showing up their conservative best. Stomach and upper thighs covered. Men with shirts tucked in and real shoes. No flip-flopping down the aisle, as this would affect the somber atmosphere. It really was a tragic day. Mother had been only fifty-eight years old. Her death was unexpected. No one had any time to practice grieving. The sorrow was immediate.

Colored light streams into the chapel from stained glass windows. A white podium with a microphone stands at attention. Rose dreams Mom; a gentle breeze lifting hair. We carry the memory of our mother in the bone of our cheek.

The minister is in an open navy sport coat and plaid slacks, a shirt buttoned to his collar. White hair, tanned, manicured nails, very white teeth. Rose thinks he's a concierge of some ritzy hotel posing as a minister. Maybe he had two jobs: one where he brought adventure to life, and one where he closed the book on adventure.

Rose and I sit in the first pew on the left. My friends sit behind us. Family members splatter the pews on the right. Jeremy is missing.

The minister welcomes everyone. Fifties music plays softly in the background along with big band music. Grandpa Poser had orchestrated a women's band early in his life. There is crying. I am not too certain where it is coming from.

The plastic flowers are prim. Rose said they looked real enough. Rose was high on weed. Cheesy grin and hard candies. I was grateful she came even though she claimed I was close to the lip of madness again. Weight loss. A crust of dirt circling my neck. My arm scaly from wiping my nose. Apparent attention to voices no one else hears. Maybe that is where the crying is coming from, though I doubt it. There is no place for compassion in the other reality.

After his sermon, the minister asks if there is anyone who would like to come forth and say something about Hannah's life. Rose elbows me. "God bless you and all your children," I blurt out. It feels and sounds like a helium balloon popped by the end of a branch.

God numbs my fingers and sends fireworks up my spine. I believe his presence wraps around all that are here. Except maybe the minister.

Another elbow from Rose and I step onto the stage and stand at the podium. A wick catches the fire of many matches. I have the attention of everyone.

"Mother died an alcoholic death. We tell stories until it doesn't hurt anymore." I paused thinking a tick had just jumped on me. And continue, "Jack Daniels keeps the ghosts away until . . ." My voice was steady and warm like the presence of a radiator on a cold day.

A quart is a quart. A half gallon a half gallon. Both tip nicely. Nectar for a bee. I paint Mom's toenails in the ICU. Deep red. Life support and then a flipped switch. Mother's life ends. Mom lived in love like yellow surrounding the center of a sunflower. When we love again, she will begin again. Rose says second chances are a waste of time.

After I left the podium, there were a few people who wanted to speak. A couple of them said what an amazing hostess my mother was and that she and Jeremy had thrown some wicked parties. There was always someone too drunk to not flirt with all the women and try to pull their tops off in the pool. The parties would end at two in the morning or so, so that some of the drunkenness would wear off and people could drive home.

One of the people at the podium raving about the parties paused and realized that that was one of the very things that brought my mother to an early death. Alcohol. Breakfast, lunch, and dinner, then a nightcap before bed.

The service ended with all knowing my mother was a beautiful hostess who drank too much. She took the drink, and then the drink took her.

## Coffee

Hannah, a pressed flower. It is after her service. Maybe a Tuesday. I have seen Hannah with a little brown dog I think is my schizophrenia. She carries the little dog through grocery stores and public restrooms. The little brown dog runs beside her, stops to pee when Hannah stops to smoke.

I envy this little dog. I want to consume it like aspirin consumes fever, leaving schizophrenia in tomorrow's obituary. Hannah joins me outside the diner. I tell her, "I did not know you were dying. Did you? Give me an hour and I will find you another liver. Let me tug you back. I miss you, your smoke, and your big fruit earrings. Rose says there is no time that is better than any time to die, no matter the brilliance of sunlight, the quiet of rain, or the whisper at dusk."

I shake off the talk, leave the coffee to sit in Hannah's chair, empty except for the cast of moon that bleeds onto the wood.

## Beauty

In third grade my friend Kori held a contest. We picked the most beautiful mother out of the crowd of mothers who waited in cars to collect their children. You, with your long black hair and wide smile, always won. I am telling you this now as you rest, cremated. Beauty did not follow you into the grave but sat on the point of my pen in a memory among many fixed in my head.

## Responsibility

Frankie prefers being with Paul. "Daddy needs me to pick him up when he falls down."

Paul lives in the curve of the sidewalk, which is a much softer way of saying gutter. Frankie does not know whether to sit him in the grass away from the curb and exhaust of cars, or plant him on the bench, a stone figure waiting for departure that doesn't come in the form of a bus.

## Welcome Back Giraffe

Jeremy loved the length of Hannah's neck. The stone pendant he gave her glitters. We didn't find the stone pendant with her belongings. We found Frankie's giraffe instead.

## The Walk Home

Frankie hops when she is happy. I think blue jay. We walk a straight line from Frankie's home to the mountain. What a marvelous way to end a street. You can only turn back. Open sesame doesn't work. We touch the mountain anyway. Rock hard. Being just what it is. Frankie believes one day we will find the door and walk into the center of the mountain where there are jars filled with jewelry and stones that make magic. There has always been magic just as there have always been squirrels. Just as there have always been rabbits. Rabbits and felines are of the same family.

"What would you do if someone handed you a bag of M&M'S?" I ask Frankie.

"Eat them fast," she says happily.

Don't swallow love. Kiss it and put it in your pocket or shake it loose from your sock. It won't melt if you give it away. There will always be more if given away. Conundrums of the sort are fast in coming. Dogs to bones. I had a dog once and will have a dog again.

Frankie and I turn and look down the street. House lights are just beginning to be turned on. "We like being able to see, don't we, Auntie?"

The question dimmed. I didn't say any more. A car pulled out of the drive in front of us. We waited until it backed up and then walked home.

## Sober

Frankie thinks Hannah is coming back. She is used to people disappearing for long periods of time only to return more beaten down but still with a smile for her. She begs her mother to take her to the farm as she and Rose have been living with Jonathan for a couple of months in the city.

Frankie had made friends with the little girl next door, so her attention was caught by the jump rope and dancing with her new friend, until it wasn't anymore.

She has not been told that the farm no longer exists except through a scrapbook Rose is putting together for her with photographs and little notes Hannah wrote to Frankie whenever Frankie knocked on her bedroom door and she didn't answer.

Rose cries over the notes, sifting through them and keeping some to herself. Some of them reflect the despair Hannah felt at being unable to open her door to Frankie. Later, Frankie will understand the grip that alcohol had on Hannah mixed with the terror Hannah had for sober days. Sober days didn't offer comfort but spoke instead to poverty and grief and shattered dreams whose shards would not allow Hannah to forget days spent loving Jeremy, her children, friends, and golf. Hannah forgot the moments of unhappiness that forced her to lash out at Jeremy, Rose, Hunter, and myself with a voice of black coal.

Frankie was Hannah's last love, her sane moments in a life of broken plates that promised to hold no food.

## Interviews

I was taken to St. Luke's for an interview. I always refer to the evaluation process as being interviewed. Sometime during the interview, I told the woman that I wanted to put my hands around her neck and squeeze tight. She told me that would not be good and continues on with her questions.

She asks me if I hear voices.

I respond, "Can you speak up? I can't hear you very well over the roar of the others."

The cubbyhole of the office we sit in is lit as if by candlelight. I follow her hands, which flicker over paperwork.

The woman is casual behind her thick glasses and impersonal pen. "Do you feel like harming others?" she asks.

"Only on Wednesdays."

"And yourself?"

"On Thursdays."

"Do you have thoughts of suicide?"

"Death exists only in so far as it quiets life."

She asks, "Why are you here?"

"My friend brought me."

The pen pauses in the woman's hand, her shirt takes a breath. I stop watching the men herd at the door, turn my gaze to my lap, and imagine my little dog curled there.

"The men won't let you out," I say.

"What men?"

"The men at the door."

"What door?" she asks.

"That door."

"My door?"

"Your door."

"There are no men there, Kristina."

Men are everywhere. Their ears attach to the walls. Their eyes to knobs. Their palms to grass. I think all this and it makes sense to me.

When done, I ask her if I had passed. Answer, yes.

I was not happy with the outcome. I didn't think I needed to be there. It didn't matter that the other realities were confusing me, or that I was being berated by Voices. These were common occurrences in my life that I was learning to live with. However, I hadn't slept for days. The Voices were keeping me up, and in my tiredness, I was having a hard time of fighting back. The truth was I desperately wanted to slip into the third reality so I wouldn't have to cope in the common reality. I suffered in the common reality. I didn't so much suffer in the third reality. I would become catatonic, or uncommunicative, and paranoid. This was better than the beatings I took mentally in the common reality. It is in the common reality that I obsess on suicide. God please take me, and he never does. Maybe I should venture to Alaska and sit miles away from anything in the snow. I heard that freezing to death was a peaceful way to die. A person simply falls asleep in the cold.

After searching me for contraband, they take me to the unit. Well, it wasn't the actual unit. It was the holding cell connected to the unit. The holding cell had no bars. It was an empty space in a fairly large room that only housed a couch in the middle of the room and had access to the telephone. This holding room was for people too psychotic to be on the regular unit next door.

I was not psychotic. Just elevated. I asked the psych tech, if I bit him, would it hurt. He reported this to the nurse. What came exactly next, I don't know. A white swallow appeared above the locked hospital door. The nurse jabbed a needle into my ass. Haldol. And placed me in a locked room. I went to sleep on the concrete floor alone in the room with one bird.

Mother, what was it you promised me? Or is it that you promised me nothing but a balloon filled with helium that would swing on Saturn's ring and knock Mars a bit closer to the Earth? My heart settles on the moon this gray evening, waiting for my mind to catch up. My mind is tucked in a cereal box of wild oats and a plastic prize for the next intern I meet. I left it there with the crusts of toast and strawberry jam that dripped from the corner of my mouth as I tried rapidly to talk my way into another reality, barely stopping to draw breath.

It is cool in the hospital. I wrap blankets around me.

Maybe I will tell the doctor that I am from the tip of Alaska that barely makes it to the map. Maybe he will believe this more than when I tell him I live on the periphery of light. It is all a matter of perspective. Ahh . . . it is the wisdom that you promised me. I think of this as I lay my body down to rest on the single bed with a plastic pillow that was just disinfected at noon today, when the other woman left, her new prescription in hand and me with a star the weight of shavings from a red crayon.

I will dream of helium tonight.

\* \* \*

A few days, I think, and I was transferred to the unit. I didn't like the unit and made a mental note to never come back to St. Luke's. Meals were served at one long table. I had to sit between two people. This was entirely too much. I didn't want to be close to anyone. I don't remember attending groups or doing anything really. I attempted to read a book, but hadn't the concentration it would take.

Although it appeared that I got nothing from my visit at St. Luke's, the truth was that I left feeling much better. The Voices had mostly diminished, and I felt I was able to think with a clear mind. I was taking meds as prescribed again and was participating in life outside my house. At this time, I was still living with my grandmother. Soon, my father would come to town, and my grandmother would move to an assisted living place called the Beatitudes. My father and Betty would take up residency in my grandmother's house, his childhood home. I would buy a condo.

## Wood Floors

Mom had left Rose, Hunter, and I a chunk of money. I used mine to put a down payment on a condo downtown. The expenditures didn't stop at the down payment. I had the walls painted different colors; deep burgundy in the bedroom, blush in the living room and kitchen, yellow in the study. And I paid for wood floors. Light wood floors. The cost of the floor almost brought me to tears. The amount I had originally budgeted for them was way too low than what they actually cost.

This was my first place. I didn't own a spoon. I learned I loved shopping. I was particular about everything, even the shower curtains. One was a heavy white cotton cloth with a baroque pattern woven into it. The other, in the guest bathroom, was a blue plastic with colorful cartoonish fish all over it. I had a deep redwood canopy bed also in the baroque tradition. Bob and Marty had bought me a big screen television and I had a couch. What more could I need? The stainless steel refrigerator was already there, as was the washer and dryer. And I had floor-to-ceiling bookshelves built in the study. Unpacking my books brought me great pleasure. I had all my books in storage for years.

My symptoms at this time were minor. The Voices a hum. My paranoia wasn't keeping me from venturing outside. I had been teaching as an intern at Arcadia High School on Indian School Road in Scottsdale, and was now preparing to really teach for a salary. The two language arts classes I had been offered became five classes. I decided what the hell, God wouldn't give me more than I could handle. It was all green lights.

## Guy

I have a crush on Guy. Unbelievable. I telephone my friend, Brenda, and tell her I have a crush on Guy.

"No way," she says.

"Yes way," I say. "I know, I know, it just doesn't seem possible," I continue to say. "But I do."

"He's a guy, you know, a guy, guy. And a bodybuilder. I think that would turn you off."

"I've been training with him now for two weeks and I'm certain we have chemistry."

"What about Angel?"

"They're split up."

"Oh." Pause. "You're certain."

"Yes. I'm certain."

"Is it mutual?"

"I think so."

"What are you going to do? Ask him out?" she asks.

"Yes, I think."

"Oh."

My body was feeling terrible because I had done nothing physical for a real long time. I knew I hated working out and would not start unless I had someone to motivate me. I decided to set aside a couple thousand to have someone train me. I approached Angel first. She too was a bodybuilder and personal trainer.

"I'm not training anyone right now," she said. "I'm working on a master's and am too busy with that. But Guy is available. He's a great trainer."

I didn't know about training with a man. I would have preferred a woman, but I decided to take Angel's suggestion. She introduced me to Guy at the gym before my first session.

"Hi."

"Hi."

And that was the beginning. Christy, my Twelve Step sponsor, told me that love finds you in the most unlikely of places. That is certainly what happened. She says, you don't pick love, it picks you. The dragon spits flame at the castle tower. It warms the inside room and the lady comes to the window seeking a cool breeze.

I invite Guy to a barbecue at my newly purchased condo and he comes, breaking his own rules of no fraternization with his clients.

We begin spending a great deal of time together outside the gym, or maybe it just feels like a great deal of time because it seems I am with him a lot when not teaching or grading papers. He comes to the school at lunchtime and takes me to Starbucks right down the street. After training together in the evenings, we take long walks in the park. It isn't long before we become a couple. It isn't long before we have the moving-in conversation. The moving-in conversation comes quickly not just because we love being around each other, but also because it would help us out financially. He comes with two little dogs, Shih Tzus, Sasha and Brutus. I was in love with them all. Him, dogs, all.

Norman, my professor and chairperson at Arizona State University, asks me one day how many cats I have. He pegs me as a cat person, and before Guy, I actually was. I told Norman I have no cats, just two little dogs. He asks me what kind. "Shih Tzus," I say. He says they don't count as dogs. They are really cats dressed like dogs.

I have said Guy was everything I never wanted. Or at least thought I never wanted. A man. A bodybuilder. A nonreader. A television fanatic. A dog owner. And yet I fell madly in love with him. Madly in a good way. And as far as I know, he too with me.

Why Guy? Again, I am reminded that love finds us, we don't find love. If I believe this, then "why Guy?" is easy to answer; it just happened. It just happens to work. If I need more than this to really understand it, I think of things he brings to my life. He brings stability. He always seems to know what to do when I'm getting sick, or am sick. When he touches me, I quiver. He is firmly him; he does not confuse me with any self-doubt. And I get to be firmly me.

Loving Guy has taught me that I can indeed love. I have hurt a great number of people on my way to him. I was terrified to love anyone too much because I was concerned with losing myself in the relationship. I have fought too hard to learn who I am, to be who I am, to lose myself in a relationship. No one can convince me that a blue wall is really green any longer. I like toast and love red velvet cake.

I didn't know I could make someone the center of my world and still fully have myself. One plus one can equal two ones and two at the same time. I love him like I do sand between my toes and a large piece of salmon settled on sautéed spinach.

### Your Inner Thigh

Your inner thigh sends bees up my spine. I pick up your stray sock, the smell of foot thick in white cotton raises my heart rate. The hairs on my arms stand up. I imagine moving into you, a wisp of finger traces the lip of your ear while the willow tree spills leaves, showering the moist earth at its base, the moist earth you reach for, your hand greeted by wetness.

Men don't strip like women, an arm bared, a shoulder exposed, pause before losing the shirt to breasts.

For men, it's over the head in one motion, pants and underwear immediately follow with no slow zipper.

I zip down for you through the muscle to the bone and the soft places in my mind—you.

### Tender

When my head is glued on well, it is interesting to write. Or should I say not so interesting. When slightly ill, I experience a flurry of metaphor and detail. When well, I feel like I'm marching along in a line of

Marines simply putting the facts to paper in a sequence of time. I think my medications rob me of color. I have to remind myself that every time I stop my medication or alter it in some way, I end up back in the hospital. I have to remind myself that when over-the-top sick, I can't write at all. It is not always easy to recall these things.

I really believe God aids my hand at the keyboard. When really sick, there is no God, or rather, no sense of God. Writing doesn't feel divine. I slough my way through. The morning dims gray. The light at my desk hiccups. No divine, I still press on. It is just more painful. I remind myself of what Isak Dinesen said, "You write because you owe God an answer." I know I owe God. I hope that writing is good tender.

## Hi, Louisa

I write Louisa, one of the nurses who worked with me at the hospital.

Dear Louisa,

It is Sunday. One of my closest friends is celebrating twenty years of sobriety today, and I don't want to go to the party. Retreat is nothing foreign to me. I do it often. I do it well. I even do it without intending to. But I will go to the party because today I am able and it is the right thing to do.

The card this note is enclosed in I thought beautiful. I have for some time known of the poem the quote is taken from. There is much emphasis on choice in his words. I don't always identify with choice. Mostly, my illness feels larger than I. I wonder sometimes if my illness is larger than God, and then I think not. Nothing is larger than God. If all is right in God's world, I think, then why does my illness steal from me the things of this world?

I do believe in destiny. I do believe God has a plan for me. I hope I have the courage and the strength to stand solid in His plan. I always think His plan includes serving others. I pray that I be made useful to others. In times of health, I offer my smile, I offer my hand, and I offer my time. It's a great thing to bring joy . . .

Did you know that I used to be a high school English teacher? Nobody thought I could do it and then I did it, and then I became the sickest I have ever been. I still grieve the loss of that job. It was one of the greatest things I have ever experienced and I was damn good at it until my mind failed me.

I am taught to believe that God will never give me more than I can handle. Now I believe God did intend something else for me other than teaching. I just don't know what that is just yet. Maybe I will find the answer in poetry. I am certain that is where Robert Frost found the answer "that has made all the difference."

What would you like to know about me that you don't already know? I have a fondness for tulips and a fondness for my boyfriend.

Kristina

# Descent

## Truth

I taught English at Arcadia High School. I came to the school dressed in a navy blue skirt with a navy blue jacket, looking less the wallflower than I ever had in my thirties. I was radiant. The sun allowed me to make a pendant out of a bit of his arm; the moon had offered me a tooth as a setting in the pendant. It hung free in the dip of my throat. Occasionally, I would touch it when my soft roar seemed to get stuck on my tongue, which didn't happen often. The students could attest to that. The students pulled every sound I had out of me as I stretched in front of them, giving them Shakespeare and Whitman on a plate, breaking down words and meanings into sugar cubes that dissolved on their tongues.

My roar replenished itself in the baths I took at night. Steam puddled in my ears, cleaning them of any ill-begotten word that might have caught the inside curve of my lobe. The fish slept in their bowl; a single light shimmied over the water's surface and through the windows and doors of their castle nestled in the small pewtered rocks. The bananas rotted on the counter. Alley cats had sex outside my front door. It was the end of another sixteen-hour day. I did not regret the length of my work. It kept me focused on giving. I wanted to teach teenagers more than I wanted a lover or a burgundy bedroom with dark wood floors. More than my friend's Chagall in greens and blues that hung in my study. I would give the past eleven years of my life to any God that asked for them in exchange for a classroom filled with students.

Schizophrenia was a challenge, though. One that I did my best to tie back with heavy string that would not fray. The day came that I needed help. Thinking that all people loved the opportunity to be of service, especially those paid to be just that, I turned to the assistant principal, Joan, the helper of teachers. Joan was a small, robust woman smelling of lavender and green things. Joan and I had broken bread together, smothering the sourdough with butter and orange marmalade. The smell of coffee opened our eyes even wider. This day, I let Joan know that I had schizophrenia in the same tone I used when explaining to friends how to bake a cake. Preheat the oven to 400 degrees.

This scared Joan. I could tell by the way Joan stiffened her body and leaned back in her chair. I explained to Joan that the reason I came to her was that I was getting signals from other realities. I just needed to ask someone other than my students if they heard them too. It was a way of checking whether or not I should take a day off. It was a way of learning the truth when my mind wanted to roam. All the sun and all the moon could not keep me from slipping into occasional psychosis.

I explained to Joan that I had dreamt of reaching for leaves on the lower branches of elms, knowing all was possible, like wearing a pink blouse lined in fur. "I once dreamt of the truth as being as simple as my name." Joan could not follow my logic. The television images of schizophrenics cornered Joan in a crease of fear left to smolder.

Joan sent me home like she would have a teacher with a bad cold or a bit of the flu. This was good. This was appropriate.

Joan then went to my classroom. Still written on the board was my quote for the day: *Today is Wednesday, December 8, 2002. Today we live, we love, and we breathe exhaust fumes from large buses crowded with people, and we love all of them, even the ones who wear their clothes inside out, their tags showing. We love them anyway.* Joan erased the board. Tomorrow she would telephone me and tell me I was a great teacher, but I was also a schizophrenic and, as a result of that, I could not be trusted to be safely alone in the classroom with children. I would be told not to come back.

* * *

I was in my study, standing at my easel, painting an image of wildflowers rooted too deep to lose themselves to wind when the phone rang. Joan did not say hello. She simply said Kristina. And I said, yes. Joan went on to say her piece. I folded into myself, searching for truth that would allow me to put on my shoes and leave the house in search of a free bird. I hung up without saying a word.

Tomorrow would come. There would be no students. What is the truth in this? A revolver would have ended it all. It would be a good year before I could thank God that I hadn't owned a firearm. It would be a long time coming before I could make sense of what happened. Joan too watches television, but aren't people smarter than prime time?

## Attorney

The following is a letter I wrote my attorney after having been told I can't return to the classroom: "You are a great teacher, Kristina, but you are also schizophrenic and because of that we fear our students are not safe with you." I thought I would die on the spot. Had I a gun, I would have.

June 3, 2003

Dear Cheri,

I spoke with Fran today and told her that I wanted to write a letter to that doctor I saw in Tucson and say all the things I did not say because I was so taken aback by his approach and by the information he wanted from me. She told me to write you instead.

After leaving his office, I realized by his line of questioning that he may have been trying to determine whether or not I was able to have intimate relationships or bond with people, even love people. As I am certain he knows, a past like mine and an illness like mine can make this difficult. I did not tell him that the friends I have today would do anything for me, and I for them. I did not tell him that my grandmother not only has loved me no matter what, but I have loved her and love her and would do anything to make her life a bit easier. He read in the charts that at one time I had said that I was going to hurt my grandmother. He does not know that I would not have spent four years living with her if this had truly been a possibility. My grandmother would not have stood for it; I would not have stood for it. Yes, as he read, I do have a history of violence. This history is before medication and without medication. The last time I did anything that was violent in nature was eight, possibly nine years ago. Somehow I think he may have gotten the dates wrong and believed I harmed my boyfriend here in Phoenix. Not so.

I do know he was trying to determine whether or not I was safe in the classroom with children unsupervised. I know with absolute certainty that I was. I wanted to write him and ask him why he could not see my calls to crisis as ensuring nothing would happen by doing a reality check as I was taught to do. In the case of mental illness, most specifically schizophrenia, how much different is this than taking insulin so you ensure yourself and your students that you don't end up in a diabetic coma on the floor? I wanted him to know that it is I who grows paranoid of the world and not the world that needs to be paranoid of me. The only psychotic thing I have ever had happen at work is me going catatonic in the bathroom, and this was nearly eleven years ago, at the beginning of my diagnosis when I had little understanding of my illness. Why did the doctor have difficulty seeing my reality checks as a tool toward my continued stability? This insight always ensures that I am safe and that the people around me are safe.

My class often told me that they respected me as a person and as a teacher, and the feeling was reciprocated by me. Only once in the months that I taught those five classes did I have a discipline situation that necessitated my sending a student to the principal's office. From what I understand, this is an amazing thing. I did not have conflict in my class that amounted to anything more than a lost thirty seconds while a student complained about anything from having to speak in the front of the class to the fact that they didn't like my shoes. I have no memories of instances of anger toward my students or anyone else while I was teaching. It was never necessary for me to raise my voice. It was never an appropriate tool. I did not have the opportunity to tell this doctor that a student of mine told me, "Ms. Morgan, usually half the class likes the teacher and half the class hates the teacher, but we all love you and want you to stay and teach us our junior year."

I want to know, Cheri, why it is not wrong that, upon learning that I was schizophrenic and not feeling comfortable with it, the principal did nothing to be proactive in ensuring my success and theirs. I believe this would have been a relatively easy thing to do. It seems weird to me that I said something to Andi, the person who monitors all new teachers, on Thursday and did not have a call from the assistant principal until Monday. Is it discriminatory that the assistant principal said to me during that call, "You are an extraordinary teacher, Kristina, but you are also schizophrenic, and because of that we do not think our kids are safe in the classroom with you"? It is true that my mentor teacher did perpetuate my paranoia by telling me that the administration did not trust me, and the other teachers by warning me that I was being watched. I know they acted out of ignorance, but these were horribly hurtful things to say, particularly when I was told that I was performing only excellently at my job. Why is it that I am being discriminated against as a person with the diagnosis of schizophrenia?

Having received a perfect evaluation from my principal, with no derogatory remarks said about me by a teacher, student, or parent, having nothing but exemplary behavior, why is it I am being discriminated against if I should receive a bad report from the doctor in Tucson and if Scottsdale Unified School District should decide to tell my future, prospective employer that they would not hire me back?

I was and am a great teacher. All of this is terribly sad for me.

Sincerely,

Kristina Morgan

## Intuition

I know something is wrong just as I know I have a single hair that grows from my right hip. Guy is behaving oddly. He seems distracted all the time. Our lovemaking has practically ceased. At Christmas, we go to my father's. Guy spends most of his time outside on his cell phone. Looking back, everything screams "other woman." I know something is wrong, but I don't expect this.

In early January, we both got dressed up. He put on a suit and tie and I a dress. I had a poetry reading at the Herberger Theater Center. The reading was awful. I was sorry I had invited my friends to come. There was another event happening at Herberger, so many people were strolling around, not there to listen to poetry. There was no microphone. It was practically impossible for people to hear myself or the other poet.

Afterward, Guy took me to dinner to celebrate, although it had gone terribly. At dinner, I brought up the fact that I was feeling uneasy, that I thought he was acting weird. Guy asked if we could just enjoy dinner and talk about things later. I agreed and changed the meat of my conversation. This was a Wednesday night.

Thursday afternoon I'm home when Guy walks in after training his morning clients. Usually, he comes home later, so it is a pleasant surprise to see him. He takes a seat on the couch and asks me to join him. He tells me he has to come clean. He tells me that my intuition has been right on this whole time. He is seeing someone else. I am devastated. I ask who. "Angel," he says. The Angel he was seeing before me. I start crying. He tells me that he will be moving out. He says he can't continue to love both of us and live with me. He needs to figure out what he is doing.

I don't remember what I did while he was packing. He asks if he can leave the little dogs with me for now. I say yes. And then he is gone with no place to go. He tells me later that he had announced in a meeting that he was homeless and if anyone knew of any rooms for rent to please let him know. Lynn, another Twelve Step group member, had a room available, so he went there.

I am a mess. One of the worst things for me to do is not sleep. I can't sleep. The Voices become terrible. They move from room to room with me. I suddenly snap coherently awake to find myself pacing. I telephoned my case manager. Maybe all I said is that I'm experiencing a full frontal attack. I don't know. But she comes to my home. It is suggested that I go to the hospital and lie low for a while. I tell her I would rather lie in the grass outside my condo door than on the carpeting at the hospital. And who will take care of the little dogs, Sasha and Brutus? "I will," she says. I collapse to the floor in a fetal position as she gets some of my belongings together to take to the hospital.

## Hair

I have just gotten to the unit. I find a place against the wall to stand, crying. I am locked away deep in my mind, but not so deep that I can't hear the woman talking and singing to me. The nurse notices this woman trying to reach me and tells her to leave me be. The woman walks down the hall and then back to me. Singing.

My hair is long. I had thought often to cut it off. Often. But Guy loved long hair. I thought this an easy concession to make.

And then there is this woman singing to me, and suddenly saying, "Go ahead, dear, cut your hair. It will be all right." I hear her but don't respond. I continue to cry, but I tuck away what she says to me. She is back to singing. The nurse continues to warn her off.

I leave my place on the wall for my bed. It is dark in the room. Still, I can make out the body of my roommate under her covers. She doesn't move. She doesn't say anything. I am glad for this.

I burrow myself in the bed wanting to be free of the Voices that are following me like shadows on a bright day. *Fuck you, you good-for-nothing piece of lard. You need us. It won't do any good to try to hide from us. You're plagued. We are the plague.*

Covering my ears never helps. I beg for sleep. My begging is answered. I fall into a heavy sleep that allows for nothing except silence.

### Grasshoppers

I tell myself if I drink pomegranate juice the world will seem lazier than the hot tempo at which it travels, knocking down skinny children and dogs that pee in the street.

I can't see through the sun to the pond that fosters frogs.

I say this to the group therapy woman and she just smiles and nods and moves on to the next person. I wonder why I try again to be a part of the patients. I am not of them. They are not of me. Actually, this is not always true. There have been patients on the unit that mimic some facet of me. Or I mimic some facet of them. As I'm thinking of this, I really can't come up with anything, but I know that something between us must exist. I have heard the term *terminally unique* before and know that it is not healthy to be this way. I am pushed to come up with similarities.

Okay, paranoid. I am not the only one who is paranoid. I think, how does it manifest itself in me? I stay sitting at my post from where I can see everything. I think the other paranoid people stay in their beds. I would also stay in my bed if I could sleep. The Voices prevent this from happening. I need a bit of outside stimulation to focus on. The psych techs talking among themselves or to the other patients gives me this. It is not that I listen to what they say. It is more that everything comes across as a drone. A pulse. An electrical current of energy that is outside myself and helps keep me in balance and grounded.

I'm not the only one on the unit who hears voices. There are others. I'm just not certain which people, and again, I think most who do stay in their beds.

The psych techs are kind to me at mealtime. I don't have to go into the television lounge to eat at the tables with everyone else. The contact would freak me out. Too much stimulation. The psych techs allow me to eat at my post. Again, I'm so relieved by this.

* * *

I come to death with an understanding of red shoes. The air in the hospital is pleasant enough—cool, with no breeze except the draft I pick up from the man who ceaselessly paces up and down the tethered hall.

We are all offered lightweight blankets. Mine is rolled as a rag doll at the end of the bed; when I sleep, her arms wrestle my legs to the mattress to quiet the tremor that moves through me—a scream of drugs extracting the hope I covet.

Mine will be a quiet death. The red shoes slip easily on. I will walk to the edge of a cliff, spread my mind to allow for cloud—for an instant, become part of the horizon, a pink spray followed by red.

I don't get up this time. This time came the way speech comes to infants—a word in a day "da-da," not sophisticated enough to say "God help."

\* \* \*

When I sit long enough grasshoppers gather on my toes. Their wings remind me of the paper planes I made in third grade. Mrs. Montgomery was my teacher. She knew I was shy so she made me sit at the front of the classroom, an arm's length from the apple on her desk.

During math lessons I would feel the stare of my classmates at the back of my head. They were all waiting for me to write the number three on the blackboard. Even I knew two plus two equals four. Three is not a good number; it is a chair missing a leg.

There came a time like wind in kites that our class was to elect a class president. I guess some trusted my silence and recognized my kindness because I was nominated, which made me feel like a freshly opened bar of soap. George won by one vote, my vote. I didn't want to appear stuck up.

Today things have changed. I will write my name on blank pieces of paper, casting them into the river for the fish to kiss like royalty. Kissing the ruby on my right hand.

## Slippers

The hospital is a dim memory. I am glad to be home.

My study has been emptied into the living room, leaving a room for Anthony. I met Anthony at Art Awakenings, the art studio for people with mental illness. He was always very kind to me, and I loved his flamboyancy. Anthony comes Friday with his embroidered pillows and leopard slippers, fifty pounds of clothes, and a wicked laugh that stops my pacing and settles me in a chair five feet away from grief.

When I asked Anthony to come live with me, I had no idea that Guy and I would be getting back together. Guy and I did and Anthony became the third wheel. I heard him through his door one night as he talked on the phone. He referred to me often as a bitch. His venom frightened me. The next day I had the locks changed and told Anthony he needed to leave. Anthony had nowhere to go other than Tucson, where his family lived.

Anthony emailed me sometime in the month after he had left. He told me he forgave me, that he knew it was my illness, my paranoia, that pushed him out. I know that it was Guy. Anyone who ever got between Guy and me always got hurt.

I have not forgotten the kindness of Anthony. He was there for me when I really needed someone to be there for me.

## Note

Anthony,

The night wilted when you slammed cupboards, setting your tea-cups on edge and slapped the doors closed into their frames.

You called me a self-serving bitch. This I heard through the keyhole. It was not the nickname I minded so much but the venom that attached itself to the bottom of my shoe.

You spit me out into the air almost losing your teeth. I gathered myself up like folded laundry.

I didn't bother to take back your keys, but changed the locks on our friendship. Fear drove me to do this. I couldn't wait for you to throw a glass at the television interrupting the balance of my home. In this

I was "self-serving."

Splashed paint is not easy to rub off a brick wall. You colored my life with tulips then ripped off their heads, leaving me to hold the weight of a vase filled with green water and slime, the residue of death.

It stank so I did all I knew to do and emptied it, pouring the water into the earth you stepped on with your last load of belongings. You left a footprint at my door pointing toward the street where cars changed lanes and headed south.

I will remember we once made toast together before the sun rose. I live with the hurt I caused you; it is a hot towel pressed against my bottom lip. It is a blister hidden by makeup.

Kristina

\* \* \*

I never heard again from Anthony.

## Bonfire

Guy moves back in. It is Valentine's Day—what a perfect day. The little dogs are as happy to see him as I am. They lick at his ankles and wag their tails madly, faster than any toy poodle on Energizer batteries, turned to high.

I would like to say that it was as if he had never left. But that is not the truth. I still carry the pain seven years later. It is less, yes, but still there as blood would be if I pricked my finger. Sometimes, it is hard to keep pictures of them in intimate scenarios out of my head. Forgiveness cannot erase everything. My mind will turn where it likes. I can either obsess over the images and thoughts, or I can spread the butter on the toast, add sugar and cinnamon, and take a bite, tasting the loveliness of it. In the immediate moment, Guy is with me, and his love for me is hotter than the bonfire on the beach and just as bright. I know this, just as I knew when the bonfire's last log burnt out.

## Thunder of Mind

It's not the wind that catches my hair in fever. It's the rough edge of the street in broken tar, the bench the lady before me pissed on. It's the fact that I'll lie again in damp grass, wake with green stain on both elbows.

I return home and tell Guy there is a river running through the middle of the family room and the little dogs are in danger of drowning. Guy tells me to pack up, we are going to the hospital. It feels like again for the fiftieth time.

With fevered hair, I am taken to the hospital, dressed in their gowns. The street is not stolen from my mouth, replaced with tender thoughts of others too dressed in gowns.

These others offer no heart to the bad-mouthed me. They think instead to hassle my difference. My difference shows in the fever of my hair and the way I say "fuck you."

It is possible to leave the street and find no safety in the walls of a hospital trained to help. It is possible because people bring their same selves tired or not, pained or not, begging help or not to the walls. The walls cannot act alone to erase the thunder of mind, the sorrow of toes.

It will take a team of staff skilled in composure, skilled in kind but firm heart, understanding that not all patients arrive knowing which side of the napkin to place the fork. Most arrive knife in chest, pain in eye, with little mind for civilities.

The trained staff sets a fine table where all can dine despite differences and fevered hair, feast on berries and Buffalo wings that have lost flight.

I still am paranoid to be in the television lounge. So I eat standing up at my post.

## The Little Dog

Touch my hand. Five fingers. A palm—a crease of life leading to you. The little dog doesn't need a leash—she follows you to the edge and feeds on pumpernickel.

I tossed the salad. The tomatoes look particularly brilliant, firm in their skin, deep red against the green of the lettuce.

I'm writing you from a distance. My mind sickened again and you dropped me off here. The intake lady could tell we were in love. I trusted her. She wore Mary Janes and had coiffed hair. Her smile helped even more when I raised my head.

Today, I'm not mad at you for leaving me here. You are bringing me back to you. Here I connect the dot of each toe to form a foot. I stand and embrace you at visiting hours. The warmth of you lingers after you leave, and I know I will be coming home soon, just as I know the little dog would follow you over the edge but you won't lead her there.

## Dessert

I have split my bottom lip thinking about what to write regarding the red tile you offered me at dinner. I mean, I know you had run out of floor and thought I could find some more for you to walk on. It was a summer night and the palms lowered their ears plotting to take over your view of the sky. The tile will have to wait until morning. You will be okay to sleep where your feet are. Keep your boots on. Use the pillow for your ass. At sunrise, I will lay the tile around the edge of the garden. You'll enjoy coming back to tomatoes. Think of them as blushing. Remember me, my blouse off, offering melon.

My blouse off and staff is on me. I forget to put a shirt on. It is as simple as that. No, I had no desire to expose myself. I just got lost in another reality and forgot to put it on.

Everybody ate in the television room except for me. I ate at my post. I think staff let me get away with it because they know how scared I am of the television room, and I had been a patient of theirs on and off for years.

It was amazing that another patient approached me, asking for my dessert. I gave it to him just for his brashness.

## Friendship

Being sent to Friendship, I thought, was a horrible thing. First off, who would name a program Friendship? How corny and stupid. I wanted to leave the hospital and return to work, and instead they sent me to a program for the seriously mentally ill. The program met Monday through Friday, from 9:30 a.m. to 2:00 p.m. There were four groups to attend and lunch.

Each group had a theme, none of which I can remember. Forty-five-minute groups with fifteen minutes between each.

I was not feeling friendly. I was feeling like the shaved-headed woman I had been in my twenties with Gia as a role model. Gia had a smile that could make Santa's belt bust. Imagine a young woman with wild black hair, a black leather jacket, jeans, Converse sneakers, and a long-bladed knife in a room with blondes with flared skirts and open-toed heels. I was supposed to have much in common with the people in this program, but instead of noting the similarities, I remained feeling different.

The program was different than Tri-City in the sense that they didn't talk about how to bathe, or throw a rubber ball around in a circle for exercise. Friendship's representative had come to speak with me while I was still in the hospital. I had said to her as humbly as I could that I was sort of smart and didn't want to sit in groups all day that I found condescending. She assured me that the groups were split up in such a way that I wouldn't feel demeaned, and certainly I could learn from the information given me. If nothing else, it was a safe place to be for the day.

I sat in groups at Friendship, silent. I did not trust my mouth to say the right things, the things that would get me out of here and back in a classroom, teaching. When I did start talking, I talked about the electronic device in my head. I felt that eye motion acted as a keyboard and my tongue, a mouse. I was certain there was a dial at the base of my head. I talk to God on channel 5, to others on channel 2. My Voices rotate the dial to channel 8 and the air fills with heavy static, leaving me short of breath.

I come to Friendship and sit in groups while my hair continues to grow. I am asked to rate my symptoms on a scale from one to ten, ten being the worst. This confused me. I thought, what is a symptom if I live with it every day? When did it become like my head turning both ways before I drive into traffic? Why not say brown on days I feel thick, and blue on days that I move slowly? Purple when delighted, and green when in thought. There are days that I am orange, meaning too loud to sit still in a quiet room.

I am a rainbow. I do color the sky when clouds clear and offer gold to anyone who happens to notice me.

I am a long-haired woman who is concerned with the wiring in my brain and the dial on my head and the government agent who slides sideways around the corner in the next room, but not so much that I miss the pulse of the common reality.

They do notice me at Friendship. They do extend a hand to me. They do look out for my best interest. I was to learn these things over the weeks that I was in attendance. Friendship allowed me to learn of the possibility of being in the world. Bonnie, one of the staff at Friendship whom I was particularly fond of, always reminded me of possibility.

I knew I was alive—I learn that at Friendship and I learn it from going to grocery stores and coffeehouses, the libraries, and parks, and movie theaters. I learn I am alive from the chocolate sauce on the top of the ice cream sundae I just ordered.

I didn't complete the program at Friendship in one try. When I started talking, I talked about the strength of my desire to join my mother in the fourth reality. My mother was dead—I would not cop to that when sick. I believed, when sick, that I could travel to the fourth reality, safely, and return to the common reality when done visiting with my mother. Staff at Friendship asked me how would I get to the fourth reality, and I told them by swallowing a bunch of pills along with a quart of Jack Daniels. Saying things like this got them awfully excited. They did not want to send me home to die. When sick, I didn't think of this as a way to die. I saw it as a way to travel through realities. Friendship sent me back to the hospital to spend more time eating pancakes. To put it mildly, I was not happy with this.

## Logic

Friendship has a doctor, Dr. Zenner, whom I met with on Thursdays, every other week. I loved my time with Dr. Zenner. He followed my logic. I could tell him that the clothes were still drying on the line, or that the cow couldn't jump over the moon. He was young and brilliant, full of energy and quick wit. I felt the time I spent with him was spiritually based—I could be exactly who I was, and it was all right.

I slowly got better in the groups. I began to listen to the other members and to identify with some of their struggles. I became willing to offer suggestions. I became willing to talk about myself without electricity, putting the dial in my brain to rest.

I also began to cry. Teaching was the best thing to happen to me. Losing my job caused tremendous grief. I learned how powerful grief was. Losing my mother hadn't caused such grief. I think I was numb at the time my mother died, unable to experience a range of emotion that included sadness and vulnerability.

## Shoes

After Friendship, I was enrolled in a program called Art Awakenings. Art Awakenings was a place for people case-managed by the county's psychiatric care, with mental illness, to come and do art. They offered drawing, painting, ceramics, writing, playing in a band, and more. There were groups that taught you how to do certain art and open studio time. I participated in the open studio.

My life moved into color. Staff members offered me paint and a canvas. I painted a girl twirling a baton. God watched from the bleachers. Her red dress rose over scabbed knees and her smile parted, revealing a clean row of teeth. I came and I came to open studio. My paintings grew to four feet in length. And I still did my large charcoal drawings.

Art Awakenings was also a great place to be in community. I made friends. Most importantly, I met a beautiful African American woman named Saashely. She taught me to be dedicated to my art, to apply my passion to all that I did. Years later, and we are still friends.

I am no longer a part of Art Awakenings. It came down to drawing and painting, or writing. Both require huge amounts of time. I decided to stick with writing. I could have used studio time at Art Awakenings to write, but found I became too distracted by the hum of conversations and the music playing from the CD player.

Why write? I like what Isak Dinesen said, "I write because I owe God an answer." And in answering God, I find myself placed in life. Which comes first, having a breakfast of English muffins slathered with butter and orange marmalade, or writing myself into the zone? Which comes first, shaking hands with someone or writing the word *cat*? I think it is all intertwined.

I have been writing since I was a little girl who fit beneath a bed. When upset, I would run away to under my bed after writing my parents a note, trying to make myself understood. I always wished they would come find me. They never did. I was left to roll out from below the bed and pick myself up onto my feet.

I stopped writing in my midtwenties. I returned to writing in my midthirties. Why the time in between? One day I was attempting to write a novel when I realized I had much life to live. I decided it was more important to fall into life than to try to write about what was yet to be.

Part of "yet to be" included getting sick. I first tumbled in my late twenties and was diagnosed as schizophrenic in my late thirties. It took me a long time to believe I had schizophrenia and sometimes, at forty-five years old, I still don't believe it.

Mental illness fuels my writing in a way I could never have imagined. It allows me to write of an alternative reality while ill. This writing saves my life. I can be on the page what I can't be standing in socks. I can be on the page barefoot in search of shoes, which to date, I have always found. My shoes have real soles and because of this I am so grateful.

## Lucy

The day begins with a loud call for breakfast that catches the corners of the hall in bright sound, reflecting the sun of early morning light. Early morning light dusts the fluorescent bulbs that blink randomly on their way out. An electric death.

The patients drag feet, socks along carpeted floor, the rustle of medication in their bones.

Lucy leaves her room, her body a slow glow of Thorazine. At breakfast she will lift the spoon slowly, dribble milk down her chin, reach for the paper napkin that dissolves in her hand. This morning marks her third day inpatient. The world is not ready for her yet, not ready for her to stand as Jesus in the food mart, preaching the gospel of bread for the poor. Even the poor have a dollar and a half. Even the poor shy away from her lambasting. Passion comes too early in the dawn. The children stick their tongues out at Lucy. She no longer wants to bite them off. She is intent on Jesus wanting kind souls to speak the word of candy necklaces lying sweetly against skin. I can tell whoever she is talking to on the telephone agrees with her.

## Movement

A typical day on the unit doesn't exist. One would think that it would be the same droll of a day as it was yesterday, and as it promised to be tomorrow. The only predictable thing is chow time and the distribution of medication. No matter how psychotic, how depressed or anxious a person, everyone shows up to eat. Breakfast, lunch, and dinner with two snack times—one at 10:30 a.m., the other at 8 p.m.

The nurses are always on top of medication. At check-in, a Polaroid is taken so that the nurses would know they have the right person. Everyone also wears name badges around their wrists so the nurses can check that too. I imagine it would be horrible to give the wrong meds to someone. Most of the meds on the unit are potent. Some days, I would think, toxic. I would think that I was being poisoned and I couldn't understand why the government would go to such lengths to kill me. The worst thing I had done in my life was to eat all the frosting off Dad's birthday cake. Oh, there was the time I walked to my therapist's house at three in the morning, offering flowers. I knew it was not a good idea for me to know where my therapist lived just from such moments. I would become driven to do something that made perfect sense to me, only to discover it was bad timing. The intention that early morning was good, but disruptive and frightening to Emily. She asked if I needed a cab. No, I said. It was only a two-hour walk home.

And then there was the time I stood over Taylor's girlfriend with a hammer while she slept. Put that to the Voices. A test to do the right thing by them, but the wrong thing by my character. Deep down, I knew I would never smash someone in the head with a hammer. Still, Taylor's girlfriend changed the side of the bed she slept on. I was glad to learn that Taylor trusted me, and I still had a home to live in.

One of the nurses told me the government had more important things to do than monitor me. There were days I believed that. And days I didn't. It never made a difference if I had eaten mashed potatoes or not. Like Scrooge, I think poor digestion can really cause some eerie things to happen. Look at the Twinkie defense of the guy who killed Harvey Milk. That was a sad moment in history.

So today, Bobby, a young man with a blond flat top and large round earrings in the lobe of each ear who had arrived two days ago, leaps through the square window of the nurse's station. It barely yields his shoulders, the width of pressed flowers on a spring day with a decent size of heavy paper. His scrawny ass follows. He thought I was tucked between boxes of Haldol. Bobby wanted to propose to me before I forgot him—before the nimbus became too thick. I thought I was worth only the weight of my smile. Wanting to propose to me was a sweet gesture, an uninformed sweet gesture, like eating pad thai and not expecting the hot spices.

This afternoon I draw wine and cheese the color of cranberries, the color of Nurse Helen's fingernails, the color of tongues on a friendly day.

After I'm done, I place the drawing under my bed. The paper can't hide under my bed, its edges stick out; the wings of a dove from a nest too small.

"Kristina," the Voices call from the lounge. "Kill the television or become a media whore." I go to investigate. The woman in the commercial looks clean under the spray of the shower. Water cups her shoulders in welcome—a feather butter flying its way down skin.

I return to my room. The wine and cheese drawing is balled up on my bed, killed by creases I can't smooth out. The young woman who sleeps in the bed one over, laughs. The hands that cover her mouth are dirty with charcoal. She has refused to give up her name, or cough. This laughter is the first I hear from her.

Jane Doe. Her presence sucks the room up. I am alone in the vacuum of my rage. My rage is like the strength of thin wire used to lop off the heads of clay cockroaches.

Her long, greasy hair provides me with handles. I wrap her hair around my hands like boxers do white tape before sliding on their gloves. A ball of yarn couldn't be tighter.

I yank her out of bed, a yank as long as a leg.

Was there a shriek? No shriek? But then the Voices drop behind my ears like a hearing aid on the fritz. I hear ten, and then twelve, and then three, a hundred, two hundred. No sheep has ever been so fierce. Before I decide what to do next, a psych tech is in on me, his hands around my waist, which only tightens the grip I have on her hair. The weight of me is pulled back into his chest. The weight of her is pulled into me. She smells like shit. My wrists are plagiarized in a grip like my own. I pray they have to cut me out of her.

A needle prick in my ass. Slowly, I calm. The pain of my picture being ruined is fierce. I think the only way I have to prove myself worth anyone's time is to draw pictures and show them off.

Jane Doe isn't to come within twenty-five feet of me. The rooms are not wide enough. I still remember how it felt to wrap her greasy hair around my hands. Hydrogen peroxide fizzles. My wounds cool like rose petals in winter. The heightened awareness of skin to movement. A slight breeze from the opened door. Light breath. A whisper harnessed. Heaven is just so far. I leave her alone. She isn't worth it. Please see I have a good heart. Without the drawing, I can still be kind. I can be worth a hello. Then there is always the possibility of another drawing. I cover my feet in socks and dream.

## Cocoa

The hospital gown is not flattering and catches breeze from the movement of other people. I stand still as a hinge. No words leave my mouth. How will they know my heart has stopped working since noon? I protect it the way a child does her first hat.

There isn't enough room in the hall for the tall man to shout, but he tries. It doesn't get him the extra cup of cocoa he craves.

The doctor will try to shake loose my shadow and fail. I seek sleep in the gown and am left with wrinkled linen creating patterns on my back.


## Hats

When my hands are locked at the knuckles, I cannot plant alfalfa. It is things like this I think about in the hospital. What alfalfa has to do with anything, I'm not certain. I think about the goat my grandfather bought to eat the grass and weeds in the corral. The goat refused to eat these things and instead wanted to eat only hay. My grandfather wasn't about to keep the goat as a pet and pay for its food. The goat got sent back from where it came. I was sad. I liked the goat.

It is cold in my skin. In two hours my shadow will appear obvious. It will reach the door before I do and find it locked. I send my shadow in to meet with the doctor. I do not want to appear too bright. Too bright, and he thinks I need to lessen the amount of Wellbutrin they give me. The antidepressant has saved my life many a time. I would rather my mind be too stimulated than have to deal with depression. Depression is a blanket that folds itself around my head making everything muffled and far away. I cannot see to walk forward into a life that is worth living. Depression will steal life every time. This I know.

I have little to nothing to do with the other patients. I don't know how to talk to them about picnics on the lawn. They embrace one another. Share feelings back and forth. My feelings are a Frisbee I don't throw, but keep clutched close to my chest.

I sit at my post, in the chair at the table to the left of the nurse's station. I write with pens my doctor said I could have. No other patient has a pen. They have little golf pencils. I wonder if they know they too could ask their doctor for a prescription to have a pen. It is good they trust me to not write on walls or stab someone with ink.

Every time I check into the hospital they take my pens from me until the doctor can write an order. I cry every time. I panic every time. Once, Charley, one of the case managers, came to my rescue as much as he could by giving me full-length pencils. His gesture was kind. I still wanted my pens.

## Olive

I write about Olive. Olive is one of the characters I have brought to the page to give me companionship. I write of her totem—the wind looks to the totem and breaks through the open mouth, rests in the "know" of pine, the smooth pine at the back of the throat. There is a low hum of wind. It is this sound that draws Olive out, not a kick to the shin. Not a soft thump to the wrist but a hum of wind no louder than a sock tossed to the floor in a tired gesture of the day's end. Olive lifts herself from the hopscotch. Chalk softens her feet; blue chalk the color of the bridge on the playground. In a long steady stride, she moves toward the totem on which rests a wren that bears her name, Olive. Tonight, she will sit with other children, eat potatoes, share stories about being lost long enough to find wind.

A psych tech calls my name, asks me if I want my lunch tray. I walk forward and take it from her hands. A roast beef sandwich, lemon pie for dessert. There is dessert with every meal other than breakfast. What a cool thing.

## Flight

I was given a job as peer support. As peer support, it was my job to visit the hospital and talk with the patients, giving them hope that they too can live outside the institution, or simply inviting them to have conversation, making the time pass.

Robert would tell me it wasn't possible to know too much as he is ravaged by the minds of others whose thoughts he reads as he pulls on his dreadlocks, fingering the puzzle piece that makes Africa.

It is true I, like others with badges and keys, am paid to talk with him. He sees past this, calling me Sunshine and Disney. I don't tell him I feel heavier than this, but allow him to enjoy my smile.

He refuses medication, believing that God intended him to hear the subconscious minds of people. Without the chatter, he would be confined to his single self. He is larger than this, he tells me, and I believe him.

I believe him when he tells me that he just lost his grandmother, wife, and child. "People do crazy things when loved ones die," he says. For him it meant driving 150 miles per hour down the interstate hoping to take flight, clearing the stars, headed for the moon, which his wife worshipped, all while cops chase him, film him, place him on television, cuffing his leap toward faith.

He sits on vinyl couches in the hospital reading *Lolita* and the dictionary, listening to the minds of others and talking with me, waiting for his time with the judge, whom he must convince of his sanity. When committed to the hospital against your will, it generally takes about ten days before you see a judge. This way staff can monitor behavior and report to the judge, also.

I came Wednesday afternoon to unit seven and found him gone. He must have convinced the judge, unlike the doctors, that his grief did not need to be medicated, and that reading people's minds was like mail that didn't require postage or a response, just mild hellos that claimed his attention when the world could not, allowing him to dress his vulnerability and keep suicide sitting in a locked box at the edge of forgetfulness.

### Thirst

We have determined I have a key to the hospital units. I am there as a peer support. In the hospital, there is little landscape in which to orient myself. I finger the vinyl of the chair and knock on the wood of small tables.

I am the men and women who don't talk with me but hover in the near distance. I am the young man whose fear widens his eyes; the vacant stare of headlights on high beam whose light stream disappears at Dark's edges, leaving him the only one who is not blinded by the road map without streetlamps. The staff cannot go where he is. He sees the corner signs and takes a soft left.

I have given him the name Patrick. Patrick's arms are tucked inside his shirt, crossed over his chest, leaving his sleeves limp against his sides.

The old woman with gray hair that reaches her waist waves at nothing I can see as she picks her feet up and down, up and down, with no forward motion. This doesn't mean her journey stops at her toes.

Another woman is frozen in prayer at the corner of the couch. Her devotion extends past the locked door. She eats air. I can see and hear it dragged into her body, past her clasped hands. I don't know what it means to hold space for so long. I am thirsty just thinking about it. Her lips are not parched.

How do I explain to anyone the seduction I feel to be lifted out of the common reality, joining them in meaningful slumber? I know not what else to call their awayness.

The problem with leaving is that life outside moves on. I would wake and find things gone like days I could have spent loving the inside of my home and the people I break bread with.

Is leaving worth this? Is leaving worth the struggle of coming back to half-filled cupboards?

Truth can only be had so many times before seduction steals my scarf, leaving my throat cold and me with no voice and headlights that do not shine on anyone.

\* \* \*

I only spent a couple of months with this job.

## Good People

I spent a few years after losing my teaching job coming and going out of the hospital as the doctor tried to get my medications right so that I would have the help of them to keep me solid to the ground, home in my house, loving the little dogs.

I always went to the same hospital. They knew me. They treated me well. Really well. It can be said that I loved them for their kindnesses. I loved them for their patience. I simply loved them because it is easy to love good people.

## Teacups

My mind matches the weight of rain. Rain slaps on front windows of cars speeding. There is no speeding here in the hospital. The windows look out on parked cars.

My mind is axed open. Realities roll through me down to my toes, affecting my walk. When I was in first grade, my friend pointed to Scott. She said Scott was going to grow up and be crazy because he walked on his toes. I was paranoid. I always made certain my heels firmly palmed the ground.

Experts attempt to reach me with a faith in pills. Once, I refused their pills. They threatened to court-order me to take pills. I took their pills. It is true, the pills help me. I hate to admit this. Instead, I puff up and tell them that if I were pregnant they wouldn't be giving me pills. They say I'm not pregnant so my point is moot. I say please take my T-shirt from me and fill my hands with blue sky, the weight of rain.

The head nurse makes her rounds. When she comes to me, she says I'm not special. She tells me this because I have pens while the other patients don't. My doctor has written an order for me to have pens and paper. Without poetry, I lay in bed haunted, or pace the floors dazed at the fact that my body just won't die. Please don't take my pens away. I promise to not write on the walls. My doctor's order trumps her; I am allowed the pens. I am glad the head nurse doesn't work the floor. I don't have to speak to her ever again. I think *fuck her and her welcome.*

Scabs are forming hardy skin covering my vulnerabilities. I recognize that fragility, like the lip of a porcelain teacup, is something I live with. But I also recognize that the porcelain is strong, is protected, is well loved, and has been passed on through generations without chips. Do not leave the teacup in the cupboard to stay safe.

Voices follow me—a rabid dog looking for purpose, slavering at the mouth. This is true, but the truth does not stop with dogs.

Please listen deeply. There is truth as heavy as the moon held up in the palm of the sky. I don't want to be the teacup in the cupboard.

## Birds

The sun has not dreamt itself awake yet. I cannot hear through the open window the excited nature of birds announcing dawn.

The microwave has quit its pulse. I hear Guy pull his bowl of oatmeal from its stomach the other side of the bedroom door.

As with most mornings, I stretch my body the length of the horizon across the bed. Somewhere in the dark are the little dogs. I imagine their eyes opened to the soft dark as are mine and wonder which God they embrace instinctively upon awakening.

Breeze flutters through the window, strokes my shins first. Guy cracks the door open and whispers *I love you,* knowing I hear, knowing I'll pretend sleep, knowing he won't resist that first impulse to tickle the arch of my foot.

He doesn't. I laugh. Time pauses, and then there are birds, always birds.

## Rain

Often I wake to a cluttered conversation carried on by people I can't see.

Guy has left for the morning, leaving his side of bed in an open yawn. I look to the little dogs. Their bodies lay like thick socks at my feet. They don't hear what I hear, or at the least, they show no interest.

I can't make sense of the air but rise anyway, my naked body a shimmer of life. The six feet that I am dresses in shorts, a T-shirt, and rubber flip-flops. It is the dogs that motivate my movement. They must be walked on leashes. This ritual spills me into the morning like the sun curling around dawn.

The Voices berate me: *Look to die today, motherfucker, you know you want to.*

I dream of silence, imagining it looks like ice in a blue cup.

Walking the dogs wakes me to the rhythm of traffic outside the gate of our complex. I can hear birds settled in the branches of lemon and olive trees, unlike the false bodies of crows that collect themselves in the corners of my bedroom.

Waking is one of the most challenging things I do in a day. I no longer roll over when the time comes to rise.

The dogs are cute. Their paws tap the pavement, *clickety, click, clack,* as we stride together.

Thank God for their need to poop and pee. It is always the basic things that lend me to the day. I tell the Voices that cup my ear that they are mist in the rain. The rain is a heavier sound that soaks me even on a dry day. I don't worry so much anymore that false things will burden the truth. The truth is like rain; it is heavier.

## Swim

I went for a swim on the hospital carpeting. It took three men to lift me. The fourth man convinces me there is no water by laying a square of paper on the floor. Indeed, the paper soaked up nothing.

I don't carry my tongue around in my back pocket. Words come to be poignant, pointed, lovely, loosely, straight from the gutter of my throat, from the slope of an unfettered mind. The easy cascade of honesties is refreshing after a day of filtered gratuities.

It is a week since my last shower. The nurse told me I stank as she hugged me. Remember, you don't like puppy smell.

All it took was that and a bar of soap. I forgot how good it felt—a warm lather, a dry towel.

## Coffee

The air in the hospital is pleasant enough—cool with no breeze except for the draft I pick up from the man who ceaselessly paces up and down the tethered hall. We are all offered lightweight blankets.

Hope is an odd thing. It is in the wristband I wear. My name typed clearly. I am not a Jane Doe. Even I know my name begins with Kristina.

The drugs are meant to squash my awkward thinking, clip the wings of the visions I have, take from me the additional current of electricity my brain runs on. To date, they fail as coffee being poured through a Styrofoam cup with no bottom. They simply leave me feeling drugged. Pause. My thinking. I have no thinking. Isn't the ceiling a nice white like the wall? I stare at both for hours with no thought but white.

The wind outside is said to be beautiful. It tugs on the petals of pansies, leaves a quiet dust on furniture, threads through the hair of people I love. The palms take a bow.

I wonder if, in this drugged state, my little dogs will recognize me when I get home. I know that I am who I am if they know that I am.

Guy visits daily, expects I am getting better, listens for quivers in me, notes my smile and changes in conversation. I have stopped talking about government invasions. The birds leave my hair alone, but my mind still gives way to the Voices I hear. My heart breaks for what will be. My heart breaks because I think I can be no different. I think I will never have a wonderfully spiritual life combined with emotional health.

Somewhere a peach orchard is burning to root. A girl pedals like hell toward a mountain, clips a rock, loses her balance, breaks her neck, and is found after the coyote has left. Somewhere a peach orchard is burning to root.

## Doughnuts

Outside this hospital between large arches there is a city filled with people eating the custard out of doughnuts. I have no information with which to report this, confidently, but in a vague cloud of a dream, I saw the man's mustache was sticky with cream. His friend had pushed her hand through the doughnut to wear a bangle. The woman had a dog as a pet. The bangle didn't last long, maybe two slobbery bites. The dog was satisfied.

## Comb

Purple corn and it is a day when the world flattens. Without a bend, a curve of sphere, water collects at my ankles inside the house. I have left the front door open—what does it matter when the lock has been twisted?

You moved into me. The butter on the kitchen counter softened in the time it took us to suck each other's toes, cradle our scars, grow dizzy and drenched with sweat after ripping open the seams of the mattress. We rocked. The lightning did not scare us off but brought us close like the eraser on the end of a pencil. I have now had time to chew it off and spit it out. You have left again, after another woman. This amazes me. This time around I thought we were so happy. The voice on the phone that told me you were fucking his girlfriend was one I didn't recognize. I was glad not to know him. I was glad the phone conversation was a short one.

Grandmother sold me on pens. Ink is bolder than lead. You pulled my signature from me when you left. I pray that my next love will not take more than a dirty sock. Yesterday I wrote a check to the TV repairman. He took the television away. The commercial breaks were killing me. It is in idle time that you loved me the most. I am sorry that you thought all I did was fill our pocket with nickels. It cost a quarter to speak to God. I would have handed you a quarter had I known.

Tomorrow I will move from this place. It is too crowded with you. It smells like you. Freshly cut grass is the other side of the trellis. I will pack Tupperware that is microwaveable. Maybe I will take the comb you left behind.

## One Room

I rented a room from my friend, Deborah. I had sold the condo downtown. With this move, I decided I would not pay for storage, so I was left with only everything that could fit in an eleven-foot by eleven-foot space. It was a sad time. I had said good-bye to Guy after learning he had cheated on me again. My grandmother was dying. I literally left behind hundreds of books. The library I had built since high school was no more. The only books I kept were poetry collections and art books. I bought a beautiful floor-to-ceiling mahogany bookshelf that fit wonderfully in the corner of my new room.

My little dog, Brutus, came with me to Deborah's. I strapped a bit of my heart to his back and he gave me little kisses. The move was hard on Brutus. He was used to having other little dogs around. Guy had the other dogs. Now it was just him. I could tell he was depressed. He had stopped eating. I change from one dry dog food to the next. It didn't help. I called the vet asking what they suggested I do. They told me to mix a little bit of baby food in with his dry food. I did this. Chicken paste baby food, and it worked. Four years later, and he still insists on a bit of baby food.

## Recognition

The earth broke in front of me. I could not grab the sun; holy shit!—I'm glad it will be over soon. Life is not a canister filled with gummy bears. End this conflict with skinny therapists who dismiss me because I say red is more than red. Don't they see death lingers in the crevice of earth at whose lip I stand? The sun throws me no handle but slips behind the line of roofs marched up against the mountain. I am left to wish for ears that have been taught exactly how to hear. The earth did break in front of me. I could not grab the sun.

## Sonic Rain

No open lake and feverish open doors. Following and ferocious. Culture wraps a scarf around my head, identifying, tattooing, directing, profiling. I run through the shadows of hills, cast off at a loss. My heart's pump, loudly triumphant, silencing nothing—not a trombone for humanity, but a pipeline for the personal. It beats hard. I prolong introductions. Splice. One artery to another. Spliced. Following flowing, ferocious. The poet Howe, I salute on open water.

I had a bad night. They jacked me up on Haldol. We have a nation that pushes medication for everything. My mind is slow to come back to pancakes and syrup. I had gotten up in time for breakfast. I had to remind myself to trust the nurses and the doctor. They all had my best interest at heart. On good days, this I knew. On bad days, I still swore I was slowly being poisoned.

How do you say goat? The Billy goat got a hoof stuck in the rocks during the grip of thunder. I saw it from the hospital window; how lightning blew out the evening, made everything clear, frightening the goat with a loud clap. Too many medications. The goat got loose with the next loud clap and ran off into the edge of a tree. Gretel's legs tangled in her gown. I thought to help, but the distance between her and I was too great, was out of ear range. My parallel universe allowed for the goat. I could have run with him to the edge of the tree. The finality of tree left me to think. Gretel sat until the nurses found her sobbing. I wanted to tell her not to worry, but I knew how hungry the corners of the hall were—they stole sense and left all that fell into them a bit more vulnerable to sonic rain, a bit more vulnerable to wing nuts loosening the mind. Code blue.

## Bones (2007)

Grandma Morgan was my best friend. She told me not to be sad when she died. We had many conversations about her dying. I told her I wouldn't be sad only to learn not being sad was impossible. Grandma didn't want me to crack up because of her dying. I really wanted to do that for her, but like dew in winter, it is impossible to keep it from the grass.

My grandmother had moved from her home into the Beatitudes, an assisted-living community. She had her own apartment, two bedrooms, furnished with her own stuff. Aside from talking on the phone every day, sometimes twice a day, we spent Thursday afternoons together, having lunch and going grocery shopping, and gabbing like two close friends gab. It was not easy to watch my grandmother's health failing.

One Thursday, I showed up and she was completely out of it. She was very confused. I ended up taking her to the emergency room. There they determined that her blood cell count was bad and that she would need a blood transfusion. The transformation of before and after was amazing. They ran tests to see if they could learn why her blood cells were so off. As it turned out, she was diagnosed with bone marrow cancer. My grandmother would simply say, "My bones are bad."

Now part of our Thursdays was taking her to get a shot every other week. The shot was thousands of dollars. Thank God for good insurance. She had Medicare and insurance through the bureau. The FBI took good care of their own, even the widows of former agents.

My grandmother's health continued to get bad. It got to the point where she could barely walk and started using a walker. She no longer left the house. She no longer bathed or dressed herself. I know she wanted to be in her own home as long as she could. It was decided that I move into her second bedroom. And I brought little Brutus with me. And hospice came on board.

At this time, I was a student in Arizona State University's master of fine arts program in creative writing. My mind had been behaving rather tamely. I was able to attend classes and put hospitalizations aside for months. I believe it was my third year, the year I was to graduate. My professors cut me great slack. They knew my grandmother was dying. They knew I needed to be with her. They allowed me to miss class.

This was also around when I met Lucy. She was a part of the hospice program my grandmother was involved with. Our crush on each other was almost immediate. Lucy would become a tremendous support for both my grandmother and me. And yes, we would become lovers.

I did miss classes, but I also hired caretakers to be with my grandmother for short periods of time so that I could go to class.

My grandmother quit taking her shots. She was tired of living the way she had been living and was hoping death would take her quickly. Dying from the ailments of old age is different than dying from suicide.

At least it is really clear in my mind, and it certainly was clear in my grandmother's mind.

The day came when we both knew I could no longer take care of her. This was a horrible moment for me. I knew my grandmother would have preferred to die before having to move again. A bear nestles into hibernation and sleeps for the winter. It was my grandmother's winter and she couldn't hibernate. She was painfully aware of this every morning she opened her eyes.

To move into a hospice facility, my grandmother either needed to be close to death, right at the door, or her caretaker, which was me, needed to have broken down. Hospice tagged it as caretaker breakdown. I felt shame. I tried not to feel shame. I knew I was doing the best that I could do.

Good fortune was with us. Hospice moved my grandmother into a facility that was directly across the street from where I lived. I could have thrown a stone and had her catch it.

Only one of her three sons was living locally: my father. I was still considered her caretaker even though she was in hospice, meaning the family still counted on me to give them updates. I knew they were counting on me determining how close to death she was so they could be certain to see her before she died.

Although my grandmother was in hospice, she seemed awfully perky and comfortable. A hospice nurse told me that just before death, the patient may seem to be doing better. Coming to death had its own rhythm. This particular hospice nurse suggested I tell the relatives to come now.

So I did, and they came.

## Death

I loved my mornings with my grandmother. I was at her bedside by six every day so she wouldn't have to wake up alone. In her sleep, she sensed me there and shortly opened her eyes once I had seated myself at the end of her bed. We didn't talk much. I didn't stay long. It was simply a time our spirits could mingle with each other and leave us radiating in love.

Grandma did complain a great deal to me about the fact that they were forcing food on her. She didn't want to eat. I told her she didn't have to eat. They said she would die. I said isn't that why she's here? Somehow they did discover she loved strawberry milkshakes, so that is what she ate three times a day.

\* \* \*

At lunch, Grandmother asks me if her legs purr. "No, hurt, Grandma, hurt."

She says, "That's what you'll remember about me, about me being sick," her eyes look to the window, and for a moment I am left to sit with her while not sitting with her; her attention on the tree outside is like that of a five-year-old tying her first bow.

I remember oatmeal cookies, root beer floats, Chinese jump rope, the organ, and chopsticks. Go Fish, Old Maid, poker. The sun behind her head and the laughter on the lawn, sectioning grapefruit, sugar on my tongue, walking to the sound of Grandma's feet.

I remember me sick, her caring for me, her blowing breath into my tired spirit and always insisting that she be the one to return the empty grocery cart to its dock.

She begins to drink her milkshake. The tremor in her hand is noticeable.

"So my legs purr, do they? I wouldn't have thought that possible. But then, Kristina, you remember we've been to the moon and back. We've flown in the stars. We've mated flowers and come up with new flowers."

\* \* \*

Friday nights I usually go to a meeting at five-thirty. This particular Friday night I decided to go see Grandma instead. I knew she had had a hard day because of contracting a bladder infection. I brought little Brutus with me to see her. She loved visiting with Brutus.

During this visit, she was pretty out of it. She was in and out of sleep. I asked the nurse on duty if she had been given anything for the pain of a bladder infection she had contracted. He said they had tried but she wasn't able to swallow the pill. I didn't get this. "What do you mean she wasn't able to swallow the pill?"

"She doesn't stay awake long enough to take it."

I thought that was ridiculous.

Mostly we just held hands that night. She said to me right before I left, "Where are we going to find you another guy?" I told her no worries and kissed her cheek. Even in the state that she was in, my grandmother was being my grandmother by asking about the welfare of others. She was always concerned with the welfare of others.

I was home maybe fifteen minutes when the nurse telephoned. "I'm sorry to tell you this, but your grandmother has passed away."

"What do you mean? I just left her!"

"I'm sorry for your loss."

"I'll be right there." I left my house and ran to my grandmother's bedside. Grief overtook me. A snake wrapped itself around my chest and squeezed. My heart ached. The flowers that lined my window ledge bowed. I knew my grandmother had been exhausted, wanting to die for a long time. I had no idea that I wasn't ready to lose her until that night.

Before leaving my house, I had telephoned my father and asked if he would please telephone everyone else. He said sure, and that he would get to the nursing home as soon as possible. At the time, he was local. He was actually living in my grandmother's home, the home he had grown up in. I also called Lucy.

The nursing home staff left me alone. I don't recall ever having cried as much as I was crying. Lucy showed up to be with me. My nose was running shamelessly. She took tissues, placed them under my nose, and told me to blow. I won't forget this gesture.

The ambulance showed up. It was time for me to let my grandmother go. Lucy didn't want me to be in the room when they lifted my grandmother onto the gurney. Dead bodies can do weird things; she said something to that effect. So I stood in the hall.

The ambulance person paused once they had removed my grandmother, pushing her into the hall. He told me he was sorry he had to cover her face; it was simply out of consideration for the other people in the nursing home. I said I understood.

Although Deborah, the friend I had been renting a room from for several months, was home, Lucy insisted that I come spend the night with her. I grabbed a few things, grabbed Brutus, and joined her in her car.

On the way to her house, I telephoned Norman, my advisor at Arizona State University, letting him know my grandmother had died. He sang a Buddha song to me over the phone. I was amazed at how soothing it was.

I don't remember anything more of the evening. Sleep stole me quietly. I believe it was a God thing that brought me to my grandmother's bedside that evening. I will be forever grateful for the time I got to spend with my grandmother right before her death.

## Photos

My grandmother's service was October 7, 2006. She died September 29. Making her funeral arrangements was easy because my grandmother had already taken care of most of it. She was to be cremated and placed in an urn beside my grandfather at Green Acres Mortuary in Scottsdale.

My father wrote the obituary and I provided the picture for the newspaper. I also wrote something and provided the same picture for the handout passed out at the service. A friend of mine had shot hundreds of pictures of my grandmother and I in the last year of her life. I love the picture we used for her service and obituary. I get to look at it every day, as it hangs on my bulletin board by my desk.

My father, as the oldest son, stood at the podium first after the minister had finished his part. Dad spoke a little about my grandmother, his mother, and then invited her granddaughter and best friend, me, to say a few words. I read two poems I had written for my grandmother, both of which I read to her before she died. Here is one of them.

## Virginia Isabel

The shop keeper tells me elephants symbolize infinity
as he bags the wooden calf.
I know you dislike fresh flowers, say they hold death in their
stalks.
I offer this wood instead. It holds the heat of my palm in its belly.

I am hoping to collect you from your afterlife like cotton does
alcohol.
You say to bury the calf with you. Let it be your guide back to me,
to the place on my shoulder where the soft weight of you will sit.
*Did you know weight could whisper?* you ask. *If you say,* I answer.

We have agreed that I will serve marshmallows at your Memorial
in large bowls,
keeping the day light, allowing children to play jacks in the center
of the room.
Many will speak to your five feet of pillar, the way you twinkled in
darkness.
I don't know how I will keep the flowers out. Imagine calla lilies
walking on toe.

We spend Thursday noon at the grocery store, pause in the
cookie aisle
to look at all the Oreos. Red stuffed. Green stuffed. Double
stuffed. Amply stuffed.
It is an American thing, this takeover of choice. For a moment,
you worry about time, consider yourself stodgy, think you keep
me too long. Sadly, it is an American thing . . .

these notions of aging, of the aged. How can I assure you my
time is never better spent?

It took years of life for me to see that your shoulders now slope
forward,

bear the weight of your blouse just as they have borne the strong breeze

of the people that have depended on you. You have kept shoes on feet

that would blister without you. I bought you the blue slippers for Christmas.

You show me the spots on your hands. I think of the beauty of bark.

I know you are tired of being an old woman. If I could pull age

from your hair I would.

You walk before me, turn to see why I have stopped. The light of the low sun

envelops you. It is hard for me to see. I wonder how my vision will be without you.

Will I still be kind in your absence? You have shown me how to take off a glove

and sense the bite of God deep within others. I do see the lily pads supporting frogs

as they settle on the pond. Life can be like this.

It will be hard not to miss you. Have you ever tried to move an arm

after it has fallen asleep? It takes another arm to wake it up.

It is good that you have taught me to use all of me. I will remember the way the sun

lit you from behind, and how your smile strengthened mine that Thursday noon.

\* \* \*

It was quite something to have all my relatives gathered in the same place. My father had asked his friend, the owner of the restaurant around the corner from Dad's house, if he would be willing to open at noon so that we could have a reception after the funeral. He was willing.

Several of my friends accompanied me to the reception. We sat together at one long table. Lucy was present. People didn't know she was my girlfriend. I thought that too much information for the day. My friends shielded me from Hunter. Hunter had done some terrible things to harm me. She is my baby sister. I spent much time in our growing years trying to be of help to her. Still, she screwed me and people close to me over and over again.

I tried to understand that she was sick. She did have mental illness just as I; the big difference between our recoveries is that she was still an active drug addict. Psychotropic medications do not work if a person is doing drugs or drinking.

Of course, Rose was there with her partner, Jonathan, and Frankie. As it turned out, Rose and Jonathan had stayed together and had a stable, loving relationship. It was good to see them. Although Mesa is just thirty minutes away, I have only been to their home once. Rose remains furious with our father. She still feels totally betrayed by him because he divorced our mother and married another woman. It has been over ten years since, and Rose is still eaten up by it. It is hard to see Rose in the pain that she is in. Rose was the one closest to our mother. She lived with her up until the demolition of her home, just before she and Frankie moved in with Jonathan.

My Uncle Bill and his family came from Pasadena, California. It was good to see them, just as it was good to see my Uncle Jack and Barbara, in from Detroit, Michigan. I correspond weekly with Barbara through email. This made my grandmother happy. She was glad to see me keeping in touch with some of my immediate family, with some of my blood relatives, although she knew I had a huge extended family with my friends. In recent years, I have begun a relationship with my father. I am glad about this. The telephone works well. We talk about books and football. He fills me in on the activities of my niece and nephews. And I like to hear about his wife, Betty. I am trying to be supportive of this relationship. My father is my father, after all.

## Illness

After my grandmother's death, my illness did take its toll on me. I wanted to be with my grandmother and my mother. The Voices promised me that I could visit them in the fourth reality, and then return to my feet in the common reality. Death. Everyone around me told me that if I overdosed to join them, I would not be coming back. People close to me asked me when the Voices had ever told me the truth. I remained convinced I needed to travel to the fourth reality. The Voices by now were constant.

## Graham Crackers

It's after another breakfast on the Sandia Unit of the hospital. Pancakes. My favorite and the best reason I can see for coming to the hospital. I'm sitting at my post. I'm at a table to the right of the horseshoe where the psych tech sits. They call it a horseshoe because it is shaped like the letter U, like a horseshoe. I have a chair to sit in, although sometimes I will stand for hours. I am also directly across from the telephones. There is not such a thing as privacy on the unit.

I am too tired to think of ink. To think of word. To think of pen, scratching its way across freeways, between cars deadened to their role in pollution and war.

So much depends upon concern for the squirrel that just got flattened on Route 10.

Felix is yelling at his wife again over the telephone. Felix is a skinny man, dragging around an IV post. I don't know if he is dehydrated or in need of some weird sort of drug that has to be administered through an IV.

He's demanding that she come see him again and bring him more clothes. And then, amazing as it is, he screams at her for having no sex with him. Their sex life is hanging in the still air where everything just got dryly quiet.

"No, no. Don't hang up, you bitch. Listen to me. Just listen. They've got me locked up and wearing hospital gowns that flash my naked ass. I'm going to cram my fist down your throat if you don't change your tone with me. I know you love me, just act like it. Oh, oh, you are acting like it? C'est la vie," and Felix hangs up.

He looks around at all of us. I make the mistake of talking under my breath. I say, "Your wife comes twice a day every day and you can't see how lucky you are."

He looks at me and screams, "Freak! You fucking freak. What do you have to say about anything? Look!" and he points to the world I'm creating out of ripped-up pages of magazines rolled into little balls. Staff has given me a large tray to place my little balls of color on so that I don't put the balls all over the counters.

I turn my head. I don't say anything. And really, I never say anything. Why I was moved to speak in this instance is a dilemma to me.

Staff asks Felix to go to his room and cool down. After a "fuck you," he goes.

I return to writing. Head down. Lost in my hair. I see no one. But Grandmother. I see Grandmother and I want to write to her to tell her how much I love her. Grandmother fills my mind and I write:

Grandma, you with curls the color of whipped cream, your face, soft cotton creased by age the length of tall pine. Tall pine with a bend in your spine. The five feet of you that of a baby kangaroo that jumps in purple thistle. You with eyes that melt meanness out of young dogs and children. You with eyes that offer full cups of soup, and eyes that dress people in love. You with arms the length of nursery rhymes and hands the color of light oak that shake with generosity and kindness. You with the thighs the strength of ducks and legs that walk supermarkets in tiny shoes of blue. You with a mind of crossword puzzles, with a mind that gracefully erases the wrongdoings of others to return to the arms of nursery rhymes and loose eyes of twine. You with a heart of a llama, with the heart of Grandfather on the day he threw the first ball to the boys. You with a heart that brings the sun to the front porch of your feet and the moon as still as a dried tear on your palm. And you the gardener, always the gardener that weeds out the coolness in me allowing my heat to move me lovingly along in a world that will be a bit less with you gone and then a bit more when I remember the fire you gave me from your hand that shakes like falling petals, falling in the light wind of a day of red sunsets.

"Fucking freak," Felix is back. I don't look up from my paper. Grandma has her arms tight around me. With no response, Felix loses interest and walks away.

It will be snack time soon. I look forward to graham crackers.

## Leaves

It is not the other side of the day at 2 a.m., but that dead time that lays its callused head on rock, hoping to find comfort in flagged stone centuries old, cut by water into slab.

I am creased between the weary sky and sullen stars whose brightness lies dim on some other side of the world.

I lie in dim, dream sleep, dream of anything really that will allow me to be rid of the physical sense of life to suspend myself from the bodily pain of having bugs chew my bones. They say there are no bugs. They say there is no government, yet I know the officials stand sullen and still, back to wall, looking straight through to the other side of the room where pansies grow fields of color. The pansies wink at me like old men trying to comfort me with their wisdom.

Sleep. Speak sleep. It sounds like breath being blown slowly through a paper cone.

I know not how to rest when the Voices are louder than my own breath. Louder than the sound scuffing feet make, socks sliding over carpet.

In here are people prepared to help me let go of the agitation of tight pants, slip me into cotton, the cotton of dream state where for miles my mind can jog softly down the freeways of other worlds and not be hurt or standing in the world of 2 a.m. at the edge of a cliff wanting to jump, knowing I could fly if gravity would just stay still for a minute. Dream of sleep, then jump, always to float in the safety of the subconscious. It is waking that is the challenge. My body caught in the sensation of life, twisted this evening into a knotted string of twine.

\* \* \*

I actually go sit in the television lounge for group therapy.

The therapist asks how I feel. I answer, "The trees are bent, shed leaves. I need brooms to sweep them up."

The therapist moves away from me and begins discussion with someone else.

Can't she hear my ABCs, hear that I'm dying over a missing broom? Grandmother liked her porch swept clean. Stay listening to me long enough to learn that a broom ties me to leaves, ties me to Grandmother, ties me to the grief of Grandma, to my heart. Broken pieces of my heart mix with leaves.

Please help me be less silent. Don't forget about me because I speak on slant. Speak to the wind that lifts arms. My arms gather nothing. I am afraid of this nothing.

It used to be bundles of tulips, paper bows of silk, bellies of Buddhas, buttons of God.

The weight of my chest freezes me in place, keeps me from eating.

I am, once again, afraid of the television lounge.

## Custard

We all wish, don't we? Maybe the answer to that question lies awake in bedsheets just before lights out. If I wish for myself, is it the ultimate good for everyone because I am pleased, or is this selfish? Should I first wish for the ultimate good of others so they are pleased and will have kind words to say?

\* \* \*

I hold my head low to my chest, letting the long curls of my dark hair provide a curtain for my face. My heartbeat is too soft for my ear to hear. I want to hear it. I want to be reminded that I am not lifeless in my blue jeans and French top. A hospital gown covers my clothes for warmth and a layer of clean. I have not bathed in six days.

Many people mull around and sit near me. Our vulnerabilities are magnified by the stark panel lighting above. One woman is still in a chair, her legs wrapped around her belly. She cries. I don't know why. Nor do I ask her. I'm not interested in any kind of connection. The electrical current running through my body is already too strong for me to handle. I want nobody else's current touching me.

Four people stand at the counter waiting to receive medication. Their feet are common to each other. They all wear hospital-issued socks. That is where the common stops. One is fat. Two are thin. All different shades of skin and tossed hair and one bald man. We would normally not meet.

We troll the halls of the hospital hoping to find salvation. Salvation may be found in a cup of custard at dinner. The smoothness of it coats a throat taut with tears. In just that moment, life is right. How many moments of custard can be found on the unit of a psychiatric hospital? In this hospital, I say many. I have been many times to this hospital. The staff have never let me down.

A hello outside on the streets to a stranger can't rival a hello coming from the man who hasn't made eye contact or spoken to anyone in four days. I'm glad his hello is not to me; I am still battling electrical currents. Kind feels so far away that I wonder if I will ever be able to return to it. Staff passes me a note. It says simply, "When I see you—I know you. When I hear you—I remember." I'm not certain what is meant by these words, or what there is to remember, but it is good I accepted the note, and good that I read the note. The note is coming to me outside the reality I currently occupy. Things don't usually get in and out so easily.

The woman crying stops. She is left wet and exhausted. She is not ridiculed but is helped up and placed in new clothes. Dry clothes.

As in any small, enclosed group of people there are conflicts of personality. Here the conflict is honest, is not sugar-coated. A woman says, "Stuff your cigarette up your ass," and means just that. He is taken aback, and decides to retreat to the opposite end of the floor.

Dinner is called. They bring my tray. I must lift my mouth.

## Small Gestures

My mind slipped into a blue hue that matched the sky settling on the sidewalk. (The sidewalk is not meant to put a stop to the blue but is meant to encourage people to move north for as long as it takes to meet God.)

I am not able to lift my head under the weight of fluorescent lights on the hospital unit. I studied mice as they chew on the toe and heel of my shoes. I was with Guy again (I had ended things with Lucy, proving once more that anyone who gets between Guy and me always gets hurt), and he stomps his foot to convince me the mice are not really there. The mice escape his heavy foot. (Two nonexistent things cannot act on each other without belief.)

It is my smile that has most noticeably changed. My lips are heavy enough to fall to the ground to be eaten by mice. Sadness hangs from the cuff of my boyfriend, brushes my cheek as he reaches for me, tilting me into his chest. (My hollowness scares him. His love for me remains. He trusts I will return to my skin.)

There is comfort in trusting that all will be well but not enough to scatter the mice not enough for the hue to offer breath, liven my mind in soft ways. (A bulb wrapped in cloth glows when the light is switched on rather than startling my eyes with a sudden explosion.)

Guy brings a hairbrush with him the next visit. Tenderly, he brushes the snarls from my hair. The blue hue in my mind rolls out my eyes in tears, dropping on the heads of the mice, killing them.

Guy picks up the dead mice one by one as I watch and tosses them into the trash. His gesture does not convince him that really there were ever mice, but allows her belief with no harm.

Slowly I awaken to life that allows for sadness, allows for human kindness to lift her lips, beg for a smile in the way that a child is left to say bye-bye.

## Inner Tubes

Ache will leave the hospital with me today. But so will strength and canvas shoes. Please forgive me, Grandma for not being as strong as we wanted me to be. I did break down, missed a month of life. It is not too late for me to pick up the reins God hands me again. Love guides me back toward the lake that is me, that is you, that is countless others. We all have rafts and inner tubes.

## Medications

In the psychosis of a dark mind, strong lights shouldn't have to stay dim. This has been a challenge for my prescribing psychiatrists; they have to lessen my impaired thinking without squelching the fire within that drives me. Oftentimes, I think medication prevents me from writing at the depth I wish to write at. I have to be reminded that I can't write at all when claimed by psychosis. I don't envy the doctors' positions. I'm just glad that, over the years, I have had doctors who really listen to me, who don't want to medicate me to numbness, but seek to allow vitality to burn free also.

# Reclamation

## Magic

The professors I encountered in the MFA program at Arizona State University went far and above to help me get through the program. They were there for me when I lost Guy, and they were there for me when I lost my grandmother. At one point, I thought I couldn't show up any longer. Sorrow over Guy was directing my actions. I told my professor that I couldn't continue. I cried with him and he didn't dismiss me. Later that evening I got a call from that professor letting me know the following semester was paid for by a grant I had been given. I cried again.

\* \* \*

The day of my defense was magical. A defense in the Creative Writing Program is me reading from the manuscript I had created while a student in the program.

I began with the following:

> We are all here. Amazing. Thank you all for coming. Glad you found a parking space. I thank all of you, and the professors who have worked with me. The ASU professors are not only brilliant, well-published writers, but passionate teachers. They are as passionate about their teaching as they are about their writing. And more than simply see me through

academia, they saw me through loss, and death, and loss . . . to this day. I am so grateful.

Karla, the program manager, took an interest in my art and suggested I display it today. So, after the reading there will be a reception in the language and lit building, two buildings north from here, where cake will be served. I have maps and Meghan, please stand, Meghan, offered to lead the way too.

I want to give you a heads-up and let you know that I am not a very practiced reader. The words and images that live inside my head, inside my body, I hear. But I don't know how to take the emotional energy of the poem and present it to you verbally. I know I read fairly flat with no infliction. I don't know how to fix this. But I do promise you my best.

I have written a book of poems from the perspective of a woman living with mental illness, which is not a stretch, since indeed I am a woman living with mental illness. The stretch for me came when I was moved to write poetry that has nothing to do with mental illness or the struggle with it, but has to do with normal griefs and joys we all experience. Can I step outside the self-centered nature of illness and write about dogs with loopy ears or the way wind catches hair? Can I see you without seeing me first?

\* \* \*

The day was magical because all of my group of friends had come: the professional mental health workers, my Twelve Step program friends, my friends who had no affiliation with anything but were just my friends, and relatives flew in. Uncle Bill was there; so were my Uncle Jack and Barbara. And my aunt who is local, Aunt Gina, showed up and gave me an amazing thick silver bracelet whose inscription read, "Live the Life you Love." And Guy was there, dressed in a blue suit, looking very handsome.

I was nervous. I told the audience that if ever I needed a drink, I needed it now. They laughed. It broke the ice.

I read for half an hour and was given a standing ovation when I finished. Magical. Yes, magical.

## Post Reading

One thing for certain, someone handed me two dozen yellow roses, their stiff cups of petals promising to live for several days like a stiff upper lip.

I studied the photographs of the event hoping to catch you armed with friendship—I was told yellow roses meant nothing less. You would think I could remember the exchange—I was too busy being nervous and distracted by all the hellos.

Mother, were you there in cotton slippers, cheering me silently on in an alcoholic haze? I don't know if I believe the dead travel in shadows. There was a draft in the room smelling of lilac and bourbon. I'm thinking you could be found in that fold of air.

Norman told me all would be well. He said he could see my aura. It was strong and calm. The rock stands still in the river being polished by the tenseness of the water.

My father was not in the audience unless somehow he snuck in behind the roses. I'd like to think he would bring them, arms full and extended, unlike pocketed hands and a gesture of invisibility.

## Infidelity

I've written beneath the skin on your back where you can't reach with a lance. Your infidelity stole months from me as I walked shocked through winds that didn't exist, bent at the heart, blinded in the mind. Something akin to flattening a honeybee before the bee makes it back to its hive. Is that what you did for me? Gave me reason to offer nectar as freely as I draw breath? The return was marvelous, like the first stroke of paint on a blind canvas. A dark sky blazed awake by the thunder it carries.

I wasn't invisible in my grief. I brought you to the page, dragged you through ink. Poetry is not private. It gathers at an open door, explodes into an empty room, decorates the floor, the walls, the ceiling, offers seating on bright cushions.

And now you are back. Do I swallow my fine print?

No.

I simply begin again with your head tucked at my chest, my willowy arm pressing you to me, pressing you in place like a piece of shattered glass to an ornate frame bordering a mirror. Your deep sigh sends a crow south. A monkey climbs the pole of a lamp, makes it flicker on. The shadow on your face becomes my shadow after I have let you see the scar above my left eyebrow.

## Guy

I hurt Lucy. I should have known this was going to happen. My ties to Guy are just too strong. In psychological terms, we have both worked on the issues we have needed to work on. It took time, but I have indeed forgiven Guy.

Guy is perfect for me. The stability he offers now is amazing. He hangs in and stands with me when I am sick. He hangs in and stands with me when I am well. He inspires me to chew my symptoms into small bites I can spit out into a napkin. When the beetle is on its back, it needs someone to turn her over. Guy does this. It doesn't matter how many times he must flip me. It doesn't matter to him that I have terrible recall and he is always having to tell me stories over and over. He doesn't mind if we watch the same rerun of our favorite TV show three times.

We are at peace with each other and in good standing.

## Stay and Color

Because of being Seriously Mentally Ill, I qualify for Social Security disability benefits. Money is transferred into my account every third day of the month. I am very grateful for this money, although it is too small of an amount to live on. I thank God that I am able to work part-time to supplement my income. Even this is not enough. Guy contributes; this is how we get by.

Mental health benefits for the indigent are not enough in this state. I can't tell you what would be enough—maybe a place to live, food, and therapy. Maybe work programs that are tailored to the individual. I recognize that I am one of the fortunate few. I will credit the benefits offered when it comes to my medication. I take quite a bit, and through health insurance and the county's mental health system, they are paid for. I have no idea what I would do if they weren't. I do have a psychiatrist and I do have a nurse. And I do have a spiritual mentor and life coach.

\* \* \*

The medicine that has helped me the most is Clozaril. I used to visit the hospital every third month. Since being on Clozaril, it has been three years since I was hospitalized—another miracle in my life. I can use all the dental floss I want to use.

The Clozaril is not without its side effects. The medication makes me horrifically tired. I take all of it at night because it affects the way I communicate and makes me feel totally out of it. If I had no place to be in the morning, I would sleep from eight in the evening until three in the afternoon the next day. I know this because I have done this. Because of holding a job, I am forced to get up in the morning at six. This is no easy task, and I thank God that I am motivated to get my ass out of bed and to my job on time. I believe that medication is 70 percent of what makes me healthy, and my actions, 30 percent.

I have come a long way from the person who couldn't get out of bed for two years except to eat cheese Danish that my grandmother always supplied. I didn't eat meals with my grandmother because I felt that if I ate the meals she made, I would be responsible for cleaning the dishes. My depression took me to a place where washing the dishes was impossible; it was simply too much work.

It saddens me when I see people placed on medication thinking that the meds are the end-all be-all and they don't have to do anything but sit back and let them work. Medication will not place a person into life who just sits back, no matter how long they wait. A recliner is not always comfortable. Backs stiffen with hours of no motion. I still occasionally have a stiff back. I have learned to stretch sooner than later. I thank God for this. Sometimes it is not in me to call for help. God knows this and sends sparrows. Light reflects off their beaks. I forget about the mud.

* * *

The day comes where I find my feet and put socks on. I'm not absolutely certain how this happens, but it does happen. I find the chain to the moon and wrap it tightly around my waist. The sun circles even in the dark. I am the place in which something has occurred. Cities dwell in me forcing me to be tall. An iron pole runs up my back, forcing me to look through windows. I say stay and be color.

### Invention

I breathe in the sky of many friends and find peace I wished for my mother in the common reality of the earth. Mom has been dead for several years now. I often conjure the last moment I saw her eyes open and her attempt to sit up; the moment I told her I knew she loved us. She laid back down as if an iron jacket had been removed from her shoulders, allowing her to float on the way down to her hospital-issued pillow. She would not come to again.

I want what lies beneath my madness. It is warm there. Thick there. Strong there. It is a place where Guy can rest his weary head on my shoulder, nestling into my long curls. I want the time I touch Guy to always be electric and new. This can be as long as my heart pumps blood to my mind, reminding me that madness is just a temporary thing. Whipped cream on coffee can be skimmed off, leaving coffee full and warm. Guy visits me where the birds dance hearts in the air above. Love and happiness lace my bones like liquor soaking cake.

Writing this book has been a way of coming home. Being a poet is a way of coming home. Writing illuminates my world. I hunger for clarity, storytelling, poetry, all of which help me see. Without it I lay in bed haunted or pace the floors dazed at the fact that my body just won't die. Anything that isn't true in this book is a happy invention. I celebrate the happy. I celebrate the truth.

## Note

Dear Self,

It is cool today. Sunlight heats the window but doesn't warm the house. How many times have I stood in the center of a room wanting heat to warm you from the outside and discovered that warmth must radiate from the inside out in your search for things sacred and holy? I reach for you through the mist of consciousness and come away with hands full of leaves. It has been a beautiful fall.

I marvel at the fact that you have lived in the center of your life free from hospitalizations for one year now. I have trusted your psychiatrist enough to feed you medicine that eases you into wakefulness, keeping you planted in your feet. Broken glass may have been thrown in your path, but you have remembered to lace your shoes, not fearing to walk through distraction.

I have been gentle and fierce with you at the same time. Gentle in that sometimes I turn to the Voices only you hear, easing out the sounds of the common reality, and I don't berate you for your lack of attention. People who love you understand that sometimes you are sloppy in your engagement with them. It is important to remember that people who don't love you can still be kind. I have allowed you to sleep extra when there is no place for you to be and not called you lazy. I know the medication makes you tired. I have been fierce in dragging you out of bed on days you work, demanding you don't be late. God knows how amazing it is that you have held a part-time job for two years now. I am also fierce in my demand that you exercise and not eat cake all the time.

As a youth, you sat on a porch in the mountains with bits of bread at your feet, coaxing the squirrels and chipmunks to come close and feast. You sat still so as not to scare them. And they came. And they ate. Today, I am that squirrel. I am that chipmunk. You coax me out of myself, convince me it's safe, allow me to feel the spirit of life nestle in my coat pocket. I pull peppermints from my pocket and offer them to Ken, the postman, Sheila, the clerk at the store, and Sam, the gas station attendant. You teach me that there can never be too many peppermints, and I believe you.

I am safe in your hands: a baby bird that falls from its nest and is willing to drink water from the eyedropper.

I thank you for your persistence, for your nudges, for your unfailing desire to seek all that can be and shake off like loose rain all that cannot be. We are in this together. I go forth. I go forth.

Loving you,

Kristina

## Vows

Guy and I had a wedding ceremony minus the priest. In our eyes we are married. In the eyes of the law we are not. There were specific reasons why we had a ceremony as such. I wanted to include my vows to him in this book.

> I stand next to you and breathe you in. I am delighted you are mine. I have traced the ball of your bicep to the curve of your arm with my fingers, loving your strength. Your strength is not just in your body, but in your mind; you love me well with your heart and mind. I am happy knowing this. Our love is part of what makes me long to live. It will beat out my madness.
>
> Guy, my love, as a poet you know that I am a wordsmith. However, when I sit to write you, language seems to walk away, leaving me speechless. In my speechlessness I am

awed by the peace that settles over me when holding you in my mind and heart. My love is constant, like the petal of a flower I have glued inside my favorite book. We are creating our story. We have history. The trials that we've had have made us stronger as a couple. I really believe this.

Your spirit is a warm wind that circles through me, leaving me to blush or to smile, leaving me to feel my body electric. I will always be grateful to you for the time you have spent with me and the time you will continue to spend with me.

Today I offer you my hand, my trust, my friendship, and my love everlasting. You can count on me to not waver in my love for you. You can count on me to not take you for granted and to keep your best interest in mind.

There's always a chance a person will rust before the glue binds the two, but as for you and as for me, we are bound eternally.

Today I become your wife spiritually, mentally, emotionally, and physically. I will be your wife in word and action.

May your days be filled with kindnesses and love for others. I love you beautiful. Thank you for being mine.

## Structure

The day is crisp and ready for me to draw breath. It is 2010. I hate admitting that the medication is working. I still wish I didn't have to take any and will sometimes think I have to stop because the government is prescribing placebos, so why bother? Or I think that all the pharmacies are going to be blown up and I might as well wean myself off them now instead of having to stop abruptly. I have been med compliant for two-and-a-half years. It is hard not to see the connection.

My spiritual mentor, Jan Black, and Guy both tell me they can see my well-being in my face. They say I am transparent. I don't get this. I think I'm good at hiding my symptoms, and I am to a point. The Voices still vibrate around me, but they are a low hum of sound with no real language with which to berate me or command me.

My paranoia about leaving my house is more intense now. The part-time job I've had for the past three years was eliminated due to budget cuts. For three weeks now, I've not had to be anywhere I don't want to be. I have not had to leave my house. But I do leave even though I think the house will burn down if I'm not in it. I do leave because I know isolation is not a good thing. I do travel to other realities when left alone for long periods of time. I need things to engage me other than my own art.

Monday through Thursday, I spend eight to noon at my computer either writing or reading submissions for the literary journal *Hayden's Ferry Review*. At noon, I have lunch. After lunch I dust the house or clean the bathroom, wash dishes and take out trash. At one-thirty, I meet Guy at the gym and he trains me. On Friday mornings, I volunteer at the Virginia G. Piper Center for Creative Writing on Arizona State University's campus. I volunteer to do the same things I did while working the past three years for them. Sean, the assistant director, reminds me that now I'm in a position to say no to any projects they give me. I chuckle at this. I can't imagine saying no since I am trying to be as helpful as possible. Occasionally, I will schedule lunches or coffees with friends throughout the week. The reason I've laid this all out is to make a point of the fact that I must have structure. I must be accountable or else I drift easily to the other realities. Life is not worth its weight if I'm not actively involved. God will not do for me what I can do for myself. Yes, my spiritual beliefs remain strong.

## Interview

Wednesday, I have an interview with the department store Macy's. I'm really excited about it. I joked with Guy and said since they sell Converse sneakers, don't you think I could wear Converse to my interview? Not, he answered. I already knew this. I had to go shopping to buy something other than T-shirts and jeans. I had to look for a pair of shoes. I scored; I found all I needed at the consignment store My Sister's Closet. A jacket, two silk skirts, two pairs of shoes, $125. Score.

I've asked Christy if she would help me practice for my interview. One question I know they usually ask is what about me gives me trouble or what about me don't I like? What character defects do I have? I've thought to tell them that I'm a brand person and believe that you get what you pay for. I've thought to tell them that I drink so much water that I have to pee often. I can tell them that I am gullible and I trust easily and that I don't discriminate very well. I could also tell them that I know I have expectations of my co-workers. I know this because after having asked someone from my Piper House job for help working on a project, I got told no. It was a small thing I had asked and I was shocked to be told *no, I won't help*. I thought, what happened to teamwork? This person could ask me to do anything, and I would do it. But give her an opportunity to be helpful, and she turns it down. Again, I was shocked.

## New Family

As time progressed in my life like time does, I grew away from my family of origin and created a family from friends and the program I am involved with. I also became tight with a few friends I had met while in class at Scottsdale Community College and Arizona State University.

Mom is dead. Dad moved back to Arizona from California and is living with his wife, Betty, in Maricopa.

Occasionally, I will get reports about Hunter from my father. She is in jail. She is out of jail. She is in Virginia. She is moving back to Phoenix. She lost custody of two of her kids, Decker and Morgan. She is trying to get custody of the youngest, Kurtis. The drama that is Hunter is endless. I am happy to not be a part of it.

Rose and I have rekindled a relationship. I am very happy about this. Rose is living with Jonathan and Frankie in Gilbert, Arizona. Rose thinks she is not able to outlive the past. I think, *Is she sutured to it like a butterfly to cardboard at rest forever in a glass case?* I hope not. She has much to offer. She is the kind of person who would give you her shoes should you need to walk forward and don't know how to because of no shoes.

## Vision

Today is beautiful, is amazing. I can easily be brought to tears of joy. I have Guy, who loves and adores me and whom I love and adore. We have two little Shih Tzus whom we love parenting. I have many friends.

The day is a bright white button-up shirt I wear easily in public and can discard at home. The day offers me soup, the kind that is thick and not clear broth, and even though I don't know everything that's in it, it tastes rich, tastes good, tastes like heat on my tongue. I trust that it is good for me. There doesn't always need to be a reason for me to walk forward—I just do it anyway and reach a smile once again.

So I end with a note to God: *Dear God, please help me believe that breathing in and out requires no work, only a steady diet of waking. Today I do wake. Today I do wake.*

## ABOUT THE AUTHOR

Kristina Morgan lives with her life partner, Guy, and her two Shih Tzus, Chloe and Shadow, in Scottsdale, Arizona. She has published poetry in LOCUSPOINT, *Open Minds Quarterly,* and the *Awakenings Review.* She received her master of fine arts degree in poetry from Arizona State University in 2007. She currently works for Phoenix Public Library.

# Other titles that may interest you:

## White Out
*The Secret Life of Heroin*
A MEMOIR BY MICHAEL W. CLUNE

With black humor and quick, rhythmic prose, Clune's gripping account of life inside the heroin underground reads like no other as we enter the mind of the addict and navigate the world therein.

Order No. 4678 (Softcover)
Order No. EB4678 (E-book)


## A Legacy of Madness
*Recovering My Family from Generations of Mental Illness*
TOM DAVIS

The story of a loving family coming to grips with its own fragilities, *A Legacy of Madness* relates the author's journey to uncover, and ultimately understand, the history of mental illness that led generations of his suburban American family to their demise.

Order No. 3897 (Softcover)
Order No. EB3897 (E-book)


## Get Me Out of Here
*My Recovery from Borderline Personality Disorder*
RACHEL REILAND

With astonishing honesty, *Get Me Out of Here* reveals what mental illness looks and feels like from the inside, and how healing from borderline personality disorder is possible through intensive therapy and the support of loved ones.

Order No. 2138 (Softcover)
Order No. EB2138 (E-book)


Hazelden books are available at fine bookstores everywhere.
To order from Hazelden, call **800-328-9000** or visit
**hazelden.org/bookstore.**

*An excerpt from*

# White Out
## The Secret Life of Heroin

a memoir by Michael W. Clune, published by Hazelden

**From Chapter 1: Memory Disease**

Now watch what happens to the addict. I'm sitting there at Dom's, minding my business. Henry's kind of talking, I'm kind of listening. Then I see a white-topped vial. Wow. I stare at it. It's the first time I've ever seen it. I know I've seen it ten thousand times before. I know it only leads to bad things. I know I've had it and touched it and used it and shaken the last particles of white from the thin deep bottom one thousand times. But there it is. And it's the first time I've ever seen it. The first time I encountered dope isn't somewhere else, it isn't in the past. *It's right over there.* It's on the table.

Something that's always new, that's immune to habit, that never gets old. That's something worth having. Because habit is what destroys the world. Take a new car and put it in an air-controlled garage. Go look at it every day. After one year all that will remain of the car is a vague outline. Trees, stop signs, people, and books grow old, crumble and disappear inside our habits. The reason old people don't mind dying is because by the time you reach eighty, the world has basically disappeared.

And then you discover a little piece of the world that's immune to habit. There's a little rip in my brain when I look at a white-topped vial. The rip goes deep, right down to the bone, to the very first time. People love whatever's new. Humans love the first time. The first time is life. Life is always fading. The work of art is to make things new. The work of advertising is to make things new. The work of religion, the work of science, the work of philosophy, the work of medicine, the work of car mechanics. Their tricks all work, a little bit, for a little while, then they get old. The addict, alone among humans, is given something that is always new.

It's not the feeling of doing the drug that stays new. The drug high starts to suck pretty quickly. Pretty soon it sucks so bad you quit. Never again. Then you see a white top. Or even imagine you're seeing one. And it's the first time you've ever seen it. Addiction is a memory disease. Memory keeps things in the past. Dope white is a memory disruption agent. The powder in the vial is a distribution technology. It carries the white down the tiny neural tunnels where the body manufactures time. Dope white turns up in my earliest memories. I remember Mom's white teeth. My future whites out.

I'm cured now. Ten years. How? How did I escape my white mind and body? How did I exit the white pollution of the past and the future, the white mind where every thought and feeling is a long or short road to the white tops? I'm outside. I'm free. But how? Can you run from yourself? Try it. It's impossible. But I did it. I ran out of myself. How? Once you get a glimpse of something that never gets old you'll never be able to live like the others. I don't want to give too much away. There's a flaw in my memory. Luckily there's also a flaw in time.

Dom wakes up. He pulls himself together in a literal way. His eyes kind of go back into their sockets. He is a big hearty man. The syringe is still in his neck. It makes him look kind of military, like he's a soldier from the future. Henry, with his missing arm, looks kind of military too.

"I'm going to get the white tops, Mike," Dom says. Henry stands up. "Get the walkie-talkies, Henry." Henry goes over to an open black gym bag, takes out one walkie-talkie, takes out another, then takes out a gun.

"When I'm halfway there," Dom says, "I'm going to say OK through the walkie-talkie. When I get there, I'm going to say OK. When I get the stuff. When I get halfway back. Mike, if more than five minutes go by between when you hear from me, give Henry the gun, open the door for him, and get out of his way."

"Yes Dom." I say it in the deferential high-pitched voice I used to reserve for cops or teachers. Now I use it with everyone. "I want you to be careful Dom. I really care about you." I pause. "I don't know if I ever told you this, but I really like you. I want you to take care of yourself. When you come back, we should talk about getting you some help."

Language is a total luxury in a white out. A full sentence is like a Rolex. I'm still straight, but already feeling really luxurious. I feel like blowing my nose with twenties. "I'll even drive you to get help, if you want."

"OK." Dom says through the walkie-talkie. "OK." "OK." "OK."

. . .

The ancient Mongols believed the soul lives in the head. So when he captured his most hated enemies, Genghis Khan would have their eyes ears nose and mouth sewn shut before they were decapitated, so their soul could not escape the death of the body. My memory would probably seep out through my neck in a white fog.

It was three months later. I knocked on Dom's door. Rain was pouring from heavy brown clouds. He opened, looked furtively around, then stood aside as I went in. He was holding his gun. "I got troubles, Mike." I nodded.

"Fathead says Dom fucked up the package," Henry squittered. Dom squittered. A rope of spit hung from his lip. "But it sure was nice Henry," he said.

"They say if you was to lay out a man's veins all in a straight line they'd go from Baltimore to Philly," said Henry, "And old Henry'd be one of them old-time railroad workers, driving a spike in every three feet."

"And I've been working on the railroad too," said Dom, "All the live-long day."

I gave Dom eighty dollars in folded tens and twenties. That's what it took, day in and day out, just to keep that white light shining. And if it ever dimmed the devils came out. Now the white light was so dim they were sticking their little paws and claws for whole seconds inside me, like children testing the water at the beach. The day before I'd bitten down too hard on a forkful of potatoes and taken a big chip out of my front tooth. I guess I'd thought the potatoes would be harder. I didn't used to make that kind of mistake.

Dom took the money and Henry opened the closet door. He moved a coat from over a hole in the floor, and pulled a bundle out of the hole. Then he pulled five little white-top vials out of the bundle and tossed them to me. I got shy with desire. Ran to the bathroom. When I got out of the bathroom the dimming white light was bright again inside me and the devils were burning to death in it.

When I got out of the bathroom Fathead was standing in the hall between Dom and Henry with a big hand over each of their shoulders.

"Hey there Mike!" he said brightly. He moved his hand to Henry's neck and gave it a little squeeze.

"Ow, Fathead!" Henry honked.

"I said hey there Mike." I kind of stood there.

"Hey Fathead."

"Why don't we go back into the kitchen where we can all sit down? You still have chairs back there, right Dom?" He gave Dom's neck a friendly squeeze. Dom didn't make a sound.

We all trooped back to the kitchen and sat down. Dom's eyes were a little bloodshot, and his skin was even whiter than usual. Next to him, the off-white aluminum refrigerator in the corner had a healthy human glow. I hadn't noticed it before. It looked kind of friendly. Like it wanted to tell me something.

"Let me tell you how to get that permanent white, son," I imagined it saying. "Just slip your head in here and have them boys shut the door real real hard on your neck."

"That's a real nice refrigerator, Dom," I said.

"Thanks, Mike," Dom mumbled. His big black-and-blood eyes opened on me like dogs' mouths.

"Maybe tomorrow," Fathead said, "you should see if you can sell that refrigerator, Dom. Maybe you could get two hundred dollars for it. Then, if you found twenty other refrigerators and sold them for two hundred each, you could pay me what you owe."

Fathead was a powerfully built white man about forty-five years old. The previous winter he'd been released from prison after serving eleven years. He'd made some good contacts in prison, and when he got out he started dealing. He'd bunked with Dom in prison for a couple years. Dom had gotten out first, but they stayed in touch, and Fathead began fronting him packages the past spring. Fathead had a huge habit, which he'd had since his twenties.

He'd kept it going straight through his prison years. His pride was that he'd never once gone through withdrawal in the whole eleven years. This was a unique, almost impossible achievement. Even the street dealers from the nearby projects who had only contempt for addicts had respect for Fathead. He was also some kind of religious freak, which I think they also respected. I did too, kind of.

Now he prepared to shoot up in front of us. Almost lazily, demonstrating that this was pure fun, that the white fire was always burning strong in him and never went out.

"Men," he said, emptying a large vial into a spoon, "there are two forces in this world. What are they, Dom?"

"God and the creature," Dom whispered through papery lips.

"God and the creature," Fathead repeated. He closed his eyes. "And the creature, the creature must be induced."